CROMER
LIFEBOATS

1804-2004

CROMER LIFEBOATS

1804-2004

NICHOLAS LEACH
& PAUL RUSSELL

TEMPUS

First published 2004

Tempus Publishing Ltd
The Mill, Brimscombe Port
Stroud, Gloucestershire GL5 2QG
www.tempus-publishing.com

British Library Cataloguing in Publication Data.
A catalogue record for this book is available from the British Library.

ISBN 0 7524 3197 8

Typesetting and origination by Tempus Publishing.
Printed and bound in Great Britain.

Contents

Preface

Situated on cliffs above the North Sea on the north Norfolk coast is the small town of Cromer, a favourite holiday destination for many. Often described as the 'Gem of the Norfolk Coast', with a population of around 7,500, it offers visitors gardens, parks, cliff-top walks and pleasant sandy beaches. Its buildings are laid out on narrow streets which surround an imposing fourteenth-century church, the centrepiece of the old fishing village which has grown in importance since the end of the eighteenth century. This importance is reflected in the size of the church, the perpendicular tower of which, at 160ft high, is the tallest in Norfolk. Since the railway came to Cromer in the nineteenth century, it has become a well-known holiday resort famous for two things – the crabs, caught by the local crab boats operating from the east beach, and the lifeboat. For two centuries a lifeboat at Cromer has been ready to go to the aid of ships in distress off the north Norfolk coast and help people in difficulty in the dangerous waters of the North Sea. The coxswains and crews who have manned the lifeboats have a record of gallantry second to none.

Much has been written hitherto about the lifeboats of Cromer, particularly the twentieth-century exploits of the town's lifeboatmen, who did so much to make Cromer arguably the most famous of all Britain's lifeboat stations. Indeed, the town is perhaps best known for the exploits of Henry Blogg, often described as the most famous of all lifeboatmen, coxswain from 1909 to 1947, and unique in being awarded the Gold medal for gallantry on three occasions. While this book looks at his many rescues, it also provides in one volume a comprehensive history of the Cromer lifeboat station during two centuries of lifesaving, and coincides with the station's bi-centenary. All of the lifeboats are covered, as are many of the rescues they have performed and the people involved with the station. All connected with it can be justifiably proud.

The importance of the lifeboat to Cromer is amply demonstrated by the fact that the town is littered with lifeboat-related features. Not only is there the lifeboat station at the end of the pier and the ILB house, but the lifeboat house, built in 1902 at the East Gangway, houses the Henry Blogg lifeboat museum and a wealth of lifeboat photographs and artefacts. In the church is a stained-glass window depicting two lifeboats; in the Henry Blogg memorial garden was the tabernacle of the barge *Sepoy*, until it was removed to go in the lifeboat museum; the secondary school's badge incorporates depictions of both the lighthouse and lifeboat; Henry Blogg Road, Heartwell Road, Bailey Road and Dixon Road are all named after lifeboats; a bust of Henry Blogg looks seaward from the East Cliff; a number of the pubs and restaurants have lifeboat photographs on display, including the Red Lion, The Albion and the Lifeboat Café; on the wall of Blogg's house, Swallow Cottage, in Corner Street, is a plaque; and in The Old Cromer Cemetery, the grave of James Davies (1826-1893) has a lifeboat on the headstone. As if this was not enough, a facsimile of a compass is planned for the forecourt of the pier with points indicating the locations of all the medal-winning services. Cromer is, truly, a lifeboat town.

Acknowledgements

Many people have assisted with the preparation of this book and the authors are grateful for their help. At the RNLI's headquarters in Poole, Brian Wead, Sarah Baumer and, in particular, Valerie Kirsch of the Rescue Records Section provided service details; Barry Cox, RNLI honorary librarian, assisted in the library at Poole; Peter Stibbons, of Poppyland Publishing, Cromer, provided photographs, general assistance and encouragement; Frank Muirhead, curator of the lifeboat museum, kindly allowed access to a wealth of historical information and photographs; others connected with Cromer Lifeboat Station also assisted, including Peter Howard, the station's public relations officer; Richard Leeds, lifeboat operations manager; Richard Davies, ex-coxswain; and John Davies, current coxswain. Jenny Sheldrake, at the *Eastern Daily Press* in Norwich, helped with photographs. The staff at Norwich Millennium Library assisted with research in local records. For assistance with photographic material, many thanks to Tony Denton, Dave Gooch, Jeff Morris, Peter Edey, Philip Simons and Roger Wiltshire.

Nicholas Leach
Paul Russell
December 2003

A stained-glass window in Cromer Church is one of many lifeboat-related items in the town celebrating the work of the lifeboat. It was installed in the mid-1960s, and features the Henry Blogg *and* William Henry and Mary King *lifeboats. (Paul Russell)*

1

A Dangerous Coast

The lifeboat station at Cromer was established through a combination of different factors: the geographical location of the town on the Norfolk coastline, the physical dangers of the seas off that coastline and the growth in the number of vessels using those seas all played a part, as did the presence of the necessary finance and an organising group in the town. In considering the geographical location, the coastline around Cromer is dominated by sandy beaches and soft clay cliffs that offer little resistance to the North Sea, the force of which is constantly changing the shape of the coastline. As the sea gradually reclaims land, anything that stands in its way is under threat. Some villages, such as Shipden, which stood to the north-east of Cromer during the Middle Ages, have been completely swallowed by the sea. Originally, Shipden was the beach landing place for the area, but the land on which its buildings stood was eroded between the twelfth and mid-sixteenth centuries so the area now lies about 400m offshore under the North Sea.

Cromer was first mentioned as a town in 1262, but an inland one. With the coastal erosion and the disappearance of Shipden, the shoreline reached the foot of Cromer's cliffs and in-shore fishing became the mainstay for the local people. During the sixteenth century, constant efforts were made to keep a pier and harbour in working order. A description of the area dating from 1536 stated that Cromer's inhabitants 'endeavoured at great cost to maintain a small harbour... but in vain'. By 1565, householders in Cromer numbered 117, of whom forty-eight were mariners or fishermen. In 1582, the people of Cromer were granted permission by Queen Elizabeth I to export 20,000 quarters of wheat, barley, and malt for the upkeep of their town, and towards the rebuilding of an 'ould decayed peere' there.

Although coal was brought ashore, Cromer was not engaged in trading on a large scale due to, as a contemporary observer explained, 'there being no convenient harbour where ships might ride in safety'. Between the beginnings of the coal trade in the late thirteenth century and the coming of the railways, collier brigs and round-bilged vessels of between sixty and 100 tons would drive ashore on a flood tide on the beach to unload. The coal was taken by horse-drawn wagons up tracks cut in the cliffs and distributed around the villages in the immediate hinterland. As the industrial revolution gathered pace in the eighteenth century, the number of small colliers bringing coal from north-east England increased. A number of merchants prospered from the coal trade, including Henry Sandford, owner of both a coal yard at the top of the gangway and the coal ship *Commerce*, and Jeremiah Cross, of Overstrand, whose coal yard in Brook Street was supplied by his ship *Wensleydale*.

The landing of coal on the beach stopped almost overnight when the first railway came to Cromer. The East Norfolk Railway from Norwich reached North Walsham in 1874 and the extension to Cromer opened in March 1877, connecting the town with the Great Eastern's main lines to London Liverpool Street. Although the coal trade had ended, the townsfolk found a new way of making a living as Cromer became a fashionable health resort and the town consequently prospered. The *Encyclopaedic* magazine of 1803 published a letter praising the town's qualities as a resort: 'In no bathing place in England is a temporary abode more reasonable than in Cromer.' Expansion continued throughout the nineteenth century with the development of the sea front, pier and promenade, as well as the construction of many hotels. Cromer grew from 676 inhabitants in 1801 to 1,272 in 1836 and by the end of the century the population had reached 3,781.

The two most prominent pieces of architecture in Cromer are the pier and the church. The first record of a pier or jetty at Cromer dates from the late fourteenth century when, to pay for the structure, Richard III granted powers to exact duties on merchandise being landed. By the middle of the eighteenth century a wooden jetty had been built, and this was replaced in 1845 by one consisting of stone, constructed at a cost of £7,000. This jetty was wrecked when a collier rammed it in 1897 and so in 1900 work on a new pier began. Built by Alfred Thorne of Westminster, it was officially opened on 8 June 1901 and was intended originally for passenger paddle steamers calling from London. Since they ceased calling, it became an attraction in its own right and is still popular today. In the centre of the town the Church of St Peter and St Paul dominates the town and the sea, with its tower, standing 160ft tall, making it by far the most prominent building.

While the town of Cromer was developing so was the nation's industry, and the east coast had become an extremely busy shipping lane as the most direct line of communication between the important industrial centres in the north-east and the thriving capital. During the industrial expansion that took place between 1750 and 1850, trade was dominated by the movement of coal from the north-east ports of Newcastle and Sunderland to London. In 1779-1784, forty per cent of coastal shipping was devoted to coal carriage. In fact, the coal trade was the largest single activity of coastal shipping for much of the nineteenth century. As well as coal, vessels carrying a variety of commodities crowded the North Sea shipping lanes using the channels along the Norfolk and Suffolk coasts. It was not an uncommon sight in the nineteenth century to see hundreds of vessels moored in Yarmouth Roads ready to enter port. An eyewitness account from 1838 stated that as many as 3,000 ships could often be seen at anchor in the Roads. Such a huge expansion in the number of ships, all at the mercy of wind and waves, inevitably meant an increase in the number of lives lost at sea.

During the early years of the eighteenth century, the dangers of the seas off East Anglia were evident to Daniel Defoe, who commented that, 'the sea-side on this coast... is particularly famous for being one of the most dangerous and most fatal to the sailors in

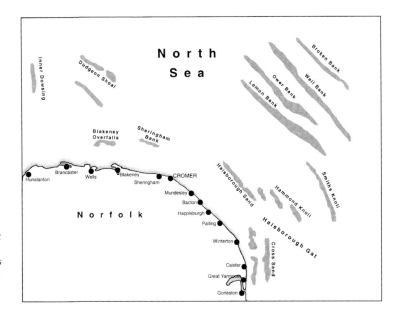

The coast of Norfolk showing the places from which lifeboats have been operated, together with the outlying sandbanks.

all England, I may say in all Britain; and the more so, because of the great number of ships which are continually going and coming this way, in their passage between London and all the northern coasts of Great Britain'. Unsurprisingly, wrecks were all too common. As early as 1692, a fleet of 200 colliers was caught in a storm off Winterton, to the north of Caister. Unable to turn for the safety of Yarmouth, 140 were driven ashore and smashed to pieces with as many as 1,000 lives lost. Such events prompted Defoe, on a visit to Cromer in 1724, to call the area 'The Devil's Throat'. On New Year's Day 1779, forty-one vessels were wrecked on the sands near Great Yarmouth with significant loss of life. During a storm on 30 October 1789, when eighty fishing boats were lost between Yarmouth and Cromer, 120 bodies washed ashore. And in February 1836 another storm claimed no fewer than twenty-three vessels, which were stranded on Yarmouth beach alone, and these were just some of the many ships wrecked at this point of the coast.

The natural dangers of the seas off East Anglia, and Norfolk in particular, were considerable. Inshore, the process of longshore drift affected the coast of East Anglia by shifting sand and other material along it, causing the mouths of rivers such as the Yare to silt up and beaches to disappear. Offshore, the area is characterised by a series of sand ridges running parallel to the coast, in between which are relatively deep channels that offer safe passage for shipping. These shipping channels today are artificially marked, but centuries ago sandbanks hidden beneath the sea presented a serious danger to the unwary mariner. To the south of Cromer and thirteen miles offshore, lies the notorious Haisborough Sand with Hammond Knoll nearby. Further offshore and to the south of Hammond Knoll is the Cross Sand, a long bank divided into the North, Middle and South Cross Sands. Between and around these banks are navigable channels, deviating from which would usually prove fatal to vessels. The ever shifting nature of these sandbanks makes them notoriously difficult and hazardous to navigate.

While the East Anglian coast and the seas off that coast were dangerous, small coasting vessels of the nineteenth century, often unseaworthy, contributed to their own demise. Not only were they reliant upon and at the mercy of weather, wind and tide, but many were operated by inexperienced crews who found navigation difficult, a problem compounded by the inaccuracy of charts. Passing sandbanks was fraught with difficulties, particularly at night when the exact position of known hazards could not be determined with any degree of certainty. The perils of the sandbanks off the East Anglian coast, combined with poor navigation systems, badly maintained ships and winter storms produced a situation in which many boats were lost. Yet despite their dangers, the sandbanks off East Anglia had to be negotiated as they bounded the important trade routes. With shipping being the main method of transporting goods, eighteenth- and nineteenth-century shipowners and masters suffered when their ships were wrecked with a heavy loss of both crews and cargoes. Contending with these problems brought about the introduction of several safety measures, including improvements in navigation as well as the establishment of lifeboats.

The first attempts to improve the safety of ships at sea involved the construction of beacons and lighthouses to mark the major navigational hazards. Navigation was difficult during the day, but seafarers could keep in sight of land and be fairly sure of their position, particularly if they were familiar with a route such as that between the Tyne and the Thames. Approaching Norfolk, however, particularly when southbound, was particularly hazardous, and so lighthouses were established at Hunstanton, Cromer, Happisburgh and Winterton, with floating lightvessels marking the major sandbanks off the coast.

The first lighthouse to be built in Cromer was one of five paid for by Sir John Clayton in 1669. He chose a site at Foulness, a headland just to the east of Cromer long since washed away, but due to the fact that shipowners refused to pay him any money the fire was never lit. Help for seafarers was, however, provided by a beacon lit on a column attached to the church tower, which served as the main light up until 1719. Then George I issued letters patent to the owner of the land at Foulness to maintain a lighthouse and so Nathaniel Life, a merchant and shipmaster, and Edward Bowell organised the construction, by Edward Browne of Ipswich, of an octagonal brick tower which gave out its first light in September 1719. Life and Bowell were empowered to raise dues of one farthing per ton on general cargo and a half penny per chauldron (1.25 imperial tons) on Newcastle coal.

As with all lighthouses of the time, it was lit by coal fires enclosed by glazings. But coal was a far from satisfactory method of illumination: not only was it both time consuming and hard work for keepers to maintain a continuous flame, but the open fires were also extremely dangerous. By 1792, the tower passed to the control of Trinity House, the body responsible for lighthouses in England and Wales, who installed a three-sided revolving optic which had fifteen reflectors and lamps. Although this improved the light's range, the position of the tower was in danger from successive landslips in 1799, January 1825 and August 1832. The latter fall was so considerable as 'to cause serious apprehensions for the safety of the Lighthouse itself' and as this site at Foulness was clearly untenable, it was abandoned. Further cliff falls in 1866 led to the tower slipping into the sea.

With the light under threat, the master and elder brethren of Trinity House had a new tower erected 400 yards inland in 1833, which remains standing and in use today. The tower, unusual on England's east coast in being masonry-built, is 52ft in height and about 250ft above sea level. When built, the lantern was lit by thirty lamps in three divisions placed in plated copper reflectors, giving a range of about twenty-seven miles. In 1905, a spur was taken from the town's gas supply and a new brighter light was provided. Thirty years later, the light was converted to electricity and in 1958 full electrification took place. In June 1990 the lighthouse became fully automated, controlled from Harwich.

But, despite the building of lighthouses and improvements in navigation, vessels continued to be wrecked with the consequent loss of crews and cargoes. Various remedies were proposed during the early years of the nineteenth century, one of the more practical of which was the use of a mortar to fire a line to a vessel in distress. As ships were often stranded close enough to the shore for a mortar line to reach them, such a scheme was viable. The main proponent of the mortar was Captain George William Manby, a Norfolk resident with a military background, who wrote extensively on a wide range of subjects, including shipwrecks. In February 1807 he witnessed the grounding and wreck

Cromer lighthouse, pictured in 1926. The white, eight-sided stone tower was built by Trinity House in 1832. (By courtesy of P.A. Vicary)

Above: *Cromer lighthouse after the new keeper's house had been built and with golfers completing the scene. (By courtesy of P.A. Vicary)*

Right: *The Haisborough lightvessel, pictured in 1934. The lightvessel was stationed at the Haisborough Sands and warned vessels of danger, and also often helped the local lifeboats by informing crews of the positions of casualties. At times, the lifeboats would assist the lightvessel's crew by bringing ashore injured or sick men. (By courtesy of P.A. Vicary)*

of the gunboat *Snipe* at the mouth of Great Yarmouth harbour, when sixty-seven men lost their lives. After seeing this tragedy, he began developing and improving the lifesaving mortar using knowledge of artillery he had acquired during his military service.

After experimenting with various weights of shot, he finally adopted a 5.5-in brass mortar which projected a 24lb shot carrying a 1.5-in rope about 200 yards, even against the wind. The mortar and wooden bed weighed 3cwt and could be carried on a specially built cart. The mortar was generally successful in helping to save lives from shipwreck and was used at various points along the East Anglian coast. In August 1810, Manby organised a series of experiments on the beach at Cromer, showing 'his newly-constructed grapple-shot, attached to a line, from a mortar, for the purpose of giving relief to vessels in distress on a lee-shore, and where the sea washes up far upon it, or a distance from land', as explained by the *Norfolk Chronicle & Norwich Gazette*. The advantage of his invention, as the newspaper went on to report, was that 'a more instantaneous communication may be formed with the vessel, and pilots conveyed with certainty and dispatch, when every other effort is impractical; thereby the lives of our brave seamen preserved; and the valuable property of our merchants and owners rescued from destruction'. As shall be seen in the following chapter, Manby's mortar proved useful on a number of occasions and the saving of several lives can be attributed to its successful deployment.

2

Establishing a Lifeboat Station

The establishment of a lifeboat at Cromer should be seen in the context of Britain's nascent industrialisation. During the half century between the 1770s and the 1820s, as the country's industrial growth was beginning in earnest, the foundations of Britain's lifeboat service were laid as a number of places, many on the east coast, found sufficient money to fund and operate a lifeboat. The Cromer boat was one of a number placed on the east coast at this time as part of the first organised attempts to help ships and seafarers in difficulty. Although the first recorded lifeboat was at Formby, in Lancashire, and was set up and financed by the Liverpool Docks Commissioners during the 1770s, the Cromer boat's origins lay on the east coast. Here, the fastest growing port was Newcastle where the first boat designed specifically for lifesaving was built. This boat was constructed by local boatbuilder Henry Greathead in 1790 at South Shields, on the south bank of the mouth of the river Tyne, and operated from there for several decades. A second boat was built by Greathead in 1798 and stationed at North Shields.

During the first decade of the nineteenth century, Lloyd's insurance agency in London set up a fund which encouraged the building and operating of lifeboats to counter ship losses. This fund provided an impetus to early lifeboat building, and helped to pay for almost thirty lifeboats up to the 1820s, including the first lifeboat in Norfolk, which was placed at Gorleston in 1802. This boat, built the previous year by Greathead for Lowestoft and of the same type as that developed for the north-east coast, was not well suited to the conditions prevalent on East Anglia's coast. Consequently, it was disliked by the beachmen who were to form the crew, was never used, and in 1807 was sold. Although this first lifeboat was something of a failure, subsequent efforts to provide lifeboats elsewhere in Norfolk were more successful.

Vessels on the busy east-coast trade route could often be seen from the cliffs at Cromer, and it was a desire to help when they got into difficulty that led the local townsfolk to buy a lifeboat. But the idea for the first lifeboat came not from the failed operations at Lowestoft and Gorleston but from Bawdsey, in Suffolk, where the newly built lifeboat (another of Greathead's North Country boats) had successfully saved eight lives from the brig *Pallas* in February 1804. The achievements of this lifeboat persuaded a number of Cromer townsfolk to start a fundraising drive to pay for a lifeboat for their town, and these efforts came to fruition in October 1804 when the following notice appeared in various local newspapers, including the *Norwich Mercury* and the *Norfolk Chronicle & Norwich Gazette*:

LIFE BOAT

Those Gentlemen, Visitants and Inhabitants of Cromer and the Neighbourhood, who wish to encourage the establishment of a Life Boat, are requested to meet at the Hotel, at Cromer, on Wednesday, the 31st instant, at twelve o'clock precisely, when some further particulars will be laid before them, and Resolutions to promote the object submitted to their consideration. N.B. Two of Greathead's publications, describing the Life Boat and its success, are left at Leak's Library, at Cromer, for the use and information of the Town and Neighbourhood.

During the meeting, which took place at the New Inn, Tucker Street, on 31 October 1804 with the Honourable Colonel W.A. Harbord in the chair, a letter from Reverend Frank Alderton was read out in which he described the qualities of the lifeboat at Bawdsey and stated he was 'happy to have it in my power to give testimony to the excellence of it.' Discussions centred around the most suitable part of the north-east coast of Norfolk on which to establish a lifeboat and how best to fund it. A number of resolutions were passed relating to the manning, funding and maintenance of the lifeboat once it had been procured. These were subsequently reported in the *Norfolk Chronicle & Norwich Gazette* as follows:

> 1st.   That from the danger of the coast, the command of experienced seamen, and the undoubted utility of a Life Boat in cases of imminent distress at sea, it appears highly desirable to establish one at Cromer.
>
> 2nd. That from accounts laid before this meeting it appears, that the sum necessary to complete the establishment in the first instance will not exceed three hundred pounds, but that it will be expedient to raise a further sum of at least as much more, to form a fund for annual and occasional outgoings.
>
> 3rd.   That a subscription be immediately opened for the accomplishment of the above humane and worthy purpose, and promoted throughout the county as a matter of general interest.
>
> 4th.   That the following Gentlemen be appointed a Committee to solicit and receive subscriptions, and when a sufficient sum is raised, to order a Life Boat from the inventor. And that the said Committee do meet at the Hotel at Cromer, at twelve o'clock precisely, on Monday the 12th day of November, viz.

Right Hon. Lord Suffield	Mr F. Bartell
Hon. Colonel Harbord	Capt. Tremlett
Rev. Leo Doughty Esq.	Mr. Thomas Mickleburgh
Rev. Dr. Gardiner	Captain Ransome
George Wyndham Esq.	Rev. Edward Edwards
John Gay Esq.	Rev. Robert Hankinson
Richard Gurney Esq.	Mr. Joseph Gurney
Major Petre	Mr. B. Rust
Rev. Paul Johnson	Mr. John Eldred

> With power to add to their number.
>
> 5th.   That the above Committee be also empowered to take the entire management of the Fund, of the Boat and its appurtenances, to order the necessary Boat-house, Carriages etc and to reward the exertions of the seamen agreeable to the hazard run, and the alacrity shown in cases of danger.

The meeting ended with thanks being given 'to the Chairman for his impartial attention to the business, and his humane endeavour to promote the object of the Meeting'. A Committee was then formed to administer the subscription fund, to order a lifeboat when sufficient funds were available and subsequently manage the lifeboat itself. At its head were Lord Suffield, the third baron of Gunton Park, George Wyndham of Cromer Hall, Thomas Mickleburgh, a local merchant, Joseph Gurney and Benjamin Rust, a Cromer draper and grocer. And so the first tentative steps towards providing Cromer with a lifeboat had been taken.

Within two weeks of the meeting, ambitious plans had been made by the newly constituted organising Committee. These intentions, reported in the *Norfolk Chronicle & Norwich Gazette*, revolved around providing lifeboats at several points along the Norfolk coast. The newspaper stated 'that a Life-Boat at Cromer is only the commencement of a plan, which has for its object, similar establishments on the most dangerous parts of the Norfolk coast; and as far as the fund will admit, it is proposed to have Life-Boats placed on other exposed situations, to the eastward and westward of Cromer'. Raising money was the main hurdle to be overcome before such a plan could be completed, but the report remained optimistic in its tone :

> …when an appeal is made to the benevolence of this county, on behalf of so humane and important an object, the most sanguine expectations are entertained of adequate encouragement. The utility of the Life-Boat has been fully confirmed; and there is great reason to expect and believe that every subscriber to this establishment will contribute to save the valuable lives of many brave seamen.

This intention was, as will be seen in the next section, almost two decades ahead of its time.

Raising the necessary funds to buy the lifeboat for Cromer seems to have been achieved relatively fast, reflecting the prosperity of Cromer at the time. By the end of November 1804, £442 5s 6d had been subscribed to which was added, during the first three weeks of December, a further £200. By January 1805, a total of £734 12s 0d had been collected, enabling an order to be placed with Greathead for one of his lifeboats. The Committee must have either overlooked or ignored the fact that the design was unpopular with the beachmen of Gorleston and Lowestoft, no doubt preferring to focus on the success of the boat at Bawdsey. This first lifeboat was of the North Country design, double-ended, probably 25ft long by 8ft 6in broad, clinker built and rowing ten oars on thole pins. She was probably delivered early in 1805, as an entry in the *Newcastle Courant* dated 6 April 1805 stated that 'Lifeboats had lately been sent by the inventor [Henry Greathead] to the stations at Cromer and Leith'. The boat could have been either towed or delivered as deck cargo on one of the many colliers plying the east coast at the time. By the summer the boat was at Cromer and on 20 July 1805 a meeting of the subscribers was held at the New Inn to discuss the state of the fund and further regulations for the future management of the boat with W.A. Harbord as chairman.

The first Cromer lifeboat went out on service at least five times – details of any further launches were not recorded – before being transferred to Wells in 1830. During the first five years of its existence, no rescues are recorded in which it took part, but it was involved in the trials Manby undertook with his line-throwing mortar in August 1810. With many onlookers present, including members of the Lifeboat Committee, the mortar was used

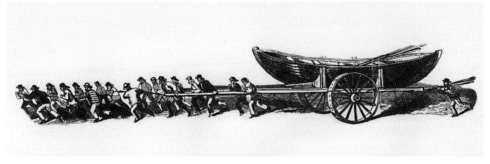

A contemporary drawing of the North Country lifeboat, the type brought to Cromer in 1804 by the local committee. The two-wheeled trolley was not supplied with the boat and no record of any launching device has been found, indicating that the boat was probably dragged and manhandled across the beach for launching.

Above: *'A Perspective View of Mr H. Greathead's Life Boat going out to assist a Ship in Distress'. This drawing, dated 1802, was produced using the model presented by Greathead to the Admiralty, and shows a boat similar to that used for a quarter of a century at Cromer. The double-ended boat with a rockered keel would have been well suited to going through the surf off the beach at Cromer.*

Above: *A model of Cromer's first lifeboat, a 25ft craft pulling ten oars with a rockered keel, probably well suited to the surf conditions encountered off the beach. (Poppyland Photographs).*

to fire a grapple and line across a rope more than 200 yards out at sea where, for the purposes of the exercise, an imaginary vessel was in trouble. The lifeboat was then launched from its carriage and rowed to the spot where the supposed vessel in distress lay. These trials were deemed a success and a contemporary account praised the 'Committee for the support and management of the Cromer life-boat'. At the same time, a request was made to Manby to devise 'a method... for getting the life-boat to and from the sea with facility and ease', reflecting the difficulties encountered when launching the lifeboat from the exposed, open beach, a problem that faced successive generations of Cromer lifeboatmen.

The mortar was employed to good effect in November 1810, after a small vessel came ashore at Trimingham during a north-easterly gale. The commander of the signal station there, Lieutenant Infield, requested the mortar equipment from Cromer, which was quickly despatched on a cart by Henry Sandford, a local merchant and member of the Lifeboat Committee. With the waves crashing around the casualty, the mortar was set up and a shot was fired. The first one missed but the second fell across the wreck's rigging and, by the means of a heavy hawser, four of the crew were saved. Within half an hour of their being brought ashore, the vessel broke up.

One of the lifeboat's earliest services – the first of which evidence has been found – took place the day after the mortar had been used so effectively at Trimingham in November 1810. A north-easterly gale had raged unabated throughout the night and when the brig *Anna*, of Sunderland, went ashore between Cromer and Runton, the lifeboat was called out. A report in *The Norfolk Chronicle & Norwich Gazette* described events: 'as soon as it was known at the former place [Cromer] the brave fellows there launched the Lifeboat and, buffeting the billows of a tremendous sea, with exertions that call for the highest praise, succeeded in saving the crew consisting of about fourteen hands and a woman passenger'. On 12 November, in response to the two incidents, a meeting of the Lifeboat Committee was held at Cromer's New Inn when rewards were made to those involved in the rescues. The Committee also considered 'other business for the encouragement of these useful establishments', and although details of their discussions are lacking, it is most likely that the funding of a lifeboat for Mundesley, a small village situated between Cromer and Happisburgh, was high on the agenda.

The Committee was aware that on the same night when such good work had been performed by the Cromer lifeboat, another brig, also named *Anna*, of South Shields, had been wrecked near Mundesley and nothing could be done to help her because of the strength of the seas. The vessel went to pieces and all ten of her crew were drowned. The Committee resolved that a lifeboat should be obtained for the village when funds permitted, and a subscription drive began. A small beach boat was fitted up temporarily as a lifeboat until a local subscription, organised by Joseph Gurney of Norwich and supplemented by a grant from Lloyds, enabled the first lifeboat to be obtained in March 1811. The boat, of the North Country type and built in Sunderland, pulling ten oars, 26ft 8in by 9ft 4in, was kept in a boathouse and initially managed by the Cromer Committee. It was used for probably the first time in 1819, going to the aid of *Endeavour*, of Sunderland, and a number of other vessels which had been driven into shallow water.

Meanwhile, the lifeboat at Cromer remained idle for a number of years and by 1819 was reported as not having been used 'in years'. It seems likely that the service of November 1810 was the only one undertaken during its first eighteen years but fortunately suggestions that it be sent elsewhere were ignored as during the 1820s it was employed on a number of occasions. The lifeboat seems to have retained a high profile as a result of demonstrations to the public held during the summer season. The *Norfolk Chronicle & Norwich Gazette* of 6 September 1823 announced that during the following week, 'the Life-boat will be exercised [and] several experiments will be made with the gun intended to throw a shot with a rope affixed to a vessel in distress'. Accordingly, on 11 September, both the Cromer and Mundesley Lifeboats, together with the mortar for firing shots to shipwrecks and the rocket invented by Mr Hase of Saxthorpe, were brought to the town which 'early in the day thronged with company of the most remarkable kind'.

On 31 October 1823, during a terrible gale, no fewer than 100 vessels were either grounded or sunk between Hull and Cromer. The lifeboat was used in a fruitless attempt to assist the coal-carrying brig *Duchess of Cumberland*, of Newcastle, which had gone ashore during the afternoon near the lighthouse in the 'tremendous hurricane'. Two mortars were brought to the cliffs as close to the brig as possible, but because the brig was too far from the shore the mortars' lines failed to reach her. The lifeboat, manned by Henry Sandford and a crew of sixteen, was launched but could not get close to the casualty, 'as the violence of the wind and fury of the waves rendered all human efforts unavailing', a subsequent report stated. The brig's captain and one of her crew took to their boat but this was soon overwhelmed and both men drowned. Within two hours of coming ashore, the vessel had gone to pieces and her crew was thrown into the sea. Two reached the shore, aided by 'the vigorous and most intrepid assistance of the spectators, many of whom plunged fearlessly into the water, and narrowly escaped being washed away or much hurt', but the rest drowned. Later the same day, at about 8 p.m., another brig, *Esther*, of Shields, in ballast, also went ashore opposite the town but this time the lifeboat succeeded in saving the crew of twelve.

The Norfolk Association

The stationing of the lifeboat at Mundesley meant that two lifeboats were operated under the auspices of one body, a significant step forward in the Cromer Committee's goal of an organised lifeboat service. During the 1820s, further developments took place as Lord Suffield, a leading member of the Cromer Committee, realised the need for 'an association for preserving the lives of shipwrecked mariners on the whole line of the coast of Norfolk', funded independently of the beachmen but relying on the beachmen for manning and operating. Suffield clearly recognised the need for such an organisation having witnessed at first hand the dreadfulness of shipwrecks, even, it is claimed, to the extent of seeing a corpse washed ashore while helping to save a ship aground at Bacton. As a result of Suffield's efforts, the Norfolk Association for Saving the Lives of Shipwrecked Mariners (Norfolk Association for short) was founded at a meeting in Norwich in November 1823. This Association took over the stations at Cromer and Mundesley and, at a meeting in December 1823, proposed to station further lifeboats at Great Yarmouth, Winterton, Blakeney, Burnham Overy or Brancaster, and Hunstanton. Lifesaving mortars were to go to Winterton Cross Light, Bacton, Runton, Salthouse, Blakeney Hood and Hunstanton.

While the Association was partially successful in achieving its stated aims, the lifeboat at Cromer remained ready to assist ships in distress, and was involved in at least two further rescues during the 1820s. In its edition of 23 October 1824, the *Norfolk Chronicle & Norwich Gazette* described the events ten days earlier when the brig *Equity*, of Scarborough, on passage from Cardiff to Newcastle with a cargo of iron, came ashore near the Cromer light, late in the evening in a north-east gale and heavy rain. As soon as the vessel had grounded, Mr Buxton, Mr Hoare jnr and Dr Lushington, 'prompted by that humanity for which they are so eminently distinguished', ran to the beach and organised the fishermen to launch the lifeboat. At the same time, the Overstrand Gun was brought to the beach, and a line was successfully fired between the masts of the vessel. As the foremast had been washed away, the line was carried by the wind over the bow of the vessel. The lifeboat then reached the brig and succeeded in saving one man from it but unfortunately got damaged during the rescue and was forced to return to the beach. A large fishing boat was then launched and brought the rest of the brig's crew, seven in number, safely ashore. The newspaper account ended by stating, 'Great praise is due to the Cromer and Overstrand fishermen for their prompt exertions.'

Almost exactly a year later, the lifeboat's services were again called upon. On 21 October 1825, the ship *Liberty*, of Boston, with a cargo of oats from London, came ashore near Cromer during the morning in a north-easterly gale that had whipped up seas. In going to the aid of the crew, which consisted of a master and two others, the lifeboat was, according to the *Norfolk Chronicle & Norwich Gazette*, 'very quickly into the water, well manned, and managed with great skill and courage, and the men were soon safely landed; the cargo is preserved though much damaged by the salt water; but the vessel is so much injured that there is little chance of her ever getting off again'.

On 30 August 1826, a meeting of the Norfolk Association was held at Cromer for what seems to have been a kind of early publicity day for the trials were certainly more for the benefit of the spectators than anything else. However, it appears that the idea of raising funds at the event was not uppermost in the minds of the Committee members who, together with several of the subscribers and friends of the Association, gathered on the beach at about 12 p.m. to witness the proceedings. Others had congregated at various vantage points to watch as the mortar apparatus and lifeboat were put through their paces. Firstly, the apparatus was inspected by the Committee members and then a series of experiments were held under the supervision of the preventive service. Shots were fired from the Runton and Mundesley mortars, and the lifeboat was launched with, according to the *Norfolk Chronicle & Norwich Gazette*, 'a view of promoting the object of the day and contributing to the amusement of those collected to witness the experiments'.

Captain Southey, the commanding officer at the local Preventative station, authorised the launch of two of his boats so that a trial could take place between them and the lifeboat. They rowed a considerable distance along the coast and, although the Preventative men had a speedier craft, the lifeboat was 'evidently manned with able seamen' as the newspaper recounted. The next part of the trials involved positioning the lifeboat 200 yards offshore and the mortar then fired two shots carrying a rope to her. Once communication had been established between those in the boat and the men on the beach, five men were hauled from the lifeboat to the beach, 'being supported in safely by the copper collars; the great utility of which was thus manifested'. The experiments were directed by Mr Wheatley and all agreed they had been 'very successful and well managed'. Afterwards, the Committee and some of the subscribers – no doubt members of the local gentry, clergy and other notable townsfolk – dined at the New Inn. It seems unlikely that any of the lifeboat's crew or mortar apparatus team were invited.

Although the lifeboat was apparently in good condition, within four years of the trials it had been replaced by a new and improved boat. On 17 August 1830, a meeting of the District Committee of the Norfolk Association was held with the Committee reportedly awaiting 'the arrival of the new Life Boat which is now in building for this station, the original Cromer Life Boat having been removed to Wells, where she has been approved of and thought better calculated for that harbour (where the Association during the last year has established another station) than the Cromer Beach'.

The second lifeboat, which like her predecessor remained unnamed, was kept on the beach at the bottom of a chine close to where the present lifeboat museum is situated. Her design closely resembled that of the first Greathead lifeboat as local builders around the river Tyne had copied Greathead's basic design lifeboat since the early nineteenth century. Reported to have cost £160, she was built by Robson of Shields, was 31ft in length with a beam of 9ft 6ins, a depth of 3ft 9ins, and rowed twelve oars. She was, like the first lifeboat, clinker built but had an airtight deck, cork inside and 'a great sheer between stem and stern'; it was possibly modified later with relieving tubes. This lifeboat was involved in at least four services, the first of which took place in February 1836 during a severe gale which battered the Norfolk coast. On 18 February the ship *Trent*, of North Shields, was wrecked and swept ashore at Cromer on 19 February. At about 10 a.m. five of her crew made for the shore in a boat but this was immediately swamped and they were drowned. The lifeboat put out to help and succeeded in saving the master and remaining crewmen.

Just over three years later the lifeboat was again called into action. At daybreak on 28 October 1839, the collier brig *Achilles*, of South Shields, bound for London with a cargo of coal, was seen in distress about seven miles from Cromer, her main and foretop masts having been carried away. The lifeboat was immediately launched with Captain Francis Pank, a local master mariner, and Mr Simons, proprietor of the Bath House, helping to make up the crew. She proceeded through very heavy surf to the casualty and after nearly two hours reached the vessel. After boarding her, the lifeboat crew succeeded in bringing her to anchor off Cromer and landed the eight men. At first light the following day, the

The Norfolk Shipwreck Association's Silver medal, awarded to Francis Pank, a local master mariner, for his part in the rescue of the collier brig Achilles *in October 1839 when he was injured. (Poppyland Photographs)*

lifeboatmen attempted to pump the vessel out but the sea was so rough that, despite their best efforts, the brig sank. During this operation, one of the Cromer men, Henry Nockels, was washed overboard but fortunately he grabbed a rope and was hauled back onto the vessel. Captain Pank was also injured when he fell between the lifeboat and the brig.

Despite the dangers involved in the work of lifesaving, the lifeboat was again in action just a few days later. On 1 November 1839, it launched to the Dutch galliot *Elizabeth Jacobi Tromp*, carrying oak timber from Memel in the Baltic to Harlingen, which was in difficulties. The lifeboat reached her just as she ran ashore on the beach and despite heavy seas saved the crew of seven as well as most of the cargo, which was subsequently stored in Mr Sandford's coal yard, but the vessel went to pieces. A contemporary report described events as the rescued men were landed:

> Great praise is due to the Cromer fishermen for their alacrity in manning the lifeboat, and we rejoice to say with such good success… An immense crowd of persons assembled on the beach to witness the landing of the boat… to witness the rescue of their fellow creatures.

In the 1840s the lifeboat was involved in the Yarmouth North Roads Regattas, during which trials of lifeboats were held. It seems that the crew was willing to row to and from Great Yarmouth for these events, quite a considerable feat given the distance. In 1845 the lifeboat was involved in a series of trials of the lifeboats 'stationed along the dangerous coast of Norfolk and Suffolk, with their hardy, intrepid, and vigorous crews', as *The Norfolk Chronicle & Norwich Gazette* for 29 July 1845 reported. Sailing lifeboats came from Great Yarmouth, Lowestoft, Pakefield, Southwold and Bacton, with pulling lifeboats from Sheringham, Cromer, Mundesley, Winterton, and Caister involved. While the sailing lifeboats were pitted against one another in a series of different tests of their capabilities, the crews of the pulling boats were tested in their skill at weighing anchor, coiling cables, manning the oars, and anchoring with fifty fathoms of cable out. Of the pulling boats involved, the Cromer boat, 'considering her small number of hands compared with the Sheringham, proved the smartest, though this was a matter of some difficulty for the judges to decide'. In the end, both boats were judged as being equal in their class, and each crew received the first prize of £4, a considerable sum for the recipients. At this time, the Cromer lifeboat was clearly in fine order although in just over a decade this state of affairs had changed.

3
The National Institution Takes Over

During the early years of the station's existence, Cromer's lifeboats seem to have been well maintained. The second boat was mentioned in two contemporary surveys of lifeboats published in the mid-nineteenth century. The 1843 Parliamentary Report on shipwrecks stated that it was kept in a lifeboat house built 100 yards from the high water mark and ten yards from the Coastguard cottages. The Report of 1851, prepared for the Duke of Northumberland and which contained a survey of the lifeboat stations then in existence around the coast, including a brief description of lifesaving facilities at each, described the boat at Cromer as being 'in good repair, safe and pulls well'. However, despite these statements the financial position of the Norfolk Association seems to have been somewhat precarious. At the Regatta of 1845, in addition to the positive comments about the Cromer lifeboat's crew, difficulties were hinted at with the remark that, 'though crews are never wanting, subscriptions frequently are'. By the 1850s the financial troubles had worsened, making it increasingly difficult for the Norfolk Association to execute its duties. Many of its lifeboats had fallen into disrepair due to poor management and maintenance and it seems that, at Cromer, even organising a crew had become a problem. A correspondent writing in the *Norwich Mercury* in 1857 complained that the lifeboat had 'not been out of its house for three and a half years up to last August, and then it was only taken out at the earnest wish of some of the visitors staying there, and the expense subscribed by them'.

Matters regarding the poor operation of the lifeboat seem to have been brought to a head on 23 October 1857 when the fishermen were initially unwilling to provide assistance to a vessel which hoisted a signal of distress off Cromer. Once they had been offered a payment, however, they put out in the lifeboat, but before reaching the ship the wind calmed and the stranded vessel was able to free itself unaided. An anonymous letter published in the *Norwich Mercury* on 31 October 1857 described this incident and asked whether 'the brave Christian spirit that risks much to save others has... departed?' Practical matters, rather than the lack of a Christian spirit, were responsible for the lifeboat's failure to launch and these explain more plausibly the fishermen's reluctance to put out. The boat had not been launched for a 'considerable time', questions remained over whether she was seaworthy, and no organised crew existed, with no coxswain or other leading figure. It appears that the Norfolk Association's lack of money had led to a situation where no rewards were available to pay the fishermen to man the lifeboat. Presumably, the fishermen had agreed to serve hitherto on such an agreement, and when money was not forthcoming they withdrew their services.

The incident on October 1857, typical of many of the problems experienced at the Norfolk Association's stations during the 1850s, showed that improvements were urgently needed. With no finance and a lack of organisation, the Association began negotiations with the national body responsible for lifeboats, the Royal National Lifeboat Institution (RNLI), which resulted in the Association's lifeboats and stations being taken over with effect from 29 December 1857. The Association had founded and operated nine lifeboat stations in Norfolk: at Hunstanton, Wells, Blakeney, Cromer, Bacton, Palling, Winterton, Caister and Yarmouth. As these lifeboats were in rather a poor condition, the national body's first task was to put them into a more efficient state of readiness.

By the time it took over in Norfolk, the RNLI had been in existence for more than half a century. Founded in March 1824 at a meeting in London as the Royal National Institution for the Preservation of Life from Shipwreck (RNIPLS), it was responsible for 'the preservation of lives and property from shipwreck'. This encompassed the funding, building, operation, maintenance and organisation of lifeboats and lifeboat stations. Initially quite successful, the new organisation added to the number of lifeboats in operation but, by the 1840s, the organisation's efforts started to falter through lack of funds. The Institution found raising money for lifeboats difficult and enjoyed only limited success in providing a nationwide lifeboat service. Its annual income dwindled during the 1830s and 1840s until, by 1850, with no public appeals made for over a decade, the level of finance available to its Committee of Management was at its lowest level. Improvements were essential if lifesaving work around the coasts was to continue, but without funds this was impossible.

Improvements to the running of the National Institution started on 2 May 1851 with the appointment of Algernon, Duke of Northumberland as president. Through his energy and efforts during the 1850s, working alongside the newly appointed secretary Richard Lewis, much-needed improvements to the Institution were implemented. During the 1850s the body was renamed the Royal National Lifeboat Institution to more accurately reflect its aims and objectives, and it began to absorb the local lifesaving organisations that had sprung up in the preceding half century or so. This included Cromer and all the other stations established by the Norfolk Association.

At Cromer, the RNLI immediately decided to implement improvements, and in April 1858 a replacement for the old lifeboat, which was by then twenty-eight years old and unseaworthy, was ordered from Forrestt of Limehouse and a new carriage purchased from T. Gaze of Mundesley. These were both ready by the end of October 1858 and the lifeboat, 34ft in length, rowing twelve oars double-banked, was brought to Great Yarmouth free of charge by the General Steam Navigation Company. It was then rowed north to Cromer under the supervision of the district inspector. On 5 March 1860, the old Norfolk Association boat and its carriage were sold at public auction for £15 5s 0d. When the inspector took the new boat afloat on exercise in November, he reported that it rowed well, and he believed that the qualities of the new boat had helped to remove much of the prejudice held by the local crew against the self-righting lifeboat then in widespread use by the RNLI.

This first RNLI lifeboat, which remained unnamed, served at Cromer for only ten years, during which time she saved five lives and is credited with six launches on service. Before she had performed any rescues, however, an erroneous report in the London press indicated that she had been capsized. On 22 January 1863, *The Times* reported that 'an alarming report has obtained circulation here [Great Yarmouth] that the Cromer lifeboat has been lost with seventeen hands. It is stated that she went to the assistance of a disabled vessel and capsized through becoming entangled with her when alongside. It is earnestly to be hoped that this report may prove without foundation.' The report was, indeed, without foundation as the boat had not been at sea that day, though quite how this story reached the papers, or where such information came from, is not known.

On 21 July 1867, the sloop *Sutcliffe*, of Harwich, stranded about a mile to the south of Cromer in a north-east gale and very heavy sea, but the lifeboat could not put out immediately as she 'was in a dismantled state... in the course of being painted', according to *The Norfolk Chronicle & Norwich Gazette*. Meanwhile, nearly all the fishermen and boatmen went to the scene of the wreck, so that by the time the lifeboat had been made ready for use there was an insufficient number of boatmen available to man her and some difficulty was experienced in forming a crew. Amongst those who volunteered to go in place of the boatmen was the Honourable Auberon Herbert, brother of Lord Carnarvon. As soon as the boat was launched she was struck by a heavy sea, which broke four of her oars, and drove her nearly broadside on the beach. But some of the crew jumped out, squared the boat, and succeeded in getting her clear of the broken water. After a long pull through a very heavy sea, the lifeboat arrived at the wreck only to find that the stranded crew had already been saved by rocket apparatus. When this incident was discussed at a meeting of the RNLI's Committee of Management on 3 September 1867, a decision was made to award the Silver medal and a copy of its Vote Inscribed on Vellum to Herbert, 'in admiration of his gallant conduct in forming one of the crew of the Cromer lifeboat… when it was launched through a heavy surf'. Why none of the rest of the crew was deemed worthy of a similar award is not recorded.

The first of only two effective services performed by the first RNLI lifeboat took place on 3 December 1867. During the morning, the brig *Wild Rose*, of Brixham, was seen dismasted off Cromer in stormy weather. The lifeboat immediately put out to help, and arrived alongside the vessel to find her with only the mainmast and top mainmast standing, and her sails blown away. However, as the ship was strongly built she had not taken in much water and so, with the assistance of two steam tugs, was towed into Yarmouth. The second and final service of this lifeboat took place on 9 April 1868, just a few months before she was replaced, when she saved the crew of five of the brigantine *Agenoria*, of Lowestoft, which was wrecked opposite Cromer Gangway after failing to ride out a heavy north-easterly gale.

The Benjamin Bond Cabbell *lifeboats*

At the time of the service to *Agenoria*, the lifeboat had 'for some time exhibited signs of decay', according to *The Lifeboat** of 1 October 1869, and so a replacement was under construction. The new lifeboat was funded by Benjamin Bond Cabbell, of Cromer Hall, who, in November 1867, had agreed to provide for 'the whole expense of renovating the station'. He subsequently sent £1,000, which covered not only the cost of the new lifeboat but also a new boathouse, slipway and sea wall extension. The new lifeboat, another self-righter, arrived in August 1868 from Limehouse, on the Thames, where she had been built by Forrestt. She was a standard self-righter, 34ft in length with a beam of 8ft 8in, pulling ten oars double-banked. Her hull was built of Honduras mahogany, diagonally planked for extra strength.

A new lifeboat house had to be constructed to accommodate the new boat and a new site was found for this building. The first lifeboat house, in which the lifeboat was kept on 'a four double wheel sliding cradle', had been built by the Norfolk Association about 100 yards from the high-water mark and ten yards from the Coastguard cottages. On taking over the station in 1858, the RNLI altered and renovated the house at a cost of £46 2s 7d. In 1864 the inspector visited the station, found the house to be unsuitable and recommended that it be replaced. A new site was obtained at the East Gangway, but it was not until almost four years later that the new house was completed. Part of its construction involved building an extension to the sea wall with a slipway across the beach. Built by local builder E. Simmons, the new house cost £476 4s 0d. This house served the station until 1902, when a larger lifeboat was stationed at Cromer and a larger house built on the same site, described below. Various alterations were made to the house over the next few years, including, in 1872, the addition of a fence erected by J. Riches at a cost of £6 10s 0d to 'prevent nuisance'. Two years later, the retaining wall was damaged by an

---

* *The Lifeboat* is the official journal of the RNLI and was first published in 1852.

The first Benjamin Bond Cabbell *lifeboat about to be recarriaged on the East Beach. Built in 1868, she was a standard RNLI design of self-righting lifeboat.*

exceptionally high tide but was repaired at a cost of £39 15s 0d. Further alterations and improvements were made to the house in 1887, again in 1889, and gas was laid on in 1895. The old lifeboat house was demolished in 1884, having been used as a fisherman's lookout room and library during its final years.

The new lifeboat was officially named *Benjamin Bond Cabbell** after her donor at a ceremony on 4 September 1868. During the ceremony, Revd F. Fitch, vicar of Cromer, read a letter from the donor expressing his regret that due to poor health he was unable to present the new lifeboat and boathouse. The RNLI's inspector, Captain Ward, described the boat at length, proclaiming the merits of the self-righting design in a speech clearly aimed at those beachmen who continued to doubt its capability:

> Like all other boats now sent out by the Institution, it was a self-righting boat. When their former life-boat was first placed in their charge, that principle was ridiculed by many, and in some places, not far from Cromer, that principle was still subject to ridicule. But the institution had watched narrowly the working of the two classes of boats, and they had found that those which were not self-righting had lost eighteen out of every twenty that set foot in them, while those which were constructed on the self-righting principle had only lost one life out of every twenty-seven. Those facts perfectly satisfied the committee of management, in London, that the self-righting principle was the best, and they had accordingly stuck most determinedly to it.

The bishop of Norwich then delivered his address, after which the boat was christened by Miss Buxton, daughter of the Dowager Lady Buxton. The *Norfolk Chronicle & Norwich Gazette* reported the event, explaining that:

> The bottle was smashed into the minutest atoms, and this was the signal for a tremendous outburst of cheering on the part of all concerned… When the cheering had subsided, eight horses were hooked onto the transporting carriage, the drag ropes were seized by a willing

---

* This name is sometimes hyphenated as *Benjamin Bond-Cabbell.* The convention throughout this chapter omits the hyphen.

throng, and the Benjamin Bond Cabbell glided to the spot where she was first to touch the sea, on which it is to be hoped she may for years to come render good service.

And so, amidst such pomp and ceremony, the new lifeboat began her service career.

During her time on station, *Benjamin Bond Cabbell* was launched on service nine times and is credited with saving thirty-one lives. The lifeboat's first launch was somewhat routine in nature. On 22 October 1869, signals of distress were exhibited by a large full-rigged ship about two and a half miles to the north of Cromer. The lifeboat was launched and found the ship *William Fotheringham*, of New York, bound from the Baltic to Shields, and then to New York. She had gone aground during the gale, had 5ft of water in her hold, and a broken rudder made her unmanageable. The vessel and those on board, with the help of the Cromer lifeboat as well as the Sheringham Beachmens' lifeboat, were safely taken to Great Yarmouth harbour.

The lifeboat was not called upon again for more than five years. Then, on 9 April 1875, she was launched through a heavy surf to help the small steam tug *Vixen*, of Shields, which had been seen at anchor flying signals of distress. Attempts were made to help and so the lifeboat remained standing by her, assisting with pumping her out, until a powerful tug arrived from Great Yarmouth. *Vixen* was then taken in tow and brought to Yarmouth accompanied by the lifeboat whose crew, having been wet through for more than thirteen hours while providing their services, spent the night at Yarmouth Sailors' Home. They returned to Cromer with the lifeboat the following day.

During 1879 the lifeboat was called upon to perform two services which proved to be the last by the first *Benjamin Bond Cabbell*. On 10 April, she was launched during an easterly gale and rough seas to the sloop *Hesperus*, of Copenhagen, which had shown signals of distress about three miles from the lifeboat station. On reaching the vessel, it was found she was badly leaking and had lost her main boom. Some of the lifeboatmen boarded her and, with their assistance, she was taken to the safety of the Humber. Without the assistance of the lifeboat, the vessel would probably have been lost.

On 20 November 1879, rockets indicating a vessel was in difficulty were seen in the direction of Foulness Shoal, about two miles east of Cromer. At about 5.30 a.m. the lifeboat was launched in a heavy snowstorm and proceeded in the direction of the ship's lights. The tide was running against them and it was sometime before the lifeboat

The first Benjamin Bond Cabbell *lifeboat on the beach. She served until 1884 and saved thirty-one lives. (By courtesy of P.A. Vicary)*

The schooner Alpha *wrecked at East Runton in October 1883. Despite the lifeboat crew attempting to go to the schooner's aid, after the lifeboat launched she could make no headway, and as a result of the crew complaining about the inadequacy of the first* Benjamin Bond Cabbell, *a new lifeboat was sent to the station. (By courtesy of P.A. Vicary)*

reached the casualty, the steamship *Moidart*, of Glasgow, bound to Odessa with railway iron. The steamer, aground on the shoal, was being swamped by the sea washing over her, but as the tide flowed she floated off and was able to anchor in deep water, disabled without a rudder or part of her stern post. The ship's captain requested the lifeboat stand by until a tug had arrived from Yarmouth. The lifeboat stood by until about 12.30 p.m., when she had to leave because of the tide. However, a lookout was kept from the shore during the night as the gale increased and when daylight came the lifeboat was launched again and remained by the ship until steam tugs arrived.

Although she remained at Cromer for a further five years after this incident, the *Moidart* service proved to be the last performed by the first *Benjamin Bond Cabbell*. The circumstances which led to the building of a new boat centred around an incident on 4 October 1883, after the schooner *Alpha* had gone ashore in a heavy gale. The lifeboat was called out but, despite considerable efforts to row her to the stranded vessel, the lifeboatmen were unable to reach the casualty against the strong wind and tide. In the outcry that followed, blame was attached to the design of lifeboat rather than the crew. A more suitable type was needed and the feeling amongst the crew suggested that the self-righter was inadequate, as reported in the *Eastern Daily Press* on 8 October 1883:

> The Cromer fishermen are very dissatisfied with the lifeboat, and are complaining loudly about it. Their opinion is that she is not suitable for the requirements, being too heavy for the number of oars, and that it is impossible to row her against a strong wind. The boat is still lying on the beach where the men left her after several fruitless attempts to row her to the wreck.

Many of the crew strongly believed that the self-righter was unsuited to the conditions at Cromer and wanted a larger boat with a greater curvature of keel, which they argued would be more manoeuvrable, although not self-righting.

During the nineteenth century, with a number of quite different lifeboat designs available, it was common for the RNLI's Committee of Management to heed the preferences expressed by those who would man the boat when considering which design was most suited for a particular station. The crew's choice often decided what type of lifeboat a station would be sent, and so it was at Cromer where the crew wanted a boat 35ft in length, with a beam of 10ft and pulling fourteen oars, to be specially designed and built for their station. After a series of meetings during which the matter was thoroughly discussed, with Captain the Hon. H.W. Chetwynd, chief inspector of lifeboats, and Mr Prowse, the surveyor, both in attendance, a decision was made about the size and construction of a new boat. The fishermen, disregarding entirely the self-righting principle, wanted a boat similar to that stationed at Cromer prior to 1858 which, a local report stated, 'was a great favourite with the men, as many of the old fishermen testify'.

Once a general design for the new boat had been agreed, on 27 November 1883, Mr Prowse, surveyor of lifeboats, visited Cromer and discussed the specific size and form of the proposed new boat with the fishermen who were to form the crew. With 'leading fishermen' Mr James Davies, Mr James Mayes and Mr Thomas Blogg on hand, the following was agreed, as was reported in the *Norfolk Chronicle & Norwich Gazette*:

> …it should have the same rack of stem and stern-post as the model which is said to represent the original Cromer lifeboat; that the length shall be 34 feet, breadth 10 feet, depth inside 4 feet, and shall be clench-built and copper fastened, with a flat keel five inches wide and four inches deep, with half-inch iron keel plate; …to row fourteen oars double-banked, and be fitted with one mast and a dipping lug-sail. The oars to row in rowlocks formed in wood chocks fitted on the gunwale, and to be steered by a rudder, or sweep oars, as shall be required; …have a water-tight deck, with copper tubes and self-acting valves for the relief of water, and ventilating hatches; …and have air-cases packed with cork, to be placed under the deck in the wings of the boat, and the remaining space to be filled with air-tight cases and other internal fittings, and other equipments required.

The RNLI apparently followed 'in every possible way' the fishermen's design sugges-tions for the new boat, which bore some resemblance to the Norfolk and Suffolk type, probably the best-known design of lifeboat to emanate from the East Anglian region, but

The second Benjamin Bond Cabbell *(ON.12) lifeboat, which served from 1884 until 1902. As this lifeboat was designed specifically for service at Cromer, and only two others were completed to the same design, it was classified as a 'Cromer'-type lifeboat. (By courtesy of Randall-Salter Lantern Collection)*

Launch of Benjamin Bond Cabbell *from the east beach. The general lines of the Cromer-type lifeboat, notably its raked stem and curved keel, are evident in this photograph. The type was also, at 10ft in beam, wider than the self-righting-type lifeboat it replaced.*

had a much higher bow, a raking stem and was of a relatively light construction. It also had a curved keel, typical of the North Country type lifeboats first built in the late eighteenth century by Henry Greathead and subsequently adapted and improved, but it was not self-righting. With a good degree of manoeuvrability, it was fitted with water ballast tanks, had ten relieving valves and the rudder was retractable to prevent damage during the beach launch and recovery procedure.

The new boat was constructed by Beeching of Great Yarmouth, and was 35ft in length with a breadth of 10ft 6in and a depth inside of 4ft. The boat was clench-built and copper-fastened, with a flat keel five inches wide and four inches deep, an iron keel plate and a belt of cork. As well as the fourteen oars double-banked, it was fitted with a dipping lug sail and was steered by a rudder or sweep-oars, as required. It had a watertight deck, with copper tubes and self-acting valves to release the water, and portable airtight cases round the sides of the boat between the deck and thwarts. Air-cases, packed with cork, were placed under the deck in the wings of the boat, which weighed 4.5 tons and drew 18in of water clear of ballast. Although well liked at Cromer, only two other boats of this design were ever built, both of which served on the north Norfolk coast, operating from Wells and Blakeney.

The new lifeboat arrived at Cromer during the morning of 25 September 1884. She was towed from Great Yarmouth by steam tug and was placed in the boathouse during the afternoon, when the old boat was taken to the railway station. She was formally named and dedicated at a ceremony on Monday 29 September 1884, an event which aroused considerable interest in the town. By the afternoon, according to a newspaper, 'the Cliffs were lined and the Beach crowded with sightseers. The Cromer Band was in attendance.' After lunch, Cliff House guests who had been specially invited to witness the proceedings made their way to the beach for the ceremony. Among those present were Edward Birkbeck, MP; vice president and chairman of the RNLI's Committee of Management, Sir T. Fowell Buxton, Bt; Mrs Bond Cabbell; Admiral Corbett, RN; H.R. Upcher; Revd F. Fitch; Commander G.C.C. Carter, RN; W.G. Sandford, honorary secretary and treasurer to the Local Committee; and many others. A platform was erected near the stern of the boat for the guests and Mr Birkbeck spoke of the new boat:

Where there exist in any locality certain difficulties or differences of opinion in regard to a lifeboat we have made up our minds to hold public inquiries, so that we may hear fairly all views to arrive at the best decision. When our Chief-Inspector (Captain Chetwynd) came to Cromer to hold an inquiry I sent him a telegram that it was our wish that the Cromer fishermen should have a boat which they thought most suited for their coast. If they did not like a self-righting one, they should have one that they thought best. Our fleet at present numbers 279 boats, of which 257 are self-righting. With regard to the expense of the boat, the late Miss Ann Egdell of Alnwick, left a legacy to provide two boats, one of which was placed at Holy Island, and we thought we could not do better than build the other for Cromer. The lady did not direct that it should bear any special name, and as a new name will be given to the boat just removed from here, we decided that this boat should bear the same name, Benjamin Bond Cabbell. In officially and formally presenting the boat to the town of Cromer I would express the earnest hope that she will give the completest satisfaction to the crews who may take her to sea.

With her son in attendance, Mrs Bond Cabbell then broke a bottle of claret over the boat, which was pulled to the water's edge and launched from her carriage, 'amid hearty cheers of the spectators and the ringing church bells, the band at the same time playing Rule Britannia'.

The second *Benjamin Bond Cabbell* lifeboat was launched on service thirteen times and saved twenty-six lives during her time at Cromer. Her first service took place on 28 January 1888, after a vessel was seen to the north of Cromer labouring heavily, flying a signal of distress. She launched at 11.15 a.m. and found the brigantine *Jane Maria*, of London, bound from Hartlepool for Greenwich with a cargo of coal. The brigantine was in a perilous state, with her decks awash and her boat had been carried away by heavy seas the previous night. Her crew of seven were taken on board the lifeboat and safely landed at Cromer.

The lifeboat's next service took place on 18 November 1893 after a sudden severe gale caught out two fishing boats. The fishing boats had gone to sea during the morning, but in the afternoon, as the sea became increasingly rough, concern was expressed for the safety of the boats which had not returned to the beach. Huge waves were rolling in towards the shore, rendering it impossible for the boats to land, so the lifeboat, manned by a crew of sixteen, was launched at 3.30 p.m. under Coxswain James Davies. She soon reached the first vessel, a large crab boat, aboard which were Alfred Lake of Runton and his two sons. The other boat requiring assistance belonged to Thomas Davies, of Overstrand, with his two sons and two others also on board. The crew of the lifeboat succeeded, with some difficulty, in getting the fishermen from both boats on board, but had to cast both boats adrift, as the heavy seas and severe gale meant that beaching was particularly difficult. The crew took her ashore just to the north of the east breakwater. In doing so they shipped two heavy seas, the first one flooding the boat completely, and before she had recovered another was upon her. Fortunately, nobody was washed overboard, although five oars were broken and the coxswain damaged his wrist. She was then beached and the rescued men were landed, although the lifeboat was further damaged after being thrown against the breakwater. The *Eastern Daily Press* ended its account of the rescue by stating:

The highest praise is due to the crew for their gallant services, which gave rise to a feeling of general admiration. As a proof of the very exceptional weather, it may be stated that the tide flowed quite two hours after the time of high water. The gale increased in violence, and continued to rage throughout the night, causing a great deal of minor damage.

In December 1894, the Cromer lifeboat was involved in a long and difficult service. At 11.50 p.m., on 28 December, *Benjamin Bond Cabbell* was launched in a strong gale and very heavy seas, with snow squalls and intense cold, after signals of distress had been seen from the schooner *Fair City*, of Gloucester. The casualty had been dismasted by the severe weather and the master had only just avoided being crushed by falling spars. He anchored and fired flares for help, hoping a passing steamer would take him in tow. When the lifeboat arrived, he declined to leave his vessel but urged the lifeboatmen to remain standing by. At about 4.30 a.m. on 29 December, with the ebb tide easing, the captain weighed anchor and both the schooner and lifeboat drifted to the south before the gale. On arriving near the Wold lightvessel, the coxswain warned the captain that they were dangerously close to the outlying sands, but he still refused to leave his vessel and asked the lifeboat to try to get help from a tug. So the lifeboat made for Great Yarmouth, passing the Scroby Sands with considerable difficulty in the severe weather, and eventually reaching Yarmouth roadstead at 2 p.m. Meanwhile, Palling lifeboat *Hearts of Oak* (ON.351) had launched and subsequently saved the schooner's crew of four as the vessel went to pieces.

The final service performed by *Benjamin Bond Cabbell* took place on 17 February 1901. She launched at 9 p.m. and found the steamship *Celerity*, of Yarmouth, bound from Rochester for Leith with a cargo of cement, and a crew of seven men, disabled after shipping water which had extinguished her fires in the gale force winds. The steamer's anchor had dragged and when she was about half a mile from the shore, she fired a flare to indicate she required help. The lifeboat stood by during the night but the lifeboatmen were unable to board her owing to the bad weather and the vessel's heavy rolling. The vessel's crew baled some of the water out and in the end managed to relight the fires extinguished earlier. The lifeboatmen then assisted in weighing the anchor and the boat proceeded, accompanied by the lifeboat, to Yarmouth. They reached the port at 2.15 p.m., by when the lifeboat crew had been exposed for nearly eighteen hours to terrible weather. Not until 5 p.m. the following day did the lifeboat finally return to her station.

The ketch Hero, *of Goole, stranded on the rocks to the north of the jetty on 3 December 1897. Her crew of four were saved by the second* Benjamin Bond Cabbell *lifeboat. (By courtesy of P.A. Vicary)*

Benjamin Bond Cabbell (ON.12) *near the pier forecourt as she is pulled along the promenade to try and launch to the west of the pier to help the Norwegian sailing ship* Esras *in March 1901. The ship's crew was eventually rescued by breeches buoy from the cliff and the lifeboat was not needed. (Poppyland Collection)*

The Norwegian sailing ship Esras, *stranded at East Runton in March 1901, with her crew being saved by breeches buoy from the cliff. (By courtesy of P.A. Vicary)*

4

Into the Twentieth Century

Louisa Heartwell

In April 1901, the RNLI's Committee of Management agreed that a new lifeboat should be sent to Cromer as the old one was deemed unfit for further service. The Committee decided to acquire the new lifeboat with the legacy of £700 bequeathed to the Institution by the late Miss Emily Heartwell, of Upper Holloway, London. Miss Heartwell stipulated that she wanted her legacy to provide a lifeboat on the east coast named *Louisa Heartwell*. Once the decision had been taken that a new lifeboat was to be built for the station, the local committee, coxswain and crew requested a 38ft Liverpool type, fourteen-oared, with a dipping lug, and an order for the new lifeboat was placed with the Thames Iron Works Company, at Blackwall, London. The Liverpool design was a non-self-righting type and was generally intended for sailing, rather than pulling. The new boat was fitted with two water ballast tanks, and two sliding or drop keels to increase her stability and improve her sailing qualities.

The new lifeboat successfully underwent her harbour trial on 19 July 1902 and just over a month later was sent to her station. She left Gravesend on 3 September and was towed from the Thames by a tug with Coxswain James Harrison and a navigating party on board. Being taken to Cromer by sea was an unusual arrangement, for pulling and sailing lifeboats at this time were more often taken to their stations by rail. She was

Louisa Heartwell on her launching carriage with sails set in a posed photograph with the crew in their cork life jackets. The Tipping's plates on the wheels were intended to make launching easier.

a sailing lifeboat, and the journey from London to Cromer was relatively short, taking her round the coast was a viable option. During the passage she gave 'every satisfaction,' according to the district inspector, and arrived at 7 a.m. on 4 September.

To improve launching arrangements for the new boat, a new launching carriage, which had been built by the Bristol Wagon Works, was sent from Bristol via the Great Western Railway. Pushing poles were also supplied, and a set of Tipping's plates was sent via the Great Eastern Railway. To house the new lifeboat, a new boathouse had to be constructed as the old house was found to be inadequate for the larger boat and carriage and so was demolished in May 1901. The process of building a new house began in March 1902 when the RNLI's Architect, W.T. Douglass, submitted a plan and specification of the new building to the Urban District Council and the Cromer Protection Commissioners for their approval. Once this was gained, work on the new house began on the same site as the previous house at the foot of the East Gangway.

Built by Girling & Smith, of Cross Street, Cromer, the new building was completed during the first week of August 1902 at a cost of £525 and, measuring 50ft by 21ft inside, was a fairly impressive building for its time. It was constructed of red brick, pointed in black mortar, with a slated roof and a lantern in the centre. The floor was laid in concrete with Staffordshire wheelways, while overhead was a small room for the use of the committee and the crew. Over the entrance, top-hung sliding and folding doors were fitted with a small door on the east side. Gas was laid on, and water was easily available nearby. This house, considered as 'a decided ornament to the parade', has remained in use in one form or another for more than a century, albeit with various modifications and improvements, including those of 1909, when alterations costing £51 7s 9d were carried out. In 1923, this house was superseded by a new house and slipway built at the end of the pier, described fully below, but it remained operational and housed the No.2 lifeboat until that was withdrawn in 1967.

The inauguration ceremony for the new lifeboat took place on 9 September 1902. Lord Suffield, president of the Cromer branch, formally declared open the new lifeboat

The lifeboat house of 1902 housed the No.2 lifeboats from 1923 until 1967 and was then used for the inshore lifeboat, subsequently becoming the Henry Blogg Lifeboat Museum, as pictured here. (Nicholas Leach)

Top: Louisa Heartwell (ON.495) during her naming and dedication ceremony on the East Beach, 9 September 1902. After the formal speeches, she was launched in front of a large crowd of well-wishers. (Poppyland Collection)

Middle: Louisa Heartwell being launched in a calm sea, possibly at the end of her naming ceremony, as many of those in attendance have cameras ready to catch the spectacle. (Poppyland Collection)

Left: James Harrison, first coxswain of Louisa Heartwell, served in the post from 1902 to 1909. (From a postcard supplied by Paul Russell)

house. Commander Thomas Holmes, RN, the district inspector, accepted the new boat on behalf of the Institution, and brought attention to the role of the crew, saying, 'the steps recently taken to improve the efficiency of the Cromer Lifeboat Station… would be of no use unless they had an efficient Lifeboat crew to take care of the boat'. He then handed over the new boat to Henry Broadhurst, MP, who accepted the gift on behalf of the local committee. A short service of dedication followed and, amid much pomp and ceremony, the new lifeboat entered service, as described by *The Lifeboat* journal for 1 November 1902:

> Lady Suffield stepped forward and said 'I have pleasure in naming this lifeboat the Louisa Heartwell, and I hope it will save many lives,' at the same time breaking the bottle suspended over the bow of the boat. Amid renewed cheers the work of launching was speedily accomplished, among those on board being members of the Local Committee and Commander Holmes, Lord Carrington, and Lady Hastings.

Louisa Heartwell was well liked at Cromer during almost three decades of service and performed many rescues, the most notable of which are described below. Her first service took place in December 1903 when she stood by the steamship *Enriquetta*, of Grangemouth, for three days. Her first lifesaving service took place on 10 October 1904, when she was launched to the steamer *Rosalind*, of Newcastle, which had its steering apparatus broken during a gale. Because of the severity of the weather, the steamer's captain could not use the manual steering gear and so the lifeboat launched to her aid at about 11 p.m. An hour later, she got alongside the distressed vessel and stood by. The tug *Yare* was summoned from Great Yarmouth and, assisted by the lifeboat, took the ship in tow. The lifeboat was credited with assisting in saving the lives of the seventeen crew on board the steamer.

On 11 February 1907, the steamship *Atbara*, of London, bound from the Tyne to Piraeus with a cargo of coal, went ashore on the Haisborough Sands. Both *Louisa Heartwell* and the Palling No.2 lifeboat *Hearts of Oak* were launched after a message had been received from the lightvessel that the steamer was aground. The Cromer lifeboat reached the casualty at about 7 p.m. with the Palling boat arriving an hour later. The lifeboats stood by until midnight, by which time it was decided to rescue the crew as the steamer remained aground. Twenty-four men were taken off and divided equally between the two lifeboats which, at the request of the master, remained in the vicinity of the vessel until daylight in case it was possible to get her off the sands. By about 7 a.m., however, the steamer had become a total wreck, so the lifeboats left. *The Lifeboat* journal commented that this was 'an excellent and very useful service, and the lifeboatmen had a very trying time, being exposed to the extreme cold for upwards of sixteen hours'.

One of the most arduous services carried out by the Cromer lifeboatmen using *Louisa Heartwell* took place on 23 November 1909, and was the first service undertaken with Henry Blogg as coxswain (see separate section below). The Norwegian brig *Alf*, of Laurvig, an iron ship of 1,066 tons, on passage from Porsgrund to Liverpool with a cargo of wood, became stranded on the Haisborough Sands. Unable to get his ship off the sands, the captain ordered that the brig's two small boats be launched. One successfully got away, but unfortunately, before the remaining crew had managed to scramble into the second boat, a wave caught it and flung it away from the ship, leaving two men still on the wreck. Worse was to come as one of the boats that had managed to get away was struck by a wave and capsized, throwing its six occupants into the water. Three were drowned but the others managed to swim to the other boat. This boat soon filled with water and the crew was forced to bail continuously throughout the night. When daylight came, they made a makeshift signal using a coat and, when a few miles off Cromer, were

The crew of Louisa Heartwell *taken during the early years of her service, with Henry Blogg, soon to become coxswain, standing at the back, second from left.*

spotted by a passing vessel, *Chanticleer*, which took them on board and landed them at Yarmouth.

Meanwhile, the brig's two mates, who had been left on board the vessel, sent up flares which were seen by the Haisborough lightvessel, which in turn signalled that help was needed. The message reached Cromer at 10.15 p.m. and at 11p.m. *Louisa Heartwell* was launched with a crew of seventeen and Coxswain Blogg in command. Once at the wreck, it appeared to the lifeboatmen that the vessel had been abandoned as her boats were gone and no one was on deck. The lifeboat was taken alongside and the lifeboatmen shouted but the two mates, who were down below looking for paraffin and material to make flares, did not hear due to the noise of the waves and the flapping of the sails. It seemed that they were too late, the lifeboatmen left the brig and began searching for the missing men.

After several hours of searching the coxswain decided it was time to return home, but as they had fifteen miles to go against both wind and tide, and the crew was exhausted after hours of pulling in the heavy sea, the lifeboat was taken to Palling and anchored until the tide was more favourable and the lifeboatmen had rested. However, at dawn, the drifter *King* reported that two men had been seen on the wreck. So *Louisa Heartwell* was taken back to the casualty, and found that it had broken in half and that the cargo was washing out. Heavy seas were sweeping right over the battered hulk, and it was the only through extremely good seamanship that the lifeboat was manoeuvred under the wreck's lee quarter. Although a sea struck her heavily on the stern, she was held in position long enough to enable the two survivors to descend from the brig's mizzen rigging, where they had been clinging, and drop to safety. The lifeboat then made for Yarmouth, where an hour after her arrival *Chanticleer* came in with the other nine hands. *Louisa Heartwell* had been afloat for fifteen hours and the crew received the congratulations and thanks of the Mayor of Yarmouth for their exertions. As Cyril Jolly noted in his biography *Henry Blogg of Cromer*, 'It had been a stern struggle but through good teamwork this difficult rescue had been effected.'

During 1914, *Louisa Heartwell* launched six times, but rendered no effective service as reports of vessels aground on the Sands proved to be without foundation on several occasions. The first service of 1915, carried out on 8 January, was to the steamship *New Oporto*, of West Hartlepool, which was stranded near the Haisborough Middle Buoy. By the time the lifeboat had arrived, the Palling boat was already at the scene and the two lifeboat crews helped to jettison the cargo. However, with the wind increasing, the sea becoming heavier and the vessel listing with about 3ft of water in the hold, the captain decided to abandon her. Between them the two lifeboats brought ashore the steamer's crew.

Ten days after this rescue, one of the most arduous and testing services carried out in *Louisa Heartwell* took place. During the night of 18 January, signals of distress were seen in the vicinity of the Sheringham Shoal, and the lifeboat was launched under Coxswain Henry Blogg. The heavy surf made launching extremely difficult with a heavy hail squall adding to the problems. Once at sea, the lifeboat proceeded in the direction where the flares were last seen but failed to find any vessel in trouble. The lifeboatmen continued to search but, failing to find the vessel in the darkness, decided to anchor until daylight. At daybreak, the coxswain sighted a small sailing vessel, the ketch *Thomas Stratton*, of Maldon, bound from Hull to Grays with a cargo of coal. Her master had burned flares for assistance during the night as she had shipped water in the very heavy seas, and had sprung a leak. Six lifeboatmen went on board and assisted with the pumps, as the ketch's crew of four were exhausted. When they got underway, a course was set for Yarmouth and at about 3 p.m. on 19 January the vessel was brought into Yarmouth Roads. The honorary secretary reported that, 'The ground was white with hail, and the cold intense, and the service was one of the roughest and hardest that had ever been performed by the Cromer lifeboat, and, further, that great credit was due to the Coxswain and crew.' In recognition of their excellent work, the crew received additional monetary rewards.

On 13 January 1916, the 860-ton steamer *Havfru*, of Christiania, bound from Goole to Amsterdam with a cargo of coal, was wrecked on the Haisborough Sands during terrible weather. The vessel was seen by lifeboatmen in the look-out at Palling, but a combination of high tide and exceptionally heavy seas made it impossible to launch the lifeboat from the beach there. A message was therefore sent to Cromer reporting the vessel on the sands, but launching *Louisa Heartwell* at Cromer was also impossible because

Louisa Heartwell under oars in a photograph probably taken from the pier, with Coxswain Henry Blogg at the tiller. This image clearly shows the layout and general lines of the fourteen-oared Liverpool class lifeboats, used by the RNLI throughout the British Isles. (By courtesy of P.A. Vicary)

Louisa Heartwell *approaches the pier in August 1930 during her last year at the station. Coxswain Henry Blogg is standing at the bow. (By courtesy of P.A. Vicary)*

of the severe weather. Although the lifeboat crew stood by throughout the day, when the weather worsened it was decided to wait until daybreak before attempting another launch. At daybreak, as the gale began to abate, an attempt was made to launch the boat, but getting *Louisa Heartwell* to sea proved an extremely difficult task, with the helpers having to go into the water up to their waists to assist in getting the boat clear.

Once at sea, the lifeboatmen headed straight for the Haisborough lightvessel, but the vessel's master had seen nothing of any wreck nor any signals of distress. The lifeboatmen decided to search the sands and about three hours after launching saw the mast of a vessel, the hull of which was completely submerged, with a man clinging to it. Approaching the wreck was difficult, but the survivor was eventually taken off. He was exhausted, having been lashed to the mast for thirty-six hours. The rest of the steamer's crew, thirteen in number, had been drowned the previous day after the vessel had stranded. Once the lifeboat had returned to Cromer, the survivor was landed and taken immediately to the Cromer Cottage hospital, which was also catering for wounded soldiers who had returned from the war in Europe.

On 16 March 1916, the lifeboat was launched with the help of local troops during a moderate south-easterly breeze to the assistance of the steamship *Lady Londonderry*, of Sunderland, bound from Seaham harbour to London and ashore on Overstrand beach. As the lifeboat was proceeding to the vessel a particularly heavy sea broke over the boat, washing the second coxswain overboard and breaking two oars. Fortunately, the remainder of the crew was quickly able to haul him back aboard and the lifeboat proceeded to Overstrand without further incident. When she reached the casualty, which was broadside on to the beach, the lifeboat atempted salvage and, with the assistance of two tugs which arrived from Great Yarmouth, succeeded in towing off the ship.

Almost a year after the *Havfru* service, the Cromer lifeboatmen and *Louisa Heartwell* were called on to perform services that tested them to the limits, saving crews in particularly difficult and testing circumstances that resulted in the award of the first of three Gold medals to Coxswain Henry Blogg. On 9 January 1917, the small Greek steamer *Pyrin* was observed riding out the heavy north-easterly gale at anchor in the roadstead off Cromer. Shortly after 11 a.m., she requested assistance and so the lifeboat crew assembled. The launch was particularly difficult as the lifeboat on its carriage had to be taken some distance over the beach before deep water could be reached. Thanks to a group of willing soldiers, many of whom waded into the water up to their waists, the boat was eventually got afloat about 11.40 a.m. The lifeboat then struggled to get clear and drifted almost a mile to the west before the lifeboatmen succeeded in setting sail and beating upwind to the distressed vessel. She reached the casualty at 2 p.m. and an hour later had safely landed the steamer's crew of sixteen at Cromer.

Just as the lifeboat was beaching on her return from *Pyrin*, an explosion occurred on board the Swedish steamship *Fernebo*, which was loaded with timber. The force of the explosion in the steamer's boilers broke the vessel in half and the two halves soon separated. Messages were received from the neighbouring stations of Sheringham and Palling that their lifeboats were unable to launch, so it was up to the by now exhausted Cromer crew to go to the aid of *Fernebo*. Blogg was in his thirties at this time, but most of the other crew was much older and calling on them for further immediate effort was asking much, but they agreed to put out again. Getting the lifeboat clear of the breakers, however, proved to be a considerable struggle and the lifeboatmen were eventually beaten back despite pulling on the oars for more than half an hour.

Meanwhile, a small boat had left *Fernebo* with six of the steamer's crew on board. Although this boat was capsized in the surf, somehow all of its six occupants were brought to safety, mainly through the efforts of the soldiers and others on the beach, with Private Stewart Holmes, of the Seaforth Highlanders, 'behaving in a particularly brave manner, and narrowly escaping with his own life in his efforts at rescue'. He was later awarded the Silver medal for his bravery.

By late afternoon on 10 January, the two halves of the steamer had grounded, one alongside a wooden groyne which projected about 400ft into the sea to the east of the Coastguard station, and the other foremast end a mile further to the east. The rocket apparatus was called upon to try to get a line to the stranded parts of the steamer, but the force of the wind was too great and it proved impossible to get a line to the survivors. Searchlights from the military authorities illuminated the scene, as more than ten further rockets were fired. At 9 p.m., Coxswain Blogg consulted with Commander Basil Hall, RN, the RNLI's district inspector, about making another attempt with the lifeboat. Hall reluctantly consented to a launch, and at 9.30 p.m. the lifeboat put off again. He described the events that subsequently unfolded as follows:

> For half an hour these splendid men made the most gallant attempt to reach the vessel – over and over again the boat was swept back into the shallow water inshore, but each time they succeeded in keeping her head on to the sea and pulling her out again into the deeper water about halfway between the ship and the shore. Bathed in the brilliant beam of the searchlight, one moment standing on the end as she mounted the crest of a huge breaker, and another with her nose buried in the trough of the sea, or completely lost to sight as a sea broke right over her, the lifeboat made a sight which will never be forgotten by the hundreds of spellbound spectators who lined the beach. I myself would not have believed it possible for even a strong and young crew to do so well with this heavy boat.

During this first attempt, five oars were smashed, three more were washed away and Blogg was forced to abandon his efforts and return to the shore. But Blogg was not to be beaten and, with his brave crew, decided to make another attempt. After a short rest, spare oars were found and for the fourth time that day the lifeboat was launched at a point on the beach where the tide had begun to create a current which swept almost out

The small Greek steamer Pyrin, *stranded off Cromer after* Louisa Heartwell *had saved her crew on 9 January 1917.*

The lifeboatmen who went to the aid of the steamship Fernebo *in January 1917, led by Coxswain Henry Blogg, who is seated in the centre, displaying their medals for gallantry. (Poppyland Photographs)*

The bow section of the Swedish steamship, Fernebo. The vessel had been broken in two by an explosion in her boilers, January 1917.

to the wreck. This time they were successful and *Louisa Heartwell* was brought alongside the wreck long enough for the steamer's entire complement of eleven to be pulled into the lifeboat, which then returned to the shore, accompanied by cheering form the crowd. It was just before 1.00 a.m. and Henry Blogg and his crew had been battling the North Sea on and off for fourteen hours.

The rescue of the *Fernebo*'s crew had been an outstanding act of courage and daring and for this extraordinary feat Blogg received the RNLI's Gold medal. In Hall's dramatic eyewitness report, particular attention was drawn to Blogg, whose crucial role in the rescue Hall went on to explain:

> More even than is usually the case, it is thanks to him that this fine service was possible. Without for a moment detracting from the part played by the rest of the crew, I feel bound to say that I believe that without him the crew could not have been got to take the boat off during the afternoon and evening of the day in question. It was his own remarkable personality and really great qualities of leadership which magnetised tired and somewhat dispirited men into launching, and when the boat was launched it was the consummate skill with which he managed her and the encouragement he gave his crew which brought their efforts to such a successful conclusion.

Blogg was presented with his Gold medal a few months later at the RNLI's ninety-third Annual General Meeting by the chairman of the Institution, the Rt Hon. the Earl Waldegrave. During the presentation, his conduct at the time of the rescue was described as 'a splendid example of the finest qualities which go to form the ideal Coxswain of a Lifeboat crew, and there is no doubt that his leadership and dominating personality constituted the mainspring of action in this fine service'. His personality and leadership skills were to be tested again and again during rescues in the coming years, but this episode marked him out as an exceptional coxswain.

Not only did Blogg receive recognition for this service, but the other Cromer lifeboatmen involved were also formally recognised, some with a new award, the Bronze medal. Acting Second Coxswain William Davies was awarded the Silver medal, twelve of the crew who went out three times received the Bronze medal, and six who went out twice were accorded the Thanks on Vellum. The Bronze medal was a new award instituted by the RNLI's Committee specifically because of the notable contributions of the Cromer crew during this service. The Institution's secretary, George Shee, explained during the presentation of the medals, which took place on 7 July 1917 at the lifeboat house, why the RNLI's Committee of Management believed the new medal was merited:

> In a case when there had been a service in which the whole crew had shown courage and dogged tenacity going out again and again, although inspired by their leader..., it was a case in which each man should have a permanent record to inspire others in the future. The Committee decided thereupon to establish the Bronze medal and the Cromer crew had the privilege of being the first to be awarded them.

On 17 November 1917, the Cromer lifeboat was involved in another fine service. At about 3 a.m., following a gale which had been raging along the coast, the alarm was raised that a ship was aground on the Sands. Launching *Louisa Heartwell* took half an hour, but once she was clear of the surf, with a newly supplied haul-off warp proving invaluable, she made for Haisborough Sands. The lifeboat crew, under the command of Coxswain Blogg, searched the area but without result, so returned to Cromer, helped by

Louisa Heartwell under sail. Her sailing abilities meant she could cover a much greater range than if she relied solely on oars and this was an important factor in enabling the lifeboatmen to reach casualties on the outlying sandbanks, such as the Haisborough Sands. (From a postcard supplied by Paul Russell)

a tow from the steamship *Jarrex*, of South Shields. Once back on the beach, however, news was received that a man had been seen in the rigging of a wrecked steamer lying five miles south-east of the Haisborough lightvessel. Blogg then asked his crew whether any of them wished to go ashore after their efforts earlier in the day when they had been at sea for ten hours. All decided to put out again, and within an hour the lifeboat had reached the wrecked vessel, the Norwegian steamship *Kronprincessan Victoria*, of Haugesund. This vessel had struck the sands during the previous evening in a strong gale and heavy snowstorm. Out of a crew of twelve, only six had survived, and they were quickly taken on board the lifeboat after spending nineteen hours in the rigging. The lifeboat was taken in tow by a patrol boat and, after a very rough passage, arrived back at Cromer, by which time the lifeboatmen had been out on service for sixteen hours. In reviewing this service, no blame was attached to anyone for the loss of life though some delay had been experienced in launching. As a result, the coxswain's house was connected to the then somewhat novel telephone system and, because part of the delay was caused by lack of efficient helpers, arrangements were made for fifteen soldiers to assist in future.

On 30 September 1918, the lifeboat was launched at 1 p.m. after a vessel had been observed in difficulty three miles north-east of the station. In the very heavy seas the lifeboat hit the groyne as she was launching, but was able to get clear without sustaining any damage. The lifeboatmen had a hard pull to get through the surf, but reached the vessel, the steamship *Inna* of Sunderland, and found another steamship, *Stanton*, trying to help by means of a line fastened to the barrel. The lifeboat got alongside *Inna* to find she was leaking and the water had put the steamer's fires out. The lifeboat passed a hawser from *Stanton* to *Inna*, but when this parted *Stanton* steamed away. The lifeboatmen then set up a temporary rig using the lifeboat's sails and one of *Inna*'s, and they drifted towards Yarmouth. When the engineer was able to get some steam, both vessels proceeded to Winterton but it was decided that, in the bad weather and darkness, attempting to pass through the

Cockle Gat into Yarmouth Roads was too risky, so they laid anchor for the night. At daybreak the steamer weighed anchor and was able to make Yarmouth under her own steam while the lifeboat returned to station after what had been another long service.

The years immediately after the First World War were relatively quiet for the Cromer lifeboatmen. They undertook only four services in 1919, the first three to vessels that had stranded on the Haisborough Sands. The last service of the year took place on 30 November when *Louisa Heartwell* was launched to aid the steamship *Réfrigérant* (ex-*War Coppice*), of London, which was aground on the Sands. When she arrived at the casualty, she found a steam drifter already on hand and four other drifters soon arrived along with the Palling lifeboat. Although the lifeboat helped with attaching a tow line, the drifters were unable to move the steamer and so tugs were called from Yarmouth. Two arrived at 7 p.m. and, with the lifeboatmen in charge of the salvage operation, helped the drifters to tow the steamer clear. She eventually refloated at 11 p.m. and the captain immediately made for Dunkirk, refusing to stop to allow the thirteen lifeboatmen and two men from a drifter, who had assisted with the operation, to reboard their own craft. One of the drifters, therefore, had to follow the steamer to Dunkirk to bring back the fifteen men who eventually returned to Great Yarmouth on 4 December.

A further series of routine services were performed in 1920, with *Louisa Heartwell* launching on a number of occasions to reach a casualty only to find her services were not needed for one reason or another. On 4 May she put out to the ketch *Ekatrauwen*, of Amsterdam, which was stranded on the Haisborough Sands, but the lifeboatmen found the ketch's crew had already been picked up by an Admiralty trawler. On 10 June she launched to the tug *Alert*, of Hull, but a passing steamer took the tug in tow before the lifeboat reached the scene. On 20 August, *Louisa Heartwell* was launched at 12.45 p.m. through heavy surf to the steamship *Bavaria*, of Cologne, and on this occasion succeeded in helping the casualty. After lifeboatmen had assisted in raising the vessel's anchor, the lifeboat stood by in worsening weather until the steamer was towed into Great Yarmouth in the evening. During the early hours of 6 September, the lifeboat went to the aid of the motor launch *Dot*, which had broken down in the surf at Overstrand. The lifeboatmen succeeded in towing the launch to a safe anchorage and landing its occupants safely.

The final service of 1920 proved to be one of the longest ever performed by the Cromer lifeboatmen. At about 8 a.m. on 10 October, the steamship *Inverawe*, of Sunderland, on her way to London with 2,500 tons of phosphate, became stranded on the Haisborough Sands about five miles south-east of the lightvessel. The Palling lifeboat was already alongside when the Cromer lifeboat arrived and the coxswains of both boats agreed in trying to save the vessel despite the heavy seas. The lifeboatmen assisted in trying to jettison the cargo, until four tugs arrived and attempted to refloat the vessel, but without success. On 11 October, when two more tugs arrived, the combined power of the six tugs now on scene failed to move the vessel. The following morning a different towing direction was taken by the tugs, but again without success and the vessel remained fast. On 13 October the tugs tried once more, and this time, with high tide at 6 p.m. and four tugs straining on the tow lines, the vessel refloated. Throughout the operation, the lifeboat had been standing by, at one point being damaged when a heavy sea carried her against the side of the vessel. An unusual feature of this service was that, on 13 October, the tide was so low that the lifeboat crews were able to walk across the sands.

Although no effective services were performed by *Louisa Heartwell* during 1921, she was called out on 12 January to a small Belgian steamer two miles off Cromer in very rough seas with extremely heavy surf breaking on the beach. Launching proved to be extremely difficult and it took considerable effort by the lifeboatmen to get their boat through the surf. Again and again the breakers threatened to overturn the boat as she drifted dangerously close to the remains of the wreck of *Fernebo*, with hundreds of anxious spectators watching. But finally she got clear of the beach and reached the steamer five miles north of the Haisborough lightvessel. By the time the lifeboat was on scene, the weather had moderated and the vessel had raised enough steam to continue on her way, so the lifeboat returned to the beach after a fruitless journey that had nearly resulted in disaster.

Launching off the open beach at Cromer had often proved difficult, as demonstrated by the above service. It was not the first time that such difficulties had been encountered. On 20 November 1910, launching had been impossible due to the heavy surf so to help improve the situation, a haul-off warp was suggested. The warp was a line anchored at sea off the beach on which the lifeboat crew could haul to get the boat through the breaking surf. Although discussions the following year concluded that a haul-off warp was impracticable at Cromer, the idea was not abandoned and in 1917 one was supplied mainly to help when launching at high tide. Although the delay in launching to the steamship *Kronprinsessan Victoire*, of Haugesund, on 27 November 1917, had been caused by a lack of helpers, the haul-off warp had proved invaluable on this occasion. Soon afterwards, in January 1918, two single haul-off warps were laid in positions carefully selected by the RNLI inspector, Commander Basil Hall, where they would not be chafed and be most effective when launching. One was laid towards the north-east and the other to the north-west so that the wreck of *Fernebo*, which remained an obstacle on the beach, was avoided and, in a north-easterly wind, the lifeboat would be kept clear of the pier. But these warps were short-lived and within six months had been removed. The west warp had proved impractical but the east warp was laid out again in autumn 1918 for use when launching at half-tide or high water. The haul-off warps were, as Commander Hall explained, only a stopgap measure as far as improving launching was concerned and had been removed by 1920. The problem of getting the boat afloat quickly and easily, however, was about to be overcome with the construction of a new slipway at the end of the pier.

In 1923 with the arrival of the motor lifeboat, described below, *Louisa Heartwell* was designated the No.2 lifeboat and was called upon much less frequently. In fact, the three services she performed during 1923 proved to be her last, with the final one, and her only effective rescue as the No.2 lifeboat, taking place on 21 December 1923. She launched at 7 p.m. that day, as the motor lifeboat *H.F. Bailey* was away undergoing overhaul at Yarmouth, to the three-masted schooner *Gotha*. Once clear of the beach and through the surf, she proceeded to the Middle Haisborough Sands but found nothing there so continued to the Wold lightvessel. As the lifeboatmen approached the lightvessel, they saw a steamer standing by a schooner. On reaching the two vessels, they found that the schooner's fore and main masts were both broken so hailed the crew but got no reply. The lifeboat was then pulled to the steamer, lying about a mile away, on board which was the crew of the schooner. The lifeboat then stood by *Gotha* until two tugs had arrived from Great Yarmouth. As the wreck was sinking and a danger to navigation, the tugs and lifeboat remained on the scene until it sank in the early hours of 22 December. The wind and tide made a return to Cromer impossible, so the tug *George Jewson* towed *Louisa Heartwell* to Great Yarmouth. They reached port at 4 a.m. and the crew remained sheltering on board the tug for two hours as it was snowing. *H.F. Bailey*, with her overhaul complete, then towed the pulling lifeboat back to station on 23 December.

On 15 September 1925, John James Davies, one of the stalwarts from the pulling and sailing era, died at the age of sixty-nine at Cromer Cottage hospital. In reporting his passing, the *Eastern Daily Press* described him as a 'lifeboat hero' and said that 'the country in general, and Cromer in particular, loses one of the staunchest seafarers who ever manned a lifeboat'.

Lifeboat service was part of his family's tradition and he was just one of many Davies to serve in the lifeboat both before and since. He took his father's place as coxswain of *Benjamin Bond Cabbell* and his sons were coxswains of the first motor lifeboats. For eighteen years, he was senior coxswain under his father, and for nine years chief coxswain and superintendent. During his time in the lifeboat he was presented with many awards for his service; on 3 May 1881, he was presented with a barometer and purse containing £10, by Sir Samuel Hoare, for saving the lives of three fishermen, and in 1894 received a medal and certificate from the Royal Humane Society. In 1901, the RNLI presented him with a set of binocular glasses, as 'An award of merit and for valuable services rendered.' He retired as coxswain in 1902 due to poor health and, to mark his retirement, was presented with a green onyx clock. He continued to serve until June 1925, when he was in charge of *Louisa Heartwell* in the absence of the motor lifeboat which was assisting the steamer *Equity*.

At the time of Davies' death, the era of the pulling and sailing lifeboats at Cromer was coming to a close. Although *Louisa Heartwell* remained on station for a further six years, she was not called upon to perform any more effective services and in 1931, after almost three decades on station, she left Cromer for the last time, an event reported by the *Eastern Daily Press* on 16 May 1931 in somewhat dramatic fashion: 'The *Louisa Heartwell* has gone! Cromer's No.2 lifeboat has been towed to Lowestoft to be sold by public auction – an inglorious end to a glorious career.' The newspaper went on to report that she 'has been the means of saving 206 lives and assisted in helping 52 vessels'. It was a rather low-key farewell to the 'Old Louisa' – a name that she was given after the motor lifeboat arrived at the station – but a few people watched from the cliffs as the old lifeboat went on her last journey as a lifeboat. At 2 p.m., the carriage was drawn out of the boathouse and across the beach under the guidance of Coxswain Blogg, the Cromer Coastguard, and numerous lifeboatmen. Shore helpers then dragged the boat to the water's edge. Just off the beach, the motor lifeboat *H.F. Bailey* waited for the tow-rope to be attached and, a few minutes later, *Louisa Heartwell* was launched for the last time. She was taken to Lowestoft where, under the RNLI's instructions, Messrs Hobson & Co sold her on 20 May 1931 by auction at the lifeboat shed on the beach for £55 to Mr N. Green. Details of her career after lifeboat service can be found in Appendix 8.

Louisa Heartwell was replaced by another sailing craft, because, according to local newspaper reports, 'it is imperative that when the present motor boat is away on service, having regard to the mileage she has to protect for lifesaving purposes, that a second boat should be in readiness'. So, on 22 May 1931, the 'new' lifeboat arrived to serve at the No.2 station and operate off the beach. She was towed from Great Yarmouth by *H.F. Bailey* and was successfully housed in the East Gangway boathouse on a new carriage. The new boat, *Alexandra* (ON.514), was a Liverpool type similar to *Louisa Heartwell*. She was 36ft in length, pulled twelve oars and had been stationed at Hope Cove, in South Devon. Whether a pulling lifeboat was needed at this time is open to question, as *Alexandra* did not perform any effective rescues, although she did launch three times to the barge *Sepoy* on 13 December 1933 at 8.30 a.m., 9.30 a.m. and 1.30 p.m., an epic rescue in which the motor lifeboat played the major role and which is described in detail in the next chapter. *Alexandra* remained at Cromer until July 1934 when she was sold out of service.

Rules and Regulations

Although lifeboat crews are made up essentially of volunteers, expense payments are made for exercise and service launches. During the late nineteenth and early twentieth centuries, when incomes were limited for many in Norfolk's small coastal communities, these payments sometimes provided perhaps too great an incentive to launch the lifeboat.

On occasions, the lifeboat would put to sea even when its services were not strictly needed if, for example, another lifeboat was better located to reach a casualty. The majority of services performed by Norfolk's lifeboats at this time were to vessels caught on the Happisburgh Sands, perhaps the most notorious of all the sandbanks off the Norfolk coast. Yet, because of the position of the Sands in relation to the lifeboat stations and the often imprecise information available about the location of a ship which required help, determining which lifeboat was most suitably placed to reach the casualty was not always a straightforward matter, particularly in the days of sail when a lifeboat upwind of a casualty was clearly in a better position to help than one downwind.

Problems arose because lifeboats were launching and the crews would claim expense payments when their services were not strictly necessary. Although overzealous lifeboat crews were also at fault, poor communications might have contributed to the problem. To alert a lifeboat to a ship in distress, signals made by the Wold or Haisborough lightvessels would be seen by lookouts on the beaches who would alert the crew to a vessel in distress. If a lifeboat was then launched, more often than not the crew had no immediate way of knowing whether the lifeboat from a neighbouring station had also put out so could justify a launch by claiming not to have been aware that another lifeboat had also put to sea.

The matter of launches deemed unnecessary became an issue because some crews would launch their lifeboat when they knew a ship was in trouble whether or not they were the best placed to help, claiming expenses for so doing, and as a result of which an increased amount of money was being paid by the RNLI for launches. The increase in payments naturally came to the attention of the RNLI's Committee of Management which controlled the release of any funds, and members of the Committee began looking more closely at whether a launch by a particular boat was in fact justified. Whether the crews launched in good faith, genuinely intending to help a casualty or whether they launched to claim expense payments is difficult to say. But during the two decades or so leading up to the First World War, expense payments became an issue at many of Norfolk's lifeboat stations.

One of the earliest incidents when a launch was questioned by the RNLI's Committee took place in June 1889. The lifeboat *Benjamin Bond Cabbell* went to the schooner *Elizabeth* on the Haisborough Sands but did not perform any service and the Committee sent a reminder to the station that the lifeboat – a relatively small boat with limited range – was not intended for service on the Sands. However, in January 1890, the district inspector found, during a routine visit to the station, that the order not to go to Haisborough Sands was resented by the crew. While the issue seems to have died down at Cromer, at stations further south along the coast lifeboats continued to launch when, according to the Committee, it was not necessary. In an attempt to clarify the situation, a series of regulations was introduced governing the launching of the lifeboats to the Haisborough Sands. The first set of rules was implemented in the spring of 1901 and covered the Caister, Palling and Winterton stations on Norfolk's south coast. But after two years in practice, the Committee considered the matter again and decided to remove the restrictions.

However, launches deemed unnecessary continued to take place. On 24 September 1907, *Louisa Heartwell* put out in fine weather to a fishing boat on the Sands although she was not strictly needed. When investigating the incident, the Committee requested that the chief officer of the Coastguard at Bacton provide more accurate information about the position of the casualty before alerting a lifeboat station, and the Cromer honorary secretary was instructed to use the recently installed telephone to 'regulate' lifeboats from adjacent stations. The Committee clearly hoped that better information would enable stations to agree between them which lifeboat was best placed to help a casualty.

At the start of the twentieth century, no fewer than eleven lifeboats were in operation between Cromer and Gorleston, with many stations having two lifeboats. The lifeboats were mostly large sailing craft specifically designed to go to the Sands, and with so many close together, regulating launches was clearly difficult and it is hardly surprising that more than one boat would launch when a ship was stranded. The problem of regulating launches became such an issue that the RNLI issued a set of rules to govern the matter. One of the services that led to these rules being introduced took place in fine weather on 12 May 1911. *Louisa Heartwell* was one of several lifeboats that launched on this occasion and, although the Committee judged that the launch was justified and decided to pay the crew, the incident indicated that some kind of policy to regulate launching was overdue.

The rules, which were to be assessed after a year, applied to the lifeboats at Cromer, Caister, Great Yarmouth, Gorleston, Palling, Winterton and Happisburgh and specified the areas each station should cover, clearly stating that the lifeboats should not launch to assist vessels that could be better assisted by a neighbouring station. The Committee explained the reasoning behind the introduction of the rules, stating that they had been:

> …drawn up with a view to preventing the recurrence of unnecessary launches by the Lifeboats of the stations concerned. The Committee of Management, while recognizing the zeal and the seamanlike spirit of the crews, have felt compelled to take steps to prevent the wasteful expenditure of public funds, caused by unauthorized and unjustifiable launches. During the last three years a very large sum was spent in this way, being two and a half times as much as the sum paid for proper and useful services. As the men are well aware, the Committee of Management do not look too critically at duplicate launches when the weather is really bad and when there is a heavy sea; but they will rigidly carry out the subjoined rules, which are issued in the true interests of the men as well as the general interests of the Institution.

The launch of more than one lifeboat in exceptionally bad weather was, of course, acceptable, but the rules stipulated that only one payment would be made in moderate weather, irrespective of how many lifeboats launched, and the decision about which crew received the payment was down to the Committee. In addition, the stations were to make greater efforts to ascertain the position of a casualty before launching and the Haisborough lightvessel was to report the wind, sea and tide on the Sands as well as the position of a wreck. The telephone was to be used to communicate and share information between the stations concerned. The Happisburgh lifeboat, a small self-righter, was confined to services near the shore, with Cromer and Palling being allowed to go as far as the outlying sands. The Winterton boat was not to go south of a line between the Cockle lightvessel and the North-East Cross Sand Buoy, which was the northern limit of the Caister station. To further improve matters, during the summer of 1912 Trinity House implemented a system of signals for lightvessels to use off the Norfolk coast to denote the position of wrecks.

Initially the rules seemed quite successful and worked reasonably well during their first year of operation. In May 1913 they were reviewed and, according to the district inspector, had proved satisfactory while not causing any serious discontent among the crews. The chief inspector was certain that their introduction had prevented some but not all unnecessary launches. On 30 August 1913, *Louisa Heartwell* launched in moderate weather even though the coxswain knew he was more than five miles further from the casualty than the Palling lifeboat. Although he explained that no message had been received from Palling, as the Palling lifeboat launched, no payments were made to Cromer.

After a further year of operation, the rules were further reviewed during spring 1914 with local committees and honorary secretaries in favour of them. The crews, however, were generally opposed to them, arguing that whatever the weather at least two lifeboats should go to the outlying sands which were dangerous because of the extremely strong tides and sunken vessels. This argument, based on the crews' experience, fell on deaf ears as the Committee continued to refuse payment when a launch was not justified according to the rules, although in especially bad weather and onshore gales payments would be made if two or more boats launched.

The problem of launching in moderate weather, however, remained, and in February 1914 Commander Rogers, chairman of the Palling branch, pointed to the difficulty in deciding which was the proper boat to launch in such conditions. As a result of this, a compass card was sent to both Cromer and Palling which explained which boat would launch when the wind was in a specific direction. So, for example, when the wind was north by east the Cromer lifeboat would launch on both tides, but if the wind was south by west the Palling lifeboat could put out. The card, although perhaps a little over complicated, was intended to help decide which boat should be launched in moderate weather, but did not impose hard and fast rules and was to be used alongside the rules already in force. It is not known whether the recommendations on this card were followed in practice.

Although the rules had been introduced with good intentions, withholding payments for a service could cause ill feeling between committees, both local and national, and crew. On 27 April 1914, the decision not to make any payment for a launch in fine weather to a vessel reported ashore to the south of the Middle Haisborough Buoy sparked a serious disagreement between the crew and the RNLI. The Palling lifeboat had launched on this occasion and the Committee stated that Cromer was therefore not justified in putting out, though the Cromer men believed they were. Matters came to a head at the usual quarterly exercise two months later, when the district inspector, Lieutenant Rigg, RN, arrived with the deputy chief inspector, Captain Rowley, RN. The lifeboat was found to be in excellent condition, but the crew would not launch as they had not been paid for this service. They claimed that on 27 April they were first to the vessel, ahead of the Palling boat whose crew had been paid. Despite the inspector promising to look at the service again and Coxswain Blogg requesting that the men 'fall in and follow me', the crew refused to man the lifeboat for the launch. During the afternoon, a number of fishermen offered their services and an exercise was carried out, after which these men were subsequently enrolled as a crew and the leader of the protesters was informed that his services were no longer required by the RNLI. Matters were further complicated when the local committee decided unanimously that the launch on 27 April was, in fact, justified, and in view of this the Committee rescinded its decision, paid the men and reinstated the original crew. At the next exercise, in July 1914, a full crew of twenty-four was available and the inspector 'found an excellent spirit amongst the men'.

During the first two years of the First World War, some of the lifeboat's launches were questioned by the Committee under the launching rules and deemed unnecessary. On 30 November 1914, *Louisa Heartwell* went out in moderate weather to a steamer stranded on the Haisborough Sands, to which both Palling and Winterton lifeboats had also launched. The Palling crew was paid, but the crews from Cromer and Winterton were not. On 8 November 1915, *Louisa Heartwell* went to the steamship *Eppleton* which was stranded north of the Haisborough lightvessel in moderate weather, but was beaten to the casualty by the Palling lifeboat which had launched after the Cromer boat and, as Cromer was not justified in launching, no payment was made. *Louisa Heartwell* launched to a vessel on the Haisborough Sands in a south-east breeze and smooth sea on 1 February 1916, with Palling No.1 and Winterton No.2 lifeboats also launching. The vessel refloated before any of them reached her, and as the Cromer boat was not justified

Louisa Heartwell on her carriage on 19 May 1920, ready to be launched for a demonstration or exercise launch, watched by a large crowd. (From an old postcard supplied by Roger Wiltshire)

in launching according to the rules the crew was not paid. On 29 July 1916, both Cromer and Palling No.1 lifeboats launched to assist a large steamer aground on the Sands in a light wind and smooth seas. As nobody was in danger, one payment was divided between the two boats.

By the time of this service, with many men being called up to the army, concerns over the possibility of raising a crew had been expressed and the matter of unnecessary launches became less relevant. Commander Basil Hall reported in July 1916 that of eighteen men then available as a crew, four or five, including the coxswain, were liable to be called up for service and it was thus doubtful if a crew could be obtained. The honorary secretary wrote to the Admiralty asking for the coxswain and bowman to be made exempt from service. In November 1916, the inspector reported that sufficient men were available but that if the crew was further weakened operating the lifeboat might be impossible, adding that 'this station is the most important one on this part of coast'. The worst effect of the First World War seems to have been the shortage of crew, and the fact that the station was operating with a depleted crew makes the *Fernebo* service, described above, even more remarkable. The situation might have got worse had war gone on much longer, but when peace was declared in November 1918, not only did crew numbers improve but the station could look forward to a new motor lifeboat and the opening of a new chapter in its history.

5

A New Dimension to Lifesaving

The advantages of steam and engine power as applied in the marine world were soon evident following their widespread introduction during the nineteenth century, and it was inevitable that these new and potentially revolutionary forms of power would soon be part of the lifeboat service. The experiments that took place when fitting first steam and later motor engines to lifeboats pointed the way forward for lifeboat development in the twentieth century. Some steam-driven lifeboats had been built at the end of the nineteenth century, but steam power was poorly suited to lifeboats and the newly invented internal combustion engine had greater potential. In 1904, a lifeboat was fitted with an engine for the first time. Although many technical difficulties had to be overcome to successfully operate an engine on board a lifeboat, once these had been solved, lifeboats powered by the internal combustion engine clearly represented the future for the lifeboat service. Initially, lifeboats already in service were converted by having an engine fitted. In 1908 the first lifeboat to be built with an engine was completed and by 1914 the number of motor lifeboats in service was into double figures.

In June 1914, the deputy chief inspector visited Cromer to assess whether a motor lifeboat could be placed on Norfolk's north coast, in order, it was explained, 'to cope with casualties like that to steamship *Heathfield* which foundered off Sheringham Shoal on 18 October 1910'. Blakeney harbour, to the west of Cromer, was seen as the only place where a motor lifeboat could be kept, but as this was not an ideal location, particularly considering the crew available at both Cromer and Sheringham, no further action was taken and when war broke out in August the matter was postponed, while further advances in the design and development of motor lifeboats were inevitably delayed by the conflict. Although the question of placing a motor lifeboat was again raised in October 1917, it was not until the following year that a decision was made by the RNLI's Committee of Management to supply a motor lifeboat to the station.

Following the end of the war, the RNLI adopted a policy of modernisation which resulted in many new motor lifeboats being built. As greater experience was gained in the operation of motor lifeboats, more reliable engines were developed to power larger and more sophisticated boats which were able to cover greater areas. Many immediate post-war lifeboats were based on old designs of pulling and sailing lifeboats, fitted with a single engine driving a single propeller. The first motor lifeboat at Cromer, named *H.F. Bailey*, was based on the Norfolk & Suffolk design of pulling lifeboat, a type developed by the East Anglian beachmen and ideally suited for work in shallow waters due to its relatively flat bottom.

The new lifeboat, 46ft 6in in length with a beam of 12ft 9in, was the third of the motorised Norfolk & Suffolk class. The other two were stationed at Walton and Frinton in Essex and at Lowestoft in Suffolk. The Lowestoft boat, *Agnes Cross*, had undertaken an exceptional rescue in October 1922, to the steamship *Hopelyn*, which had gone a long way in showing the advantage of motor lifeboats over their pulling counterparts to those lifeboatmen who remained sceptical about motor power. The steamship had broken down with steering failure off the Norfolk coast, and the sailing lifeboat at Gorleston attempted to assist but could not get alongside in the heavy seas and strong winds. The extra power provided by the motorised *Agnes Cross* enabled her to come alongside long

Cromer's first motor lifeboat, H.F. Bailey (ON.670), with her sails set. She was built in 1923 at East Cowes and arrived at Cromer in May of that year.

enough for the twenty-four men to be rescued. For this outstanding rescue, both Coxswain William Fleming, of Gorleston, and Coxswain Robert Swan, of Lowestoft, who was in command of *Agnes Cross*, were awarded Gold medals.

Agnes Cross was powered by a 60hp Tylor engine, while, as *The Lifeboat* journal for December 1923 explained, 'the Cromer boat has one of the Institution's new 90hp engines, so that, with the exception of the New Brighton Boat [which had twin 76bhp engines], she is the largest and most powerful Motor Life-boat on our coasts'. She was, in fact, fitted with an 80hp Weyburn DE.6 engine, rather than the 90hp engine described in *The Lifeboat*, but this was a significant advance. The new engine, designed by Arthur Evans, the RNLI's chief inspector of machinery, incorporated several new features including a small motor to start up the main engine from cold. However, as the boat had only a single engine, auxiliary sails were also carried. Built at East Cowes at the yard of J.S. White at a cost of almost £11,000, during her speed trial on 18 April 1923 on the measured half mile in the river Medina at Cowes she had achieved a mean speed of 8.6 knots and at a further trial almost a month later she reached 8.521 knots, with the engine running at 697rpm. The new lifeboat had a radius of action of forty-five nautical miles at full speed and carried a crew of twelve, including the mechanic.

The new lifeboat arrived from the Isle of Wight on Saturday 26 May 1923, watched by, according to the *Eastern Daily Press*, 'the greater part of Cromer's population', after a trip throughout which the engines worked faultlessly. She left Cowes on the Isle of Wight on the morning of 23 May with Coxswain Blogg, Second Coxswain George Balls, the engineer, Ernest Amis, and three other men from Cromer forming the crew, accompanied by Commander Carver, the district inspector. During the passage she called at Newhaven, Ramsgate and Gorleston, and after leaving Ramsgate also went alongside the Kentish Knock and Landsand lightvessels to give newspapers to the crew of the latter. After leaving Gorleston, the lifeboat was taken round the wreck of the steamship *Hopelyn* on Scroby Sands.

To accommodate a motor lifeboat, a new lifeboat house had to be built. The RNLI initially proposed a new lifeboat house and slipway alongside the pier, which had been completed in 1901, with access gangways. Drawings and specifications of the proposed house were prepared and submitted to the Cromer Protection Commissioners in May 1919. In July 1919, after examining the plans, the Commissioners requested that the boathouse and slipway be placed 'seaward of the pier-head and on a centre line of the pier', with public gangways on both sides so that the slipway could be used for landing purposes with access to the pier-head. The Commissioners were concerned that the new lifeboat house might prevent passenger steamers, regular visitors at the time, mooring for disembarkation alongside the pier. As these suggested alterations meant an additional cost of £910, making the total cost an estimated £5,910, the RNLI wrote to the Commissioners explaining that it would be 'costly and disadvantageous to do as they suggested'. If the Commissioners persisted, the RNLI's Committee of Management had considered abandoning the idea of placing a motor lifeboat at Cromer and finding another station on the Norfolk coast, although the chief inspector believed that this would be difficult as Cromer was the favoured option.

But as the placing of a motor lifeboat was clearly seen as a prestigious honour for the town, the Commissioners rightly wanted such a boat at Cromer and were prepared to compromise. In September 1919, in expressing the hope that the Institution would still find the site at the end of the pier feasible, they explained that a building at the side of the pier 'would materially obstruct the view of persons in the shelter and on the pier-head'. As both parties wanted the matter resolved, by November 1919 plans had been agreed for a new boathouse at the end of the pier and, on 14 November, the RNLI approved a contract with the Scottish firm Charles Brand for driving fixed piles into the sea off the pier.

The work of construction had two distinct phases. Firstly, the building of the substructure and slipway using the then relatively new technique of precasting in reinforced concrete. And secondly, the building on this reinforced concrete platform of the new station using partly preformed timber components with riveted steel roof trusses. During the first phase, the piles were moulded from special concrete and then left to harden at the western end of the promenade before being transported to the end of the pier via a wooden track specially laid to protect the promenade and the pier decking. On completion of the substructure, the boathouse subframe was constructed with rafters in the roof. Finally, the cladding of the building was undertaken using tongued and grooved boarding.

Construction work lasted for about three years and was not without incident, as working in such a hostile environment, particularly in winter, took its toll. In June 1920, the staging used by the workmen had been wrecked necessitating the construction of a new and more substantial stage. It is not recorded when the contracted work should have been

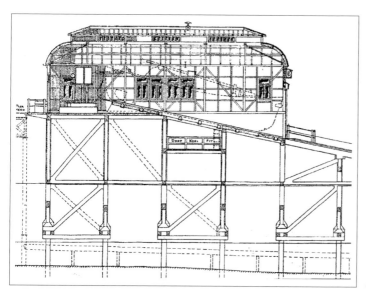

Line-drawing of the 1923 lifeboat house and slipway built for the station's first motor lifeboat, the outline of which has been included in this architect's drawing.

The lifeboat house and slipway built in 1923, seen from the sea, greatly eased the task of launching the lifeboat.

completed, but in November 1920 the RNLI's Committee of Management noted that it was behind schedule. Between 22 and 24 October 1921, a severe gale and heavy seas damaged the work that had by then been completed and, although the foundation timbers were nearly all recovered, a further gale on 1 November carried away nearly all the replacement work. A storm in January 1922 damaged the building and work was delayed a month later by bad weather. The RNLI's initial estimated cost of the work had been just under £6,000, and the Institution had questioned the tender from Charles Brand of £14,500 as being 'unnecessarily high'. However, the actual cost of approximately £32,000 reflected the difficulties involved in the construction. The new house measured 60ft by 21ft internally, with a floor of solid concrete. The advantages of the new house were explained in *The Lifeboat* journal:

> Now it has a motor lifeboat, Cromer has become one of the most important Stations on the coast, and it was this fact which decided the Institution to make the experiment – for the first time with a Motor Boat – of placing the Boathouse and Slipway at the end of the pier. Here, at all states of the tide, the boat can be launched well clear of all rocks and groynes. The pier itself runs to 500 feet from the shore, and as the boathouse is 60 feet long and the slipway 165 feet, the boat will enter the water nearly 250 yards from the shore.

On 26 May 1923, the new lifeboat was hauled up the slipway and entered the new boathouse for the first time. Some difficulty was experienced in initially getting the lifeboat into the new house but once this was overcome the first launch took place, a significant event which involved, according to the local newspaper, 'the boat charging down the 168ft slipway and reaching the water with thrilling spectacular effect'. The problems of launching over the beach, which was obstructed by groynes and debris from wrecked vessels, were now a thing of the past and the many outstanding rescues performed by the lifeboats operating from this boathouse vindicated the decision to invest so heavily in the station. The new house meant that a lifeboat could be stationed at Cromer that was larger – over 45ft in length – than any of the carriage-launched boats, with a far greater range than any pulling lifeboat, and as a result Cromer became one of the key stations on the east coast.

Despite the arrival of the new motor lifeboat in 1923, and the construction of the new boathouse, the beach-launched boat was retained to become the No.2 lifeboat providing back-up to the slipway-launched motor lifeboat. In certain states of weather, recovering the lifeboat up the slipway was impossible, and so she would have to proceed to Gorleston to shelter until conditions improved. At these times, cover was provided by the No.2 lifeboat, the importance of which is reflected by the stationing of a second motor lifeboat at Cromer in 1934, as described below.

The H.F. Bailey *Lifeboats*

Between 1923 and the end of the Second World War, four motor lifeboats served at Cromer, all named *H.F. Bailey* after their donor, Henry Francis Bailey, of Brockenhurst, a London merchant born in Norfolk. Bailey died in 1916 and directed that the residue of his estate, amounting to about £150,000, should be divided amongst various charities. A generous £10,000 was given to the RNLI for a lifeboat on the Norfolk coast, and part of this money was used for Cromer's first motor lifeboat. The inaugural ceremony for the first *H.F. Bailey* (ON.670) took place on 26 July 1923, with thousands of spectators crowding the pier and lining the shores. Sir George Shee, secretary of the Institution, presented the new lifeboat to Norfolk, and she was received by the Earl of Leicester, GCVO, Lord-Lieutenant of the county, who formally transferred her to the president of the Cromer branch, Lord Suffield, CB, CVO. The boat was dedicated by the bishop of Norwich, who said:

> For all our admiration for the splendid craft we are dedicating today, we are aware that her real usefulness in the gales we know so well on this coast will come from the fearless men who, leaving behind them all whom they love best, in agony of anxiety as to their safe return, quietly and bravely shall put out to save others who but for their efforts would be devoured by the sea.

Lady Suffield then christened the lifeboat which was launched down the slipway.

Despite a rather grand beginning to her service career, the first *H.F. Bailey* was not liked by either the coxswain or crew and after less than a year was replaced by a new 45ft Watson motor class. The Watson motor lifeboats were preferred at Cromer and a number of different versions served the station until the 1960s. During her time at Cromer the first *H.F. Bailey* was launched three times on service, the first on 19 July 1923 after a message had been received by the coxswain that the smack *Hepatica*, of Lowestoft, was in difficulty. After launching and proceeding about half a mile, the lifeboat's engine stopped so the sails were set. After a further ten minutes, the two motor mechanics and the assistant mechanic got the engine working again, and it worked satisfactorily for the rest of the service. The casualty was reached at 8.20 a.m. and was found to be aground. Two ropes were put aboard and, as there was no risk of damaging either boat or machinery, the lifeboat pulled the vessel off in ten minutes and towed her clear of the sands outside the East Buoy. She left the smack at 9.30 a.m. and proceeded to Cromer, calling and reporting at Haisborough lightvessel, and towing the Palling lifeboat until 12.10 p.m. The lifeboat arrived back at her station at 1.10 p.m. but could not be rehoused as, when the wire hawser was being hauled down the slipway, one link of the chain broke. The boat therefore had to anchor until the chain had been repaired – not a particularly auspicious start for either the new motor lifeboat or the equipment in the lifeboat house.

Further problems with the engine were experienced on 18 December 1923 after the lifeboat launched to an unknown steam trawler in difficulty. After about five minutes at sea, the mechanic reported that the engine was airlocked, so he pumped sea water into the tank. The engine was run slowly, but stopped after about fifteen minutes and the mechanic could not get it to start again. So sails were set and the lifeboat was taken to the casualty's position, but nothing was found except for a trawler fishing close to the Sands. The lifeboat went as far as the East Buoy, but again found nothing so went to the

Above; *Launch of H.F. Bailey (ON.670) after her naming ceremony on 26 July 1923. (From an old postcard supplied by Paul Russell)*

Right: *Lady Suffield, with the bishop of Norwich, about to name Cromer's first motor lifeboat, H.F. Bailey, 26 July 1923.*

Haisborough lightvessel at about 8 a.m. The lifeboat remained there whilst the mechanic tried to repair the engine but without success. The captain of the lightvessel told the coxswain that the vessel in difficulty had refloated at 1.35 a.m., and that he saw the lifeboat in the position about 2 a.m. The lifeboat left the lightvessel around 9 a.m. and reached the slipway at 4 p.m., but a heavy ground swell considerably slowed the recovery.

The last launch of the station's first motor lifeboat took place on 1 January 1924. She put out after a message from the Haisborough lightvessel had been received about a vessel on the Sands. At 8 p.m. the lifeboat found the steamship *Nephrite*, of Glasgow, which had stranded at about 3.15 p.m. Assistance was required to refloat the vessel, so Coxswain Blogg put seven lifeboatmen aboard and then went to the Haisborough lightvessel to telephone for tugs. Upon returning to the steamship, the lifeboat ran out the anchor and the lifeboat crew assisted in jettisoning the cargo. At about 1 a.m. the vessel refloated and was able to proceed under her own steam so the lifeboat returned to station. During the operation, the lifeboat collided with the steamship and nine planks were stove in just below the gunwale on the starboard bow. During the passage back to Cromer, the engine developed three airlocks and G. Garner, the RNLI's Fleet Mechanic, had to monitor the engine very carefully to ensure the boat returned safely, as the wind had all but died away. *H.F. Bailey* returned to her station at 6.30 a.m. on 2 January after a long service, and one which had again shown the engine to be somewhat unreliable.

Although the station's first motor lifeboat had a questionable reliability record, this was not the reason for her departure from the station. The main problem with the first *H.F. Bailey* was getting her to slide down the slipway from the house. Her keel, of similar metal to that in the groove of the slipway, caused such friction that when launching, more often than not the two metals would grip each other. On 15 May 1924 the *Eastern Daily Press* reported that another motor lifeboat was to be sent to the station, and published an interview with the station's honorary secretary, F.H. Barclay, explaining why a new boat was coming when the one to be replaced had been at Cromer for such a relatively short period of time:

> One can imagine the risk her crew would run in launching the boat in rough weather conditions, with seas breaking over the slipway. They and the boat would be at the mercy of the waves, helpless, if the keel stuck on such an occasion. For months every means of remedying the trouble without having to change the boat has been exploited. The lifeboatmen and the officials of the Institution have experimented untiringly, and a variety of tests and experiments with a model of the boat and various metals and weights have been carried out at the Institution's storehouse at Poplar. These efforts all proved futile, and the decision was arrived at to send *H.F. Bailey* to Gorleston where she will have only a short slipway to go down, and not straight into the open sea.

The replacement motor lifeboat was of the 45ft Watson motor type, which the Institution had originally allocated to Cromer but which the lifeboatmen had rejected in favour of a Norfolk & Suffolk type. Coxswain Henry Blogg and some of the crew went to Cowes to examine one of the Watson boats, which apparently they had not seen before, and were reportedly 'very pleased with it'. Unlike the Norfolk & Suffolk boat, which was completely open, the 45ft Watson had a small cabin and shelter for the mechanic. She had a much wider and heavier keel than her predecessor, and so she could be successfully launched alterations were made to the slipway which involved removing the metal keelway, which was embedded in concrete, and installing a system of rollers down the first part of the slipway from the house. The development of roller slipways by the RNLI came about with the advent of the motor lifeboat, as hitherto, relatively light sailing lifeboats had been operated at the majority of slipway stations. The larger and heavier motor lifeboats needed a modified slipway to ensure they could be launched safely and rollers set into the keelway have been a feature of lifeboat slipways ever since.

The new Watson lifeboat arrived on 19 August 1924 having sailed from Cowes, where she had been built by J.S. White, with Coxswain Blogg accompanied by Captain Carver, district inspector of lifeboats, and some of the Cromer lifeboatmen. Built at a cost of £7,579 16s 3d, she was, like her predecessor, appropriated to the legacy of Henry Frances Bailey and named *H.F. Bailey*. She was fitted with a single 80bhp White DE six-cylinder petrol engine, incorporating a self-contained reverse gear. During trials, she had reached a maximum speed of 8.18 knots, consuming sixty pints of fuel per hour, and had a range of sixty-three nautical miles.

The first service by the new *H.F. Bailey* (ON.694) took place on 9 September 1924, within a month of her arriving at Cromer. Four shipwrecked men from the auxiliary motor boat *Iona*, of Middlesbrough, who had been picked up by the steamship *Orjen*, were on the Happisburgh lightvessel. Coxswain Blogg asked chief mechanic G. Garner and mechanic R. Davies to get ready as quickly as possible as he thought it would be a good test for the engine. The lifeboat was launched at 7.20 a.m. and soon reached the lightvessel from which the four men were collected. The engine worked well throughout and the four men were brought back to Cromer where they were safely landed at 10.50 a.m. The official report stated that the boat was much easier to get onto the slipway than the previous boat.

The new lifeboat performed three further services during 1924. On 22 October she rescued nine from the steamship *Clansman*, of Lowestoft, which had been damaged by a violent gale. Heavy seas swept over the vessel, so the crew took to the ship's boat and the steamer later sank. The lifeboat launched at 10 a.m. and rescued the shipwrecked men, who were very cold and exhausted having been in the small boat for about five hours. On 5 December 1924, *H.F. Bailey* went to the aid of the steamship *Vojvoda Putnik*, of Split, which had stranded on the Haisborough Sands. The vessel, with a crew of forty-one, was bound for Blyth from Genoa. Together with the Palling No.2 lifeboat *Hearts of*

This excellent photograph of H.F. Bailey *(second) off the slipway in 1924 clearly shows the layout of the RNLI's early motor lifeboats. The 45ft Watson type, of which* H.F. Bailey II *was one of the last built, was one of the first motor lifeboat classes to have any kind of crew shelter. (By courtesy of P.A. Vicary)*

Oak (ON.656), the Cromer lifeboatmen assisted to pump out the steamer and in the early hours of 6 December she was refloated. The final service of the year took place on 27 December when the lifeboatmen went to the Smiths Knoll lightvessel, which had parted her cable and was about two miles out of position.

During the following year, *H.F. Bailey* performed three services. The first took place on 19 April 1925 when she went to the steam drifter *Couronne*, of Lowestoft, which had been wrecked on the Haisborough Sands while returning from the fishing grounds with her catch. When the lifeboat reached the casualty, she found three steamers already standing by. Boats from these steamers had attempted to reach the stranded drifter but had been unable to get close enough in the heavy seas on the Sands, and so the crew was taken off by the lifeboat. On 12 June, *H.F. Bailey* assisted the steamship *Equity*, of Goole, and on 14 October went to the barge *Scotia*, of London, bound for Maldon with a cargo of basic slag. The lifeboat launched at 11.40 a.m. and reached the casualty just over an hour later. Several lifeboatmen were put on board the barge and she was taken in tow by a drifter, which had arrived at the same time as the lifeboat. Twice the tow rope parted but eventually the barge reached Great Yarmouth safely with the lifeboat in close attendance.

During 1926 the lifeboat was not called on to perform any services and was not needed again until 9 July 1927. She then went to the aid of the steam trawler *Anson*, of Grimsby, which had gone aground in the middle of the Haisborough Sands. The trawler had grounded at 6 a.m. in thick fog and her fishing gear had fouled the propellers. The lifeboat stood by until the arrival of two tugs at 1.03 p.m. A towing operation began but failed to get the vessel off and had to be abandoned because of the shallow water and heavy breaking seas. The lifeboat continued to stand by until 5 p.m. when the vessel was driven right across the sands. Coxswain Blogg then passed ropes aboard and towed the vessel to a safe anchorage about a mile from the Wold lightvessel. The lifeboat then went to Great Yarmouth to send a tug to tow the trawler, and remained in port overnight.

In November 1927, an outstanding rescue was performed by the Cromer lifeboatmen, the first medal-winning service since the new pier-end boathouse had become operational. The rescue also became one of the most famous in the history of the station. The Dutch oil tanker *Georgia*, of Rotterdam, of 5,111 gross tons and 3,104 net, was bound from the port of Abadan on passage to Grangemouth with a cargo of crude oil. The 389ft vessel, built in 1908 at Newport News, was nearing the end of her voyage when she was caught by a vicious gale in the North Sea on 21 November. Her steering gear broke down, she struck the Haisborough Sands and was bumped and pounded on the Sands by the heavy seas until she was ripped apart amidships. She had kept sounding her siren as a distress signal but eventually the two halves drifted out of sight of each other. So sudden and violent had been the impact when she went aground that the radio operator did not have time to send a distress call out before the aerials were carried away. The vessel had been torn in two and, as the stern section was carried away by the gale, the bow section stuck fast on the sands with huge seas washing over it. Captain Harry Kissing and fourteen of the crew crouched in the fo'c's'le watching the after part drifting away with sixteen of their shipmates on board.

Throughout the night it drifted north-westwards, battered by the seas which constantly swept the decks. The men who gathered in the stern could only wonder whether their part would sink before help arrived or whether it would come to grief on another sandbank. The next morning it was spotted by the steamer *Trent* and the sixteen men were taken off. The steamer then made for the Haisborough Sands to try to save the men on the forepart of the ship while her radio operator called for assistance stating that help was urgently needed. The news reached Great Yarmouth about 9 p.m. on 21 November that *Georgia* was seven miles north-north-west of the Newarp lightvessel, and so the

The stern section of the Dutch tanker Georgia *sinking off Cromer, November 1927. (By courtesy of P.A. Vicary)*

Gorleston lifeboat *John and Mary Meiklam of Gladswood* put off under the command of Coxswain Fleming to provide what assistance she could.

Meanwhile, the abandoned stern part of the casualty drifted along until it was seen off Cromer at about 2 p.m. At first it was believed that the vessel's bow was completely under water and her stern in the air. Although no distress signals came from the steamer, shortly after 2.30 p.m. the coastguard fired rockets to summon the lifeboat crew and within three minutes *H.F. Bailey*, with Coxswain Blogg and his crew, was launched into the easterly gale. Although of course the bow could not be seen, the mainmast and funnel were clearly visible while the vessel's stern seemed to creep higher and higher into the air. Shortly after 3.15 p.m. the lifeboat returned and the lifeboat crew sent a message to the effect that the steamer had been abandoned, as there were no signs of life on board but one of the steamer's three small lifeboats was missing. The lifeboat then returned to the steamer to stand by and warn shipping as the broken vessel was a danger to navigation. Throughout the bitterly cold night the Cromer lifeboatmen stood by, returning to the pier on the morning of 22 November to receive some food by means of ropes as the boat could not be rehoused.

While the Cromer lifeboat was making an apparently fruitless journey on Monday afternoon to the sinking steamer two miles out, it was not realised that this was only half the vessel. Help was still being sent to the other half which remained in grave danger on the Sands, battered incessantly by the heavy seas, while the Gorleston lifeboat stood by throughout the night. A wireless message was sent from *Trent* stating that *Georgia* was showing red lights only, that further assistance was necessary, and that it was dangerous to approach the drifting tanker. At 4 a.m. on 22 November, the Yarmouth tugs *George Jewson* and *Tactful* left to try to help *Georgia* while that part of her crew which had been picked up by *Trent* were put ashore at Cromer.

As dawn broke on 22 November the Gorleston lifeboatmen saw the remains of the tanker being battered by the heavy seas. Coxswain Fleming tried to take the lifeboat alongside, making what use he could of the lee provided by *Trent*, but in the heavy seas could do nothing to help the fifteen stranded men who had by now left the fo'c's'le for the shelter of the chartroom high on *Georgia's* bridge. The Gorleston lifeboat then stood off and waited until conditions might ease. Coxswain Fleming made another attempt at midday and succeeded, at the fifth attempt, in getting a line to the wreck. A 2in rope was then pulled across by the men on *Georgia*, but just as they were preparing to leave, a huge wave picked up the lifeboat, dropped her into a trough and the rope parted. Coxswain Fleming and his crew had done all they could, with the coxswain later remarking 'we were all finished and half dead'. Weighing anchor, the Gorleston lifeboat headed for the destroyer HMS *Thanet*, one of several vessels standing by, for hot drinks and to obtain fresh water for the cooling system of the lifeboat's engine which was not functioning properly. *John and Mary Meiklam of Gladswood* had been out for twenty-one hours by the time she returned to Gorleston and the crew was exhausted.

Meanwhile, at Cromer, *H.F. Bailey* was being rehoused after standing by the stern section of the tanker throughout the night. As the lifeboatmen were clearing a rope which had fouled one of the lifeboat's propellers, the honorary secretary F.H. Barclay arrived in the boathouse with word that their services were again required on the Haisborough Sands. They left at 1.30 p.m., taking oil to pour on the sea and agreeing that they would not return without the rescued men. At 4.30 p.m., with the last glimpses of daylight left, the Cromer lifeboat got sufficiently near the wreck for the lifeboatmen to effect a rescue and just as they arrived at the casualty one of the cargo tanks burst open, spreading oil over the seas and calming them. Coxswain Blogg quickly decided, he explained afterwards, that 'the job had to be done before dark, so I went straight at her'.

Taking advantage of the relatively smooth seas created by the oil spill, Blogg steered the lifeboat close to the doomed vessel and the men on *Georgia*'s bridge got ready to jump. As they waited for the right moment, a heavy sea caught the lifeboat, turned her around and threw her stern hard against the side of the wreck. The damage to the lifeboat was considerable, but she remained seaworthy and the lifeboatmen soon recovered themselves. Heaving lines were thrown to the stranded men and ropes were made fast to hold the lifeboat in position. Each time the lifeboat lifted on a sea, one or two of the tanker's crew leapt to safety to be grabbed by the lifeboatmen. Leslie Kaye, the captain's steward on the tanker, later described the moment of rescue:

> When I saw the lifeboatmen I felt as happy as anything. They shouted to us 'Take your time, be steady, and jump one at a time.' Captain Henry Kissing was the last to jump. The lifeboatmen gave us cakes and bread and cheese and then brought us to Yarmouth. We spent our time of waiting in the wheel-house, packed like sardines in a box, smoking, talking, and sleeping when we could.

The half of the tanker on which they were sheltering would not have lasted much longer, while fumes from the oil also added to the discomfort of both rescuers and rescued.

Soon all were aboard, but before the lifeboat could get clear of the wreck a heavy sea suddenly caught the boat and carried her onto the tanker's bulwarks. Motor mechanic Davies did not wait for orders from the coxswain but immediately slammed the engines into reverse and the lifeboat moved astern, clearing the wreck just in time to avoid serious damage. Her bilge keel had been partly torn off and a hole had been ripped in her hull flooding the forepeak. But she remained seaworthy and set course for Great Yarmouth. Shortly before 7 p.m., *H.F. Bailey* arrived in harbour with the fifteen rescued men who had been almost forty hours on the broken steamer without food or drink, ending a truly extraordinary rescue. The lifeboat had made no fewer than three trips to the Haisborough Sands, and on the final one ran alongside the stricken vessel in a dangerous and daring rescue bid. The *Eastern Daily Press* for 23 November 1927 hailed the event as 'one of the most dramatic stories in the annals of East Coast shipping casualties'. *H.F. Bailey* had been away from her station for forty-eight hours from the time the stern part of the *Georgia* was seen sinking off Cromer to the time the lifeboat was hauled up the slipway.

In recognition of this outstanding rescue, the Gold medal was awarded to Coxswain Henry Blogg, and Bronze medals to the rest of the crew: Second Coxswain George Balls; the mechanic Robert Davies and Henry W. Davies (brothers); Bowman John J. Davies and John J. Davies jnr (father and son); W. Davies and Jim Davies jnr (father and son); R. Barker jnr; L. Harrison and S.C. 'Kelly' Harrison (father and son); G. Cox and W. Allen. On board the lifeboat for this rescue were no fewer than six representatives of the Davies family. The Bronze medals were presented by George Shee, secretary of the RNLI, at a ceremony held in the Town Hall at Cromer on 30 January 1928. Shee paid tribute to the Cromer crew, 'I can congratulate Cromer upon having young men who recognize the value of sea service, and are proud to be in the lifeboat.' The crew who took part in the rescue also received inscribed silver watches, with Coxswain Blogg getting a gold one. The inscription read, 'Presented to Coxswain Henry G. Blogg, Cromer lifeboat *H.F. Bailey*, for gallant service s.s. *Georgia*, 22 November 1927.' Coxswain Blogg received his medal from the Prince of Wales in March 1928 at the Institution's annual meeting in London.

Soon after this rescue, the Cromer lifeboatmen were involved in another test of their stamina and endurance, but despite their efforts did not perform an effective service. During Christmas Day 1927 a severe gale increased in force throughout the day, accompanied by squalls of snow and hail. At about 9.30 p.m. a message was received that the Union-Castle liner *Crawford Castle*, a screw steamer of 4,383 gross tons built at Newcastle in 1910, had collided with the Haisborough lightvessel during a snow squall. The lifeboat crew was ordered to stand by but stood down when subsequent reports stated that the collision was a minor incident.

However, the following day, 26 December, a request for assistance was received and so *H.F. Bailey* was launched to the steamer, reported to be two miles east of the Dudgeon lightvessel. Watched by a large crowd from the pier, the lifeboat battled her way through the hurricane force winds and heavy seas. She disappeared from view for a moment, but was soon seen again by the crowd contending with the wind and seas. At 3.30 p.m. she reached the Dudgeon lightvessel, where the lifeboat crew was told that *Crawford Castle* had collided with the lightvessel and that two flares were burned to show the steamer's position. *Crawford Castle* was last sighted by the lightvessel at 10.30 a.m. heading north.

Two Hull tugs had been sent from Grimsby and the Spurn lifeboat was also launched, while the Cromer lifeboat headed north searching for the casualty. After twelve difficult hours at sea, the Cromer lifeboatmen had not seen the steamer, which by this time was reported to have reached the Humber safely. So, as the gale was too heavy to return to Cromer or Yarmouth, the lifeboat made for Grimsby. Coxswain Blogg recalled the hours at sea: 'We were taking water aboard for ten of the twelve hours and were drenched to the skin. It was a big test for my crew, four of whom were on the young side. It is certainly the biggest test the *H.F. Bailey* has had, but she stood it well.' News reached Cromer at midnight on 26 December that the lifeboat had arrived safely at Grimsby from where the lifeboat crew returned to Cromer by train. Although no rescue had been performed, it was one of the most difficult and arduous services undertaken hitherto.

The last service performed by the second *H.F. Bailey* during what was to be her first spell at the station took place on 25 January 1928. A vessel was reported to be in distress two miles north of Mundesley. The ketch *Harold*, of London, with a crew of three, bound from Keadby to St Osyth, was found with damaged steering gear and sails. A tug from Great Yarmouth took the ketch in tow and the lifeboat escorted both vessels until they reached Yarmouth at 8.30 p.m. As weather conditions were too bad for the ketch to enter harbour, she remained anchored outside for the night with the lifeboat standing by. After seeing the ketch safely into harbour the following morning, the lifeboat returned to station.

When *H.F. Bailey* was taken to Rowhedge in 1928 to be thoroughly overhauled and repaired after the damage she received while on service to *Georgia* in November 1927, a brand new lifeboat was sent to the station. Named *H.F. Bailey II* (ON.714), this new boat was a 45ft 6in Watson cabin motor type built by S.E. Saunders at Cowes. Fitted with twin 40hp engines and twin screws, she had a radius of action of more than sixty miles and was equipped with a searchlight and line-throwing gun. She left Cowes on 22 November 1928 under the command of Captain Carver, the district inspector of lifeboats for the Eastern Division, together with Coxswain Blogg and a crew of four Cromer lifeboatmen for a passage that became rather a drawn out affair. The new lifeboat reached Gorleston at 4 p.m. on 23 November, when Coxswain Blogg and the lifeboatmen returned to Cromer. On Sunday 25 November, the old lifeboat was launched and taken to Gorleston by some of the lifeboat crew. Meanwhile, Coxswain Blogg and the crew left for Cromer with the new boat, but when they got beyond Caister heavy seas and squalls forced them to return to Gorleston again as recovering the boat up the slipway in such weather would have been impossible without damaging her. She ended up staying at Gorleston for more than a week until, on 4 December, she left at 9 a.m. and finally reached her new station, where she was housed at 2.10 p.m. in fine weather and calm seas. The crowd, which had gathered on the pier and cliffs to watch the new boat being recovered included Mr D. Davison, chairman of the Lifeboat Committee, and the station honorary secretary F.H. Barclay.

H.F. Bailey II served at the station for less than six months, during which time she launched only three times on service and is credited with saving five lives. Her only effective rescue took place on 11 December 1928 and proved to be a rather routine incident. After a message had been received from Mundesley that a vessel was in difficulty, the lifeboat launched and proceeded to the schooner *Thursonian*, of Wick, which was anchored north-east of Mundesley. The ship's master stated that he had anchored for safety but the wind had caused the vessel to drag her anchor, taking her into shallow water. Fearing that a strong easterly gale was imminent, he requested the lifeboat take off the crew of five, which was done, and the lifeboat then returned to Cromer. An attempt was made to recover the lifeboat on the slipway but, with the strong sea running, the buoy anchor dragged and they gave up. The schooner's crew was landed on the slipway, and the lifeboat was recovered later.

The other two services performed by *H.F. Bailey II* at Cromer took place during spring 1929. On 17 March 1929 she was launched to a steamship, *Corbrae*, of London, which was reportedly aground and in need of assistance. She reached the vessel and stood by until 9 a.m. the following day, but her help was not required. Her last service at Cromer, on 14 April 1929, took her to the Haisborough Sands. After launching at 9 a.m., she reached the North Haisborough Buoy at about 10 a.m., and searched to the south end of the sands without success. After proceeding to the Newark lightvessel, the lifeboatmen found the Palling lifeboat *Jacob and Rachel Vallentine* (ON.580) anchored alongside, unable to proceed against the wind and tide. The Palling coxswain informed Coxswain Blogg that the steamship *Tansworth* had reported a vessel was aground on the south part of the Haisborough Sands needing assistance, and that the crew of the lightvessel had seen a small boat, hatches, and other wreckage drifting past. Coxswain Blogg took the Palling boat in tow and again proceeded to search the sands as far as Middle Haisborough Buoy, but as nothing was found both boats returned to their respective stations.

Right: H.F. Bailey II (ON.714) off the slipway at Cromer with her mast down preparing to be recovered. This photograph may have been taken on the day she arrived at the station. (By courtesy of P.A. Vicary)

Below: Lifeboat crew and station officials at the 1928 annual Lifeboat Dinner. (From a photograph by H.H. Tansley)

A month after this service, *H.F. Bailey II* (ON.714) was withdrawn from Cromer and taken to the RNLI's storeyard for overhaul. After this, she went up the Thames to London where she was inspected by Members of Parliament and then proceeded to Selsey where, renamed *Canadian Pacific*, she served as that station's first motor lifeboat. According to the Branch Annual Report of November 1929, the crew had the option of retaining *H.F. Bailey II* as station lifeboat but they preferred their old boat, the second *H.F. Bailey*. So this boat was returned to the station, arriving on 14 May 1929 after repairs had been completed and just in time for the station's centenary celebrations. A Centenary Vellum was presented by Sir Godfrey Baring, chairman of the RNLI's Committee of Management, at a special meeting held at the Parish Hall on 19 July 1929. Up to this time, it was recorded that the station's lifeboats had launched 169 times and had saved 366 lives. During the presentation, the Vice Consul of the Netherlands for Yarmouth, G. Palgrave Brown, on behalf of the Queen of Holland, presented a gold watch to Coxswain Henry Blogg and a silver watch to each of the crew who took part in the epic service to the Dutch oil tanker *Georgia*.

On 30 October 1929, a sailing vessel was seen in difficulties about two miles north of Sheringham Shoal Buoy and so *H.F. Bailey* was launched. She reached the vessel, the four-masted schooner *Svenborg*, of Vardo, at about 12.15 p.m., and found that the schooner's fore-mast, bowsprit and jib boom had been carried away. Her captain, however, refused any assistance, saying that he would navigate his vessel to the Yarmouth

Reserve 45ft Watson motor lifeboat City of Bradford I *(ON.680) launching on exercise during one of her periods on duty at Cromer, either June 1931 or 1932. (By courtesy of P.A. Vicary)*

Roads. As the vessel was so badly damaged and the weather was squally and getting worse, the coxswain decided to stay by the vessel until she safely anchored at Yarmouth about 6.30 p.m. The lifeboat then put into the port and did not return to station until 1 November as it was too rough to rehouse her before then.

In 1931, tragedy struck North Norfolk's fishing community. On the morning of 17 February, after a number of fishing boats from Sheringham were caught in heavy seas, *H.F. Bailey* was launched at 3.20 p.m. The Sheringham private lifeboat *Henry Ramey Upcher* rescued the crew of two from the fishing boat *White Heather II* and took her in tow while another fishing boat, *Welcome Home*, was making for the shore. When about 200 yards off, she was overwhelmed by a heavy breaking sea, capsized and sank. The Sheringham lifeboat, which was a quarter of a mile away, and *H.F. Bailey*, 600 yards away, immediately went to help. Another motor fishing boat, *The Liberty*, which had just been landed, was launched again and her crew of three made a gallant attempt but the boat's engine stopped, a heavy sea filled her and she was driven ashore. Sheringham and Cromer lifeboats were quickly on the scene. The Sheringham boat picked up one man, and the Cromer boat made for the other two, one of whom was wearing a lifebelt, while the other had an arm thrown over a spar. The coxswain threw a belt with a line attached to the first man, who was hauled on board, while at the same time the bowman, J.J. Davies snr, jumped overboard to the help of the second man, who had been injured, and held him up until a line was thrown to them and they were hauled aboard. The lifeboat made full speed for Cromer, where the two rescued men were landed. The St John Ambulance Brigade attempted to revive the second of the men, John Craske, but their efforts were in vain and sadly he died. He was the son and brother of two of the three men who had made such a gallant attempt in *The Liberty* to rescue him before the lifeboats had reached him. In recognition of his gallantry, the Institution awarded a second Service Clasp to the Bronze medal to Bowman J.J. Davies snr.

Three further services were performed during 1931, one of which proved to be particularly long and arduous. During the night of 19 November, the steamship *Zembra*, of Dunkirk, bound from Hartlepool to Savona, laden with coal and with a crew of twenty-nine, ran aground in heavy fog on the Haisborough Sands. After the Coastguard had received details of the stranding the following day, *H.F. Bailey* was launched at 12.30 p.m. and reached the vessel, about four miles south-east of the Haisborough lightvessel, two hours later. The lifeboat stood by throughout the rest of the day and overnight as salvage tugs attempted to refloat the steamer. At daylight on 21 November the coxswain was asked to continue standing by during the tugs' salvage operations, so the lifeboat remained on scene until the early hours of 22 November, when *Zembra* floated off the Sands and was able to continue her voyage.

During the latter part of 1932, two services were performed to motor vessels that had got into difficulty which, while relatively routine in nature, were long in duration. On 7 August, *H.F. Bailey* put out to the motor trawler *Iverna*, of Galway, which was disabled off Overstrand. The lifeboat towed the trawler, together with its three crew, into Great Yarmouth and then returned to station after being out for eleven hours. On 3 September, the motor barge *Olive May*, of London, with a crew of four bound from Rye to the Humber laden with shingle, was in need of help after she had struck a rock and was leaking badly. *H.F. Bailey* was launched at 6.30 p.m. and towed the barge into Great Yarmouth, arriving at 2 a.m. She then returned to Cromer, arriving at 5.30 a.m. but, owing to the strong wind and sea, had to lie at moorings until 2.30 p.m. before being rehoused.

A month after this service, the Cromer lifeboatmen were involved in another impressive and daring rescue. In October 1932, the 5,000-ton cargo ship *Monte Nevoso*, of Genoa, left La Plata (Buenos Aires) in Argentina, bound for Hull, with a cargo of wheat, maize and linseed. But on the morning of 14 October she stranded in fine weather on the Haisborough Sands, fourteen miles from Cromer. Captain Angelino Salvatore and his crew attempted to free her using the steamer's engines, but when this failed he requested the help of tugs. At 9.30 a.m. *H.F. Bailey* was launched and reached the casualty at about noon to find the tug *Noordzee*, of Rotterdam, already standing by. Five more tugs arrived later and at 4.30 p.m. the first attempt to tow the steamer off the sands began. Meanwhile, the wind had gradually increased and by the early hours of 15 October a gale was blowing from the north-west with heavy seas greatly hampering the rescue attempts. In the heavy weather, the tow ropes on two of the tugs, *Irishman* and *Yorkshireman*, broke and the tow rope on *Scotsman* had to be cut.

By 8 a.m., all six tugs had cast off with the steamer on the point of breaking up having been weakened by being constantly lifted and banged on the Sands. Her engine room became flooded and the rudder and stern post were smashed by a huge sea. At this point, a signal to take off the steamer's crew was made so Coxswain Blogg weighed anchor and the lifeboat, which had been standing by for eighteen hours, approached the casualty. *H.F. Bailey* was anchored to windward and veered alongside to begin the difficult and dangerous job of transferring the steamer's crew to the lifeboat in the heavy seas. The seas were so heavy that the lifeboat was rising to the top of the ship's rail and then dropping 20ft below. The lifeboatmen encouraged the seamen to jump just as the lifeboat reached the peak of its rise. Several times the lifeboat hit the iron side of the steamer and, although fenders were used, the boat suffered damage throughout the operation. The cork fender was ripped off and everything else used as a buffer was torn to shreds.

After an hour, twenty-nine of the steamer's crew had been rescued, clambering onto the lifeboat one by one, together with one of the Dutch tug's crew who had gone aboard. At one point, a crewman had misjudged the distance when he jumped and ended up in the sea between casualty and lifeboat, but he was hauled aboard unhurt. The captain, mate, chief engineer and wireless operator, however, refused to leave and so the lifeboat set course for Gorleston with those she had saved. After the twenty-one mile passage, she reached Gorleston at about noon, landed the rescued men, was refuelled, and some of the lifeboat crew, all of whom were soaked through, changed into dry clothes. Then, without waiting to get a hot meal despite having eaten virtually nothing since the previous morning, and declining the offer of the Gorleston lifeboat to relieve them, the lifeboatmen put out again at 2 p.m. and returned to the wreck in the hope of persuading the four men still on board to leave.

H.F. Bailey reached the Sands at 4.45 p.m. but found the captain still refusing to abandon his vessel. If he needed help, he would call using his wireless which remained in working order, so the lifeboat returned to Gorleston where the crew had their first proper meal for thirty-five hours. They were put up at the Mariners' Refuge, close to the Coastguard station, so that they were ready to set out at once if the call came. Nothing, however, was heard, so at 5 a.m. on 16 October Coxswain Blogg took the lifeboat out again accompanied by two tugs and reached the wreck three hours later. The vessel had by this time broken her back and the four men had abandoned her in the steamer's motor boat. They had left two dogs behind, one a large St Bernard which was

The Italian steamer Monte Nevoso, *grounded on the Haisborough Sands with H.F. Bailey (second) and the Dutch tug* Noordzee *standing by, 14 October 1932. The tugs attempted to pull the steamer off the sands, but all efforts failed in the increasingly bad weather and the lifeboat had to move in and rescue the steamer's crew as well as one of the tug's crew who had gone on board during the salvage operation. During this service, the lifeboat was away from her station for more than fifty hours and rescued twenty-nine lives. (By courtesy of P.A. Vicary)*

The motor barge Goldcrown *ashore at East Runton on the evening of 20 November 1933, with H.F. Bailey standing by. The lifeboat, which launched to stand by as the master did not want to abandon ship, passed a hawser between the motor barge and a tug which attempted to tow the barge clear. When this failed, and as the barge was in no danger, the lifeboat returned to station after fourteen hours on scene. The barge later refloated and resumed her course. (From a postcard supplied by Paul Russell)*

rescued by lifeboatmen who boarded the wreck. The other, a small dog, would not allow itself to be caught and the lifeboatmen were forced to leave it behind.

The four men who had abandoned the vessel were picked up by a trawler and taken to Lowestoft, while Coxswain Blogg made for the Haisborough lightvessel to find out if the weather conditions would allow the lifeboat to be rehoused up her slipway. He then made for Cromer, where the lifeboat arrived at 1 p.m., nearly fifty-two hours after she had been launched and during which time she had travelled seventy miles. *The Lifeboat* for November 1932 summed up the rescue; 'It was an outstanding service, marked by faultless seamanship on the part of Coxswain Blogg, and great courage, endurance and devotion to duty on the part of Coxswain and Crew.' Blogg was awarded the Silver medal, accompanied by a Vellum signed by HRH The Prince of Wales as president of the Institution, and each of the twelve crew members were accorded the Thanks of the Institution on Vellum: George Balls (ex-second coxswain); William T. Davies, snr; Jack J. Davies (later second coxswain); Robert Davies; Charles Cox; Robert Cox; J. Davies, jnr; H.W. Davies; James Davies; A. Balls; R. Blogg, and W. Allen.

Other organisations rewarded the crew for their courage and endurance, including the Canine Defence League, which awarded Blogg with its Silver medal for the rescue of the dog. Blogg was later presented with the dog, after six months quarantine, and he christened it Monte. Recognition by the Italian Government was also forthcoming. At the annual meeting of the Cromer branch in November 1934, Lady Suffield presented Blogg with an Italian Silver medal and the remainder of the crew a Bronze medal each, accompanied by a warrant of appreciation in Italian.

Just over a year after the *Monte Nevoso* incident, the Cromer lifeboat was involved in another epic rescue. In December 1933, heavy snowstorms swept over England and parts of Wales, and the country was lashed by gale force winds of which the east coast bore the brunt. The East Anglian coast was battered by the storm and lifeboats in both Norfolk and Suffolk were exceptionally busy as the heavy weather in the North Sea tested any ships caught out of port. A three-masted vessel was lost with all hands off Aldeburgh and the Aldeburgh lifeboat *Abdy Beauclerk* (ON.751) launched but the vessel had disappeared without trace. Sheringham and Blakeney lifeboats launched to a barge in trouble off Blakeney and stood by until the evening, by which time the vessel was out of danger. At Cromer, the Dover barge *Sepoy*, of sixty-five tons, was driven ashore and in saving the two men who were on board the Cromer motor lifeboat performed one of the finest services in the history of the station. The *Eastern Daily Press* of 14 December 1933, in describing the 'thrilling rescue', stated that 'so fine was the seamanship shown by Coxswain Blogg and his crew that by way of celebration a peal was rung on the Cromer Church bells'.

When *Sepoy* first hoisted distress signals at dawn, the motor lifeboat was on service further down the coast. *H.F. Bailey* had been launched at 4.30 a.m. in response to a message from Haisborough Coastguard that a vessel was showing flares and by the time the lifeboat was most needed at Cromer, she was on her way to Gorleston. By 11 a.m., with the No.1 lifeboat away, *Sepoy* was dragging her anchors and had started drifting towards the shore. Attempts were made to get the No.2 pulling lifeboat *Alexandra* afloat, with more than 100 people assisting as a cold, biting east-south-east gale blew along the beach, making the launch very difficult. Her carriage was pushed into the water and she was got away, but within ten minutes had been thrown back onto the beach as the crew had insufficient water in which to row. Getting the boat back onto her carriage after this initial launch took nearly an hour, but eventually she was launched again and this time into deeper water. The crew rowed hard for twenty minutes, but the wind proved too strong and the lifeboat was forced to return to the beach.

On the barge, matters were worsening. The two men on board had taken to the rigging as the vessel drifted towards the groynes and, being swept by huge seas, soon came ashore. It was bitterly cold, as hundreds watched the plight of the men and the efforts of the lifeboat and the Cromer Life Saving Company to save them. After three unsuccessful attempts, the Life Saving Company fired a rope which landed across the bow of *Sepoy*. The man at the bottom of the rigging jumped to the deck and, climbing back to the rigging again, succeeded in fastening the rope to the mast. At 1.15 p.m. *Alexandra* was launched for a third time but, unfortunately, drifted over the rope that connected the barge to the shore and cut it in two. As the lifeboat was carried past the wreck, the waves took her right over the breakwater which might have ripped her bottom out and for the third and final time she was flung onto the beach near the boathouse.

Meanwhile, the position of the two men in the rigging was getting ever more precarious as all efforts to save them had failed, leaving the only hope of rescue in the hands of the No.1 lifeboat. Since 10 a.m., the Coastguard had been trying to contact the boat in vain. She was eight miles from Great Yarmouth Harbour when, at 11.30 a.m., the Gorleston lifeboat reached her to relate the plight of *Sepoy* to Coxswain Blogg. *H.F. Bailey* was nearly twenty miles from Cromer at this point, and had to battle through terrible seas for just over three hours to reach the scene. Blogg commented afterwards,

'The journey up and down was the worst in my twenty-four years experience as coxswain. At first the seas were not heavy, but the wind was bitterly cold, and the men were wet through as soon as we launched.'

At 2.45 p.m., with the barge hard and fast 200 yards from Cromer beach and the two men on board having to climb ever higher up the rigging away from the heavy seas, the motor lifeboat was seen approaching from the direction of Overstrand. Fifteen minutes after arriving at Cromer, to the accompaniment of loud cheers from hundreds of onlookers, Coxswain Blogg and his crew succeeded where the pulling boat had failed. Unable to anchor to windward and drop down to the barge, Blogg had to try to get to the lee side of the ship. With big seas sweeping over her, the lifeboat was manoeuvred alongside *Sepoy*, between the barge and the shore. On the first approach, the force of water swept the lifeboat past the wreck. The manoeuvre was repeated again but without success.

When his third approach also failed, Blogg realised that drastic action was needed in order to succeed – orthodox methods had been tried and failed so, after shouting orders to the crew and the mechanics to be ready for quick action, he swung the lifeboat, circled

Opposite above: *The remains of the wrecked barge* Sepoy *on Cromer beach at low tide on 14 December 1933, the day after the dramatic rescue. (By courtesy of P.A. Vicary)*

Opposite below: *The crew of the No.1 lifeboat H.F. Bailey on the beach after the* Sepoy *rescue, 13 December 1933, left to right: Coxswain Henry Blogg and his dog Monte, Walter Allen, H.W. 'Swank' Davies, Jimmy Davies, George Balls, W.H. 'Pimpo' Davies, Lewis 'Tuner' Harrison, Bowman Jack Davies, William 'Captain' Davies, George Cox and Charlie Cox. (By courtesy of P.A. Vicary)*

Above: *Tiles from the wrecked barge* Sepoy *piled on the promenade at Cromer, 15 December 1933. (By courtesy of P.A. Vicary)*

Right: *A lifebelt, washed ashore from* Sepoy *after the rescue, on display in the lifeboat museum, with the front page of the* Daily Mirror *giving an account of the series of events. (Nicholas Leach)*

the barge and from the lee side pointed the lifeboat's bow at the barge and drove straight at the wreck. He took the boat right on top of the barge, close to the rigging where the men were hanging and, with the lifeboat in an extremely hazardous position, her crew dragged the first man to safety. Before the second man, Captain Hemstead, could be saved, a sea lifted the lifeboat and swept her off the wreck. Blogg was forced to repeat the dangerous operation, and so for a second time he drove the boat over the barge and the crew was able to help the last man into the lifeboat.

Despite suffering damage during the rescue, with her stem broken and a couple of holes in her side, *H.F. Bailey* was driven on to the beach where the two men were landed. Blogg had decided that a long passage to Gorleston was too risky for the survivors and, with the lifeboat short of fuel, beaching was the best option. As soon as she had grounded, a dozen men ran into the sea to steady the lifeboat while others helped the survivors out. One was taken ashore on a stretcher while the captain was assisted to the Red Lion Hotel. The crowd cheered the lifeboatmen on the beach and acclaimed Coxswain Blogg, who only praised his own 'magnificent' crew.

In discussing the rescue, Blogg spoke with his usual modesty. He said 'it was easy', but admitted that effecting the rescue had been difficult because the lifeboat crew never knew just where the tide and sea were going to set. 'We ran the lifeboat's head on to the *Sepoy's* bulwarks, rammed one in, put the lifeboat back and rammed another bulwark,' said the coxswain. He added that he beached the lifeboat because he felt his crew had had enough after being at sea for eleven hours. Blogg paid a warm tribute to the crews of both lifeboats and made special mention of the 'scratch' crew, under Robert Davies, who manned the sailing boat. The rescue had been carried out within two hundred yards of the Cromer beach and, for the hundreds of people on the shore and cliffs who cheered as they saw the men jump into the motor lifeboat, Blogg's seamanship, daring and courage must have seemed awesome. The account in *The Lifeboat* summed up the events:

> It was a dangerous and arduous service, carried out in the worst conditions of weather, close in on a lee shore in a very heavy surf, where there was continual risk that the lifeboat herself would be washed up on the beach. That the two men were rescued and the life-boat herself was not wrecked was due to the perfect seamanship of the coxswain.

For this extraordinary rescue, Coxswain Blogg was awarded a second-service clasp to his Silver medal, and each of the crew was accorded the Thanks of the Institution Inscribed on Vellum: George Balls (second coxswain); John J. Davies snr (bowman); Henry W. Davies (mechanic); William T. Davies (assistant motor mechanic); James W. Davies; William H. Davies; John J. Davies jnr; Charles P. Cox; Robert Cox; Edward W. Allen; Lewis Harrison and Sidney Harrison. Robert Davies, acting coxswain of the No.2 lifeboat, was also accorded the Thanks of the Institution Inscribed on Vellum.

Refloating the damaged *H.F. Bailey* proved to be a difficult task. An assistant surveyor was sent to carry out temporary repairs to the broken stem and patch up two holes in her side. She was repaired, but getting her afloat again was long and difficult as she had come ashore at high tide. Attempts were made to float her at each succeeding high tide, but it was not until the afternoon of 16 December that she was got off. The lifeboat was then taken to a boatyard at Lowestoft where a new piece was put in the stem, chocks were fitted inside the holes and brass plates fastened on the outside. She left the yard three days later and was back at her station on the morning of 20 December, ready for service once again.

In contrast to the *Monte Nevoso* and *Sepoy* rescues, one of the more tragic incidents in the history of the Cromer lifeboat station occurred in July 1934. On the morning of 27 July, eight crab boats put out from Cromer, with a gale blowing and a moderate sea which got

H.F. Bailey
approaches the
pier at full speed,
with Coxswain
Henry Blogg at the
helm, and mast
and sails stowed.
(By courtesy of
P.A. Vicary)

H.F. Bailey
(ON.694) off the
slipway in June
1934, after picking
up the body of
Charlie Cox,
whose crab boat
overturned. (By
courtesy of
P.A. Vicary)

heavier as the men were attending the crab pots. The Coastguard watched the boats, particularly *White Heather* as she was in rougher water than the others. On board her were two members of the lifeboat crew, Charlie Cox and Gilbert Mayes, brothers-in-law and owners of the crab boat. Just after 11.30 a.m., the watching Coastguard saw the boat capsize about a mile and a quarter from the shore, and the two men were thrown into the water.

The maroons were immediately fired and seven minutes later *H.F. Bailey* was launched. Within fifteen minutes she had reached the spot where the boat had disappeared, and the lifeboatmen saw various articles from the vessel floating about. After a short search, they found the body of Charlie Cox and he was brought ashore. Sadly, all efforts to revive him by the crew, and later at the hospital, failed. As soon as Cox had been landed, the lifeboat continued the search, but could find no trace of Gilbert Mayes or of *White Heather* so returned at 2.15 p.m., having then been out about two and a half hours. The body of Mayes was eventually washed ashore twelve days later. Cox had been a member of the lifeboat's crew for almost forty years. He won the Bronze medal for his part in the service to the steamer *Fernebo*. Mayes had been a member of the crew for about thirty-five years, and won the Bronze medal for the *Fernebo* service.

What proved to be the last service performed by the second *H.F. Bailey* took place on 31 October 1935. She was launched at 6.30 p.m. after the steamship *Egyptian*, of Liverpool, went ashore near South Middle Haisborough Buoy. The lifeboat reached the vessel at 8.15 p.m. and proceeded to get a rope on board. However, before the rope could be properly made fast, or the coxswain could get on board, the steamer refloated and proceeded on her way. The lifeboat then returned to her station at 11.45 p.m. She remained there until 14 December 1935 when, with a new lifeboat due the following day, she was sent down the slipway for the last time, with Second Coxswain Jack Davies in charge, to go to Oulton Broad for further service in the RNLI's Reserve Fleet. She served as a Reserve lifeboat for more than two decades until sold out of service in 1953.

Two New Lifeboats

Just over a year before *H.F. Bailey* was replaced as the No.1 lifeboat, a new No.2 lifeboat arrived at the station. The importance of a No.2 station had been highlighted during the *Sepoy* rescue and a beach-launched No.2 lifeboat was clearly needed. So, in 1934, a new 35ft 6in Liverpool class motor lifeboat, *Harriot Dixon* (ON.770), was allocated to the station. The new lifeboat left Cowes, where she had been built by Groves & Guttridge, at 6.30 a.m. on 2 August, and called overnight at Ramsgate and Gorleston during the passage. On the first part of the trip the weather was rough, but by using both sails and the engine a good speed was maintained. Commander Vaux, the lifeboat inspector, accompanied Coxswain Blogg and his crew on the trip. She arrived on 4 August, shortly after 9.30 a.m. and, watched by large crowds, was hauled up to the lifeboat house.

Harriot Dixon had been funded from the legacy of £3,750 left by the late William Edward Dixon, a surgeon, of West Worthing, Sussex. He had died in 1921 and left the money for a lifeboat to be named after his mother and stationed, if possible, on the Kentish or East Coast. She ended up staying at Cromer for thirty years and performed a number of useful services, many in conjunction with or backing up the No.1 lifeboat. With a new motor lifeboat on station, a workshop was constructed in the boathouse of 1902 so that the mechanic could effect repairs to the boat, while electric lighting was installed.

A No.2 lifeboat had been operated since the first motor lifeboat arrived in 1923, and in 1934 the station was upgraded with the arrival of a motor lifeboat. The 35ft 6in Liverpool motor Harriot Dixon (ON.770), pictured arriving at Cromer on 4 August 1934, was launched from the beach and served the station for thirty years. (By courtesy of P.A. Vicary)

With sufficient depth of water, Harriot Dixon is launched on exercise for Lifeboat Day, 4 August 1935. (By courtesy of P.A. Vicary)

The first service launch of the new No.2 lifeboat took place on 2 April 1936, when she went to the aid of the fishing boat *White Rose*, of Cromer. Before launching the No.1 lifeboat, the coxswain advised Coxswain Leslie Harrison to stand by in readiness to assist two Cromer crab boats at 7.30 a.m. Coxswain Harrison, having collected his crew and helpers, had the No.2 lifeboat brought from her house ready to launch. As the weather became increasingly bad, and one crab boat was still out, the lifeboat was slipped from her carriage at 8 a.m. Unfortunately, the port side drag rope fouled the propellers and the boat had to be beached without being able to assist the crab boat. Many of her subsequent services were undertaken with the No.1 lifeboat, and so the following services undertaken during this era are described in chronological order, encompassing rescues by both No.1 and No.2 lifeboats, either working alone or in tandem.

The station's new No.1 lifeboat arrived shortly after 11 a.m. on 15 December 1935, with a large crowd on hand to see her hauled up the slipway. She had left Cowes on 12 December and came to Cromer via Newhaven, Ramsgate and Gorleston, with Coxswain Henry Blogg in charge during the voyage, accompanied by the lifeboat inspector Commander Vaux, Honorary Secretary E. Peter Hansell and Colonel F. Noel, a member of the Cromer Committee. As she was being hauled up the slipway for the first time, the exhaust funnel was found to be an inch or so too high to get under the top of the door, so part of the funnel had to be removed to give the necessary clearance with a new, slightly smaller funnel supplied later. The new lifeboat was similar to her predecessor, but was slightly larger at 46ft in length and 12ft 9in in breadth. Her hull was divided into seven watertight compartments, of which the engine room was one, and fitted with 142 air cases. With a crew of twelve, in rough weather she could take a further ninety-five people on board. She was fitted with the latest equipment, which included a line-throwing gun and an electric searchlight. Most significant of all, however, were her engines: twin 40hp Weyburn CE.4 four-cylinder diesel engines gave her a maximum speed of just over 8 knots and, at a cruising speed of 7.5 knots, she had a range of almost 100 nautical miles. The diesel engine offered significant advantages over its petrol counterpart, proving more economic to operate, and because less fuel was needed to travel the same distance, the effective range of a diesel-powered lifeboat was significantly greater than that of a petrol-engined one.

The first service performed by the new *H.F. Bailey* (ON.777) took place on 26 March 1936. At 7.50 a.m., the Cromer Coastguard received news from the steamship *Caduceus*

H.F. Bailey *arrives at Cromer, 15 December 1935, having set off from her builder's yard at Cowes three days earlier. (By courtesy of P.A. Vicary)*

With a large number of onlookers, H.F. Bailey *is hauled up the slipway for the first time. During this oper-ation, it was found that she would not go under the boathouse doors and so the top of her funnel had to be cut off. (By courtesy of P.A. Vicary)*

that the French steamer *Boree*, of Caen, was in distress five miles south-east of the East Dudgeon lightvessel. A second message stated that *Caduceus* had launched a ship's lifeboat to pick up the crew. At 8.40 a.m., further information was received from *Caduceus* via the Coastguard stating that *Boree* had sunk at 7.20 a.m., that two survivors were on board *Caduceus* and a search for other survivors was being carried out in very bad conditions. The lifeboat launched at 9 a.m. and set a course for the last reported position. During her passage, the lifeboat picked up a lifebelt at about 11.45 a.m. and about a quarter of an hour later came up with *Caduceus*, going alongside at the master's request. He gave the lifeboat crew all the information he could of the disaster, explaining that six men had been picked up by a Spanish steamer, *Caduceus* had picked up seven, that three dead men had been seen floating past the ship and another had disappeared. As his vessel was bound for Buenos Aires he asked the lifeboat crew to land the seven men he had picked up. After the seven men had been transferred to the lifeboat, she searched for another half an hour, but as nothing further could be done Coxswain Blogg decided to make for Wells, as rehousing up the slipway at Cromer would be impossible in the conditions.

On the morning of 7 August 1936, the 6,000-ton steamship *San Francisco*, of Havre, carrying a crew of thirty-eight and bound laden from Newcastle to Havre, ran aground on Haisborough Sands, about two miles south-east of Haisborough lightvessel. A moderate north-north-easterly breeze was blowing, with a moderate sea, and poor visibility. When news was received from the lightvessel, No.1 lifeboat *H.F. Bailey* was launched at 11.40 a.m. with E. Peter Hansell, honorary secretary, on board. Once on scene, he and Coxswain Blogg went on board *San Francisco* and, at the coxswain's suggestion, the master sent a message to Great Yarmouth for tugs. The lifeboat then took the towing wires from the steamer to the tugs, and played a part in the salvage operations which followed, not returning to her station until 6.50 p.m. on 11 August. Her actual periods on duty were 11.40 a.m. on 7 August to 4.40 p.m. on 8 August; 7 p.m. on 8 August to 5 a.m. on 10 August; and 11.30 a.m. on 10 August to 6.50 p.m. on the 11 August. The steamship refloated on the afternoon of 12 August.

During November 1936, both *H.F. Bailey* and *Harriot Dixon* were involved in a series of services to motor vessels. Between 16 and 18 November, *H.F. Bailey* stood by the steamship *Nesttun*, of Tvedestrand, loaded with wood pulp, which had stranded on the Haisborough Sands. Various attempts by tugs were made to refloat the vessel while the lifeboat remained on hand until, on 17 November, the vessel refloated. In the fresh north-westerly wind, rehousing was not possible so the lifeboat made for Gorleston, arriving in the early hours of 18 November with only three gallons of petrol left. With the No.1 lifeboat away, *Harriot Dixon* was called into action just after 6 a.m. on 18 November when the motor barge *Lady Gwynfred* sent up distress signals about a mile

The steamship San Francisco, *which the lifeboat spent four days helping in August 1936 after she had ran aground on the Haisborough Sands bound laden from Newcastle to her home port of Le Havre. (By courtesy of P.A. Vicary)*

north of the station. In very heavy seas, the boat was swept off her carriage as she was being launched. Attempts were made to get her head to sea in an endeavour to float her, but when the message was received that the casualty was ashore, the lifeboatmen recovered the lifeboat onto her carriage. The difficulties in launching on this occasion had been caused by the fact that the carriage had run too far into the water, as some of the regular helpers had been at the pier boathouse for the No.1 lifeboat so were not on hand to assist.

The same day, 18 November, at about 7 p.m., the No.1 lifeboat was again called out. She left Gorleston under Coxswain Blogg, together with the Gorleston coxswain and crew, and went to the aid of the steam drifter *Pitgaveny*, of Banff, which was disabled and drifting to the south of the harbour. The lifeboat took off the drifter's crew of ten, but sustained some damage in the process. Shortly after 8 a.m. the following day, she was again called out from Gorleston, this time taking a doctor to a sick man on board the steamship *Yew Forest*, of Glasgow, who was subsequently found to be dead. Just as she was moored after this service, another call came and so *H.F. Bailey* again went out. She picked up a fire party from HMS *Foyle* and the lifeboatmen located and extinguished a fire on board the steamship *Lindisfarne*, of Newcastle. This was the last call made on *H.F. Bailey* during a hectic few days for coxswain and crew, and she was then able to return to her station.

The station's two new lifeboats were formally christened on 27 August 1937 at an unusual double ceremony held at the pier boathouse. With Lord Suffield, president of the branch, in the chair, Sir Geoffrey Baring, chairman of the RNLI, presented the lifeboats to the station on behalf of the donors and the Institution. They were received by Lt-Col. F.A.G. Noel, the chairman of the branch. The bishop of Norwich, the Rt Revd Bertram Pollock, then conducted a service of dedication, after which the lifeboats were named by the Rt Hon. Sir Samuel Hoare, Bt, MP, Secretary of State for Home Affairs. Before performing the formal christening, Sir Samuel Hoare said:

> As a Norfolk man I am very glad to take part in this ceremony. My earliest memories are connected with rescues by the Cromer life-boat. I am glad to think, too, that my interest is hereditary. I have here a newspaper cutting of the year 1808, giving an account of the wreck of the Duchess of Cumberland, which says that 'many gentlemen of respectability, among others Mr Samuel Hoare, jun., exerted themselves at their own personnel risk.' It is very pleasant in a world in which everything seems to change so quickly to find that in Cromer these old family associations persist. Lord Suffield is the third member of his family to be

Left: *Everard's spritsail barge* Hibernia, *of London, from which* H.F. Bailey *saved the crew of three after the barge had been wrecked at East Runton, 10 November 1937. (By courtesy of P.A. Vicary)*

Opposite: *A dramatic launch for* H.F. Bailey *into a north-easterly gale on 10 February 1938 to stand by the fishing boat* Urgent, *of Cowes. (By courtesy of P.A. Vicary)*

president of the Branch, and Mr Peter Hansell, the honorary secretary, is the third member of his family to be closely connected with lifeboat work. The Royal National Life-boat Institution still depends upon the support of private people. Long may the country continue to give this voluntary organization the support necessary for it to carry on its work.

He then named the lifeboats *H.F. Bailey* and *Harriot Dixon*, and the former was launched down the slipway. *H.F. Bailey*, built at a cost of £7,307, was the fourth and final lifeboat to be provided through the estate of the late Henry Francis Bailey, of Brockenhurst, a London merchant, born in Norfolk. The boat's searchlight was funded by a gift from the Mitcham Schools, Surrey, and her compass was provided out of gifts from RNLI supporters in Warsaw and received through the British Embassy there.

The first service after the naming ceremony took place on 9 November 1937. At 8.33 p.m., the coastguard reported distress signals about eight and a half miles north-east of Cromer. *H.F. Bailey* was launched into a moderate north-north-easterly gale at 8.45 p.m. and about an hour later found the barge *Hibernia*, of London, awash amidships and sinking. She was bound from Goole to Sittingbourne with a cargo of coal, and had a crew of three. She had sprung a leak and, as saving her was impossible, the lifeboat went alongside and rescued the three men. *H.F. Bailey* then made for Gorleston and landed the survivors. *Hibernia* subsequently went ashore and became a total wreck, while the lifeboat returned to Cromer just before midday on 16 November, almost a week after launching to the barge.

During 1938, *H.F. Bailey* performed a number of routine services, the first of which took place on 10 February. She put out to two fishing boats caught out in a gale force wind, and stood by one, *Urgent*, until she was safely beached at Overstrand. On 30 May, she went to another fishing boat, *G.V.H.*, of Great Yarmouth, which was in difficulty about four miles from Haisborough. When the lifeboat reached the vessel at 9.15 a.m. she was four miles east of Palling, with her engine broken down and anchor lost. The lifeboat towed the vessel to Great Yarmouth. On 7 August, *H.F. Bailey* stood by the motor vessel *John M.*, of London, with the Sheringham lifeboat *Foresters Centenary*. The vessel had run ashore off Beeston Hill and she refloated without assistance.

The most noteworthy rescue of 1938 took place on 2 November. *H.F. Bailey* was involved in an unusual incident that resulted in a rescue from a shelled steamer in fine weather. At about 3 p.m., gun fire at sea was heard by the Coastguard and a large steamer, with an armed vessel nearby, was seen about ten miles north of Cromer. The armed vessel was the cruiser *Nadir*, operated by Spanish nationalists, flying the flag of General Franco and with the signal 'heave to or I fire' hoisted. The other vessel was the steamship *Cantabria*, of Santander, of over 5,000 tons, belonging to the Spanish government. After unloading a cargo of timber from Russia on the Thames, the steamship had left the previous night bound for Immingham but had encountered the cruiser during the voyage.

Just after 5 p.m., *H.F. Bailey* was launched to see if help was needed. As the lifeboat went alongside, it was found that of the forty or more people who had been on board, only the master, his wife and two children, and one member of the crew remained. They were apparently prepared to face death by drowning rather than be captured. The rest of the passengers and crew had left in two boats, one of which was picked up by the cruiser and the other by British steamer *Pattersonian* on her way from the Tyne to London. About twenty shells had fallen on or near the steamer and, although no one had been injured, several shells had hit the hull. The vessel had a heavy list to starboard, which hampered the lifeboatmen's task of taking off the five people. While alongside, the lifeboat sustained some damage to her stanchions and guard chain on the port side, but got safely away and was back at Cromer at 8.15 p.m. The captain and his family were landed and looked after at the Red Lion Hotel. For their efforts, Coxswain Henry Blogg and the crew were sent a letter of appreciation by the RNLI. This incident, the lifeboatmen's first entanglement with armed conflict, was just a prelude for what was about to happen. On 3 September 1939, Britain declared war on Germany and for the next six years the conflict affected all aspects of life, with demands made on the lifeboat service greater than ever before.

Left: H.F. Bailey, *seen from the pier on a fine day, takes a party of supporters for a short trip, with Coxswain Henry Blogg at the helm. (By courtesy of P.A. Vicary)*

Below: Harriot Dixon *on the beach ready to be recovered with lifeboat crew and shore helpers posing for the camera left to right: F. Davies, L.J. Harrison jnr, H. Linder, G. Cox, H.T. Davies, W.H. Davies, J.W. Davies, J.J. Davies snr, L.J. Harrison (snr), W.T. Davies, Coxswain Henry Blogg, T. Allen, R. Cox, A. Balls, W. Burgess, G. Balls and R. Davies. (From an old postcard supplied by Paul Russell)*

6

Wartime Service

During the Second World War, both Cromer lifeboats performed many notable rescues, of which a considerable number were to casualties of the war. During the period of hostilities, operations were very different to those of peacetime because, as with the RNLI's other stations, Cromer came under the control of the naval authorities. Maroons were not fired to summon the crew, but a messenger or telephone call would alert them when needed. Once at sea, few if any lightships or navigation lights were shown, and restrictions on radio communication were imposed. In addition, a gap was blown in the pier in case of invasion, but this had to be bridged so that the lifeboat house at the end could be reached. Added to these difficulties was the need for the lifeboatmen to be prepared to handle a wide variety of casualties as both No.1 and No.2 lifeboats went to the aid of ships that had been wrecked, bombed or torpedoed, as well as facing the hazards of mines, and often had to be wary of enemy fire.

During the 1939-45 conflict, the record of the Cromer lifeboat was second to none. The No.1 boat launched 183 times and saved 437 lives, while the No.2 Boat went out twenty-seven times and saved twenty lives. Both boats also launched on missions when nothing was found and many hours were spent on fruitless searches. But the fame of the Cromer lifeboat and the deeds of its life-boatmen were known nationwide even before the outbreak of war. With war, new responsibilities and challenges were met by lifeboat and crew, and publicity was often forthcoming, sometimes on a national scale. The magazine *Illustrated* on 2 March 1940 featured the lifeboats of North Norfolk with an emphasis on Cromer, under the headline 'The Lifeboat's Out' and with a portrait of Coxswain Henry Blogg on the cover. The sentiments expressed, no doubt written to boost moral and encourage those on the Home Front, read:

> In peace time the existence of a lifeboatman is relentless and hard. War necessarily adds to its hardships. War, as the Nazis conduct it, makes his life one long succession of tasks demanding all his courage and powers of endurance. His life-saving battle with the elements is made doubly difficult when such terrors as torpedoes, mines and murderers in planes are added to his combatants.

During the first three months of the war, lifeboats rescued more than 1,300 people. The Cromer lifeboat frequently put to sea. Although the bravery of the Cromer lifeboatmen during the war was widely reported, much of their work was undertaken without many of the regular crew, who had of course been called up for military service. However, it seems Coxswain Blogg was determined to keep the nucleus of his crew. The *Eastern Evening News* of 9 April 1942 reports a little recounted event which shows the importance Blogg attached to having his regular crew available. The headline read 'Blogg's threat to resign', with the article explaining the situation:

> Coxswain Blogg says he will resign from the lifeboat service rather than go to sea with an amateur crew. Two of his crew, Robert and Dick Davies, are being called up, and Coxswain Blogg made the threat at a private meeting of the crew called by Sir Thomas Cook, MP,

when asked what he would do if it were suggested that men from the Labour Exchange should be trained. Three other members of the crew will also resign, and there may be a fourth resignation if the two men are taken. Three of the crew have already been called up. Sir Thomas will meet representatives of the RNLI in London today, and will inform them of the lifeboatmen's views and those of Mr Baldwin, secretary of Cromer Branch of the RNLI, who attended the private meeting.

Blogg referred to a further communication he had received from RNLI headquarters that afternoon, stating that local lifeboat crews must be bound by the agreement made between the Ministry of National Service that lifeboatmen up to the age of twenty-one would be called up unless it was proved that their removal would affect the efficiency of the station. 'That agreement was made without the knowledge or consent of the crew, and they refuse, as volunteers, to be bound by it,' he said. It would seem that Blogg got his way, as many of the crew remained in Cromer and played their part in the many outstanding rescues that were performed.

Although the Second World War placed a greater demand on lifeboats and lifeboatmen throughout the British Isles, it also undoubtedly brought more opportunities for heroic service. The lifeboats of the east coast in particular, because of their location, often went to crashed aircraft and many calls were to shocked survivors of mined or torpedoed ships, drifting in small boats. The following descriptions encompass the most outstanding wartime rescues for which formal recognition was received as well as many of the other more routine services in which both the Cromer lifeboats were involved.

Mount Ida

The first launch of the war took place on 5 October 1939 and proved to be a fruitless search for the Cromer lifeboatmen. *H.F. Bailey* was launched at 5.30 p.m. after reports that an aeroplane had crashed into the sea. Together with HM trawler *Drangy*, she searched the area but found nothing and after more than seven hours at sea returned to station. But the crew was soon called into action in the most dramatic fashion as the second service of the war proved to be a particularly outstanding one. At 6.25 a.m. on 9 October 1939, Coxswain Henry Blogg was informed by the Coastguard that a vessel had gone ashore on Haisborough Sands, thirteen miles to the east. Twenty minutes later, the No.1 lifeboat *H.F. Bailey* was launched into a strong south-east-by-east breeze and very heavy sea. After heading towards the reported position of the wreck for more than an hour, the lifeboatmen were informed by the Coastguard via the wireless that the vessel had grounded on the Ower Bank, nowhere near the Haisborough Sands, but nineteen miles further on. When details of the revised position were received, the lifeboat was near the North Middle Haisborough Buoy and so Coxswain Blogg immediately altered course. She went south towards Middle Haisborough Buoy, across the sands to the gap between that buoy and the East Haisborough Buoy, and then Blogg set a course for the Ower, to the north-east. At about 1 a.m. the lifeboat crossed the Leman Bank, and shortly afterwards reached the vessel which was aground on the Ower.

The lifeboatmen found the Greek steamer *Mount Ida*, of Piraeus, of 4,275 tons, loaded with grain and timber, and on her way from Vancouver to Hull with twenty-nine on board. She was lying nearly head-on to the seas, offering the lifeboat no lee, and had a list to starboard. Part of her bridge had been smashed, her starboard lifeboats had been carried away, and to make matters worse for the lifeboatmen a very heavy sea was running on the bank. The lifeboat had reached the casualty at about 12.30 p.m. and approached on the port side. Before a rope could be thrown, however, the lifeboat was

The 4275-ton steamship Mount Ida, *from Piraeus in Greece, was on her way to Hull when she got into difficulty on the Ower Bank. (By courtesy of P.A. Vicary)*

struck by two heavy seas and flung back. Coxswain Blogg made a second attempt to take the lifeboat alongside, but the strong cross currents in the tide made it impossible to remain near the vessel. Blogg, therefore, decided to wait until slack water before another attempt. He took the lifeboat clear of the sands and signalled to the ship what he intended to do.

At 2.15 p.m. the tide had slackened enough for another attempt to be made, although wind and sea had considerably increased in force. The lifeboat went alongside and at least a dozen ropes were thrown to her from the wreck, but they snapped almost at once in the heavy seas. With no hope of keeping the lifeboat alongside using ropes, the coxswain had to maintain position by skilful use of the lifeboat's engines. He drove ahead as the seas broke alongside the ship and so prevented them from sweeping the lifeboat away. A rope ladder was dropped over the steamer's side and six men climbed down into the lifeboat. The seventh man, when about halfway down, hesitated, so the lifeboat crew shouted to him to jump. Instead he started to climb back, but before he could get aboard the steamer a big sea lifted the lifeboat right to the top of the ladder and the man's leg was crushed between her and the steamer's side. His comrades pulled him aboard and did their best to stop the flow of blood from his mangled leg. Then they tied him in blankets and lowered him by ropes from the steamer's port side into the lifeboat, where he was attended to by the lifeboat crew. After this incident, only six of the remaining twenty-two used the ladder, as the others slid down a rope hanging from the port lifeboat.

By about 3.30 p.m., the last of the twenty-nine men had been rescued and the lifeboat had been alongside the steamer, held in position by her engines, for well over an hour being swept almost continuously by heavy seas. During this time she had been flung against the wreck and badly damaged. Only the outstanding seamanship of Blogg, the care with which the mechanics had managed the engines and the promptness with which they had carried out the coxswain's orders had made it possible to stay alongside the steamer at all. When the last man had been rescued, Blogg decided that the best way of clearing the sands was to drive straight ahead through the seas, and he made for Cromer to land the injured man and to get him immediate medical help.

The lifeboat arrived at her station at 8 p.m., but it was impossible to land the man on the slipway, so the No.2 lifeboat, *Harriot Dixon*, was launched by tractor off the beach at

8.25 p.m. with Dr D. Vaughan on board. Unfortunately, as she was being launched, a throttle wire broke, the engine stalled, and the lifeboat was thrown right across the carriage. A hole was knocked in her port quarter, the carriage was broken, and the lifeboat launched stern first, but in spite of this mishap she got away and was used to bring ashore the injured man, the other twenty-eight rescued men, as well as the *H.F. Bailey*'s crew. The mechanic of the *H.F. Bailey* stayed on board her, together with four members of *Harriot Dixon*'s crew, to look after her while she lay at anchor. The injured man was taken to Cromer and District hospital but died of his injuries the next night. The lifeboat crew was sent home to get dry clothes and a meal as they had been out for fourteen hours.

Meanwhile, the tractor and carriage needed to recover *Harriot Dixon* had been completely submerged. Both had to be hauled out by the winch and a wire hawser, a difficult task in the darkness, wind and rain. Coxswain Blogg remained on the beach supervising the recovery and then went home. But he had only just got inside when news was received that another vessel was in distress off Bacton, ten miles south-east of Cromer. He put on dry clothes, called out the crew again, and went to the boathouse, intending to refuel *H.F. Bailey* from the slipway, but this proved to be impossible. Launching *Harriot Dixon* again was also out of the question after the damage sustained to the tractor earlier in the day, so the biggest shoreboat available was loaded with forty tins of petrol and the crew refuelled *H.F. Bailey* using these. Two of the lifeboatmen brought the shoreboat in again, narrowly avoiding capsizing in the broken water. *H.F. Bailey* stood by until they were safely ashore, and made for Bacton in a strong south-easterly wind.

The vessel in distress was the steam drifter *Vera Creina*, of Lowestoft, with ten men on board. She was on her way home from the fishing grounds and had run aground. The lifeboat reached the vessel at 1 a.m. on 10 October, but it transpired that the drifter's crew had already been rescued by the Coastguard lifesaving apparatus. The drifter herself was refloated two days later. As the lifeboat had been damaged during her service to *Mount Ida*, instead of returning to Cromer she made for Lowestoft, twenty-five miles further south, where repairs could be undertaken immediately. The lifeboat arrived there at 6.30 a.m. and her crew returned to Cromer by road, arriving at midday, by which time it had been thirty hours since they had originally set out to help *Mount Ida*. During that time, they had been at sea nearly twenty-one hours and had travelled over 100 miles.

Harriot Dixon was also damaged; six planks in her skin had been fractured on the port side and a hole in one of her air-cases. She was temporarily repaired with a patch of copper on the outside, and strengthened with timber on the inside. These repairs were completed by 12 October and she was then ready for service. The No.1 lifeboat *H.F. Bailey* had her stem badly damaged at the forefoot. Four inner skin planks, two ribs and two deck beams had been fractured. Half of the fender on the starboard side had been broken and the footwale was badly split along the starboard side. Stanchions had been bent and the guard chains broken. Repairs were completed late on 20 October and she returned to Cromer the following day to be ready for service again on 22 October.

For his actions during this outstanding service, carried out in very severe weather, a second clasp to his Silver medal for gallantry was awarded to Coxswain Blogg, and a second clasp to his Bronze medal went to Second Coxswain J.J. Davies snr; a clasp to their Bronze medals went to the mechanic, H.W. Davies, and assistant mechanic J.W. Davies; The Thanks Inscribed on Vellum was accorded to signalman H.T. Davies and the other seven members of the crew: R.C. Davies; F. Davies; J.J. Davies jnr; W.H. Davies; J.R. Davies; R. Cox and G. Cox. The owners of *Mount Ida* made a donation of £50 to the Institution. In his biography of Blogg, Cyril Jolly summed up this service by stating that, 'In many ways this rescue was Henry Blogg's greatest achievement in seamanship... Had it not been for his amazing skill in handling the lifeboat, some of the things he did on this service could have been called foolhardy. But, more than any other man, he knew just what could be done with a modern lifeboat.'

The next services were routine in comparison, but mostly involved vessels that had become casualties as a result of enemy action. On 1 December 1939, shortly after 7 p.m., a vessel two and a half miles north of the lifeboat station wished to land a rescued crew. Fifteen minutes later, *H.F. Bailey* was launched and found the Italian steamer *Santa Gata*, of Naples, on board which were thirty-two men from the Norwegian tanker *Realf* – which had been sunk by enemy action – together with two naval officers and eight naval ratings who had gone aboard when she was struck. The lifeboat took all off, landed them safely and returned to her station at 8.45 p.m.

On 21 December 1939, *H.F. Bailey* launched just after 2 a.m. to the tanker *Dosinia*, with a crew of fifty-one, which had struck a mine near the Haisborough lightvessel and had a heavy list to starboard. Forty members of her crew were taken into the lifeboat, which then stood by as the captain and officers remained aboard to see if it was possible to save the vessel. At daybreak, a mine was seen drifting about half a mile away in the path of an oncoming convoy, so the lifeboat headed for it to warn the convoy's leading ships to alter course. She then returned to *Dosinia* to find the vessel's back was broken, but the captain still wanted to try to save her. He decided to try and reach the Humber and asked the lifeboat to go with him. So the lifeboat then escorted the vessel north and, at about 6.30 p.m., when they were off the Humber, *Dosinia* was taken in tow by a tug. The lifeboat put *Dosinia*'s crew on board her again and, at the captain's request, continued to stand by until the following morning. She then returned to her station, arriving at 5 p.m. after a very long service.

In January 1940, the No.1 lifeboat was involved in various incidents with vessels that had got into difficulty as a result of enemy action. A framed letter of appreciation was sent to the station commending the crew for their services during these incidents. The first took place on 11 January after the Coastguard reported explosions to the north-east. At 10.45 a.m. *H.F. Bailey* was launched and just under two hours later found the steamship *Traviata*, of Genoa, of about 7,000 tons, eighteen miles off Cromer. She had been mined and her crew of thirty and a pilot were rowing in two boats to another vessel, the Italian steamer *Marte*. They all went aboard the steamer except the English pilot, who was taken into the lifeboat. The lifeboat then took *Traviata*'s captain round his ship to see if it was possible to salve her, but she was beyond hope and sank at about 4.30 p.m. Her crew was taken on board the lifeboat from *Marte* and the lifeboat set off for her station.

During the passage back to Cromer, a German aeroplane circled round the lifeboat and then attacked a trawler about a mile away. The lifeboat made for the trawler, HM Trawler *Holyrood*, of Grimsby. Coxswain Blogg boarded her and found that her captain was injured and her engines were out of action. One of the lifeboat crew went on board to give first aid and the trawler was taken in tow. The lifeboat towed it for three hours, during which time repairs were effected to the engines, enabling the trawler to proceed under her own power and the lifeboat to return to her station. The following day, 12 January, reports were received that lightvessel No.85 was being attacked by enemy aircraft, so *H.F. Bailey* was launched and reached the lightvessel at 7.45 p.m. No one on board the lightvessel had been injured but the crew's nerves had been badly shaken, especially as the German plane had sunk a trawler with all hands about three miles away. Two of the lightvessel's crew collapsed while the lifeboat was alongside, so together with one other man they were landed by the lifeboat at Cromer at 3.30 a.m. on 13 January.

During 1940, the reserve lifeboat *J.B. Proudfoot* (ON.694), which had served at Cromer until 1935 as *H.F. Bailey*, was on station in place of *H.F. Bailey*. She performed one effective service while on reserve duty, on 16 June 1940, to the steamship *Brika*, of

Swansea, which had gone ashore on the Haisborough Sands in the fog. At 8.05 a.m. the reserve lifeboat launched and found the 7,000-ton steamer stranded a mile east of the North Middle Haisborough Buoy. The Admiralty tug *Muria* was also on scene, and the lifeboat passed a rope from the tug to *Brika*. The tug started to tow at 2.45 p.m., refloating the steamer, which was able to go on her way. Coxswain Blogg remained on board the steamer throughout the operation, advising the captain when the tow should begin and the direction to be followed in order to refloat the steamer.

Towards the end of the year, *H.F. Bailey* was back on station and she was involved in two long drawn-out services. The first began on 15 November, following reports that a trawler was ashore near the Haisborough Gap in a heavy ground swell. *H.F. Bailey* was launched at 4.05 a.m. and found, ashore on Haisborough beach, the armed trawler *Dungeness* which had been attacked by enemy aircraft and beached by her skipper. Part of the crew had managed to land in a small boat, so the lifeboat took off the remaining eleven and then returned to station. Three days later, on 18 November, the No.2 motor lifeboat *Harriot Dixon* was launched at the request of the Admiralty salvage officer engaged in salving *Dungeness*. The lifeboat took pumps from the salvage vessel to the stranded trawler and then brought a steward ashore from the salvage vessel to buy stores for her crew. *Harriot Dixon* was again launched on 20 November, at the request of the salvage officer, to take off the pumps which she had put on board *Dungeness* two days earlier.

The second started in the early hours of 7 December when a message was received that a vessel was ashore a mile and a half south of Palling Coastguard station in a strong westerly wind with squalls and a heavy swell. *H.F. Bailey* was launched at 2.20 a.m. and found the steamer *Royston*, of Newcastle-on-Tyne, broadside on to the beach. Attempts to get alongside proved impossible as the seas under the steamer's lee were too rough, so the lifeboat stood by until daylight when a tug arrived from Great Yarmouth. A line between *Royston* and the tug was made fast, and the tug then tried but failed to tow the steamer off. The lifeboat stood by until 2 p.m., by which time it was safe to leave, arriving at Gorleston almost three hours later. Between 10-12 December, further attempts were made to get *Royston* afloat, with both Cromer lifeboats playing their part. The No.2 lifeboat *Harriot Dixon* launched at 8 a.m. on 10 December and stood by all night in strong squally winds. The lifeboat returned to station at 8 p.m. on 11 December, having been out for thirty-six hours. The No.1 lifeboat launched the following day and was at sea from 1 p.m. until 10.30 a.m. on 13 December, standing by during the night with the tug successful in refloating *Royston* at 7 a.m. on 13 December.

In the early morning of 22 January 1941, the 9,500-ton steamship *Meriones*, of Liverpool, stranded on the Haisborough Sands three-quarters of a mile from the South Middle Haisborough Buoy. Her stranding was not reported to the lifeboat crew until, at 9 p.m. on 24 January, a request came for Coxswain Blogg to go to Great Yarmouth to discuss how to salvage the vessel. The following morning, Blogg and the salvage officer went out in the salvage tug *Richard Lee Barber* to examine the steamer, with the marine superintendent of the China Mutual Steam Navigation Co, owner of *Meriones*. The tug took out salvage pumps as the steamer's No.6 hold was full of water. As the tug was approaching the sands, the steamer was attacked by German aeroplanes, but they were driven off by other ships in the vicinity and the marine superintendent immediately sent a wireless call from the tug for the Cromer lifeboat. An earlier attack on the steamer at 2.15 p.m. had wounded one of her gunners, and in another attack at 4 p.m., when bombs fell very near the steamer, no damage was done and no one besides the gunner was hurt.

The message for help was received at Cromer at 3.16 p.m., and within twenty minutes *H.F. Bailey* was launched with the second coxswain in command. She reached the scene at about 6.30 p.m. and Coxswain Blogg left the tug to take charge of the lifeboat, which then stood by. Meanwhile the wind and sea had been increasing, and the crew of *Meriones* decided to abandon ship. The lifeboat was taken through the rough, broken seas on the sands to where the steamer lay. When she had been made fast alongside, the lifeboat began to take on board the steamer's crew. Oil was released onto the water from the steamer to flatten the seas, which helped to a certain degree except that each time a sea broke over the lifeboat her decks were covered with the substance. But the rescue continued until the lifeboat had taken off about half the steamer's crew. They were transferred to the naval tug *St Mullion*, which had anchored outside the sands, and the lifeboat returned to the steamer. A further forty members of the crew got on board the lifeboat before the ropes parted again, so she took the survivors to the tug *Richard Lee Barber* before returning to the steamer. Again she made fast alongside and this time rescued eight officers, the only men left on board, who had before leaving the steamer shot the two horses.

It was now about 1 a.m. and the lifeboat had on board, besides her own crew, the eight officers of *Meriones*, the ship's doctor and an injured man on a stretcher. A course was set for the Cockle Gat, but in the darkness, rain and sleet, the coxswain was not certain of the position and, knowing that a heavy sea was running, thought it more prudent to anchor until daylight. So the lifeboat waited in the bitter cold for five hours until daybreak, when the position was fixed as two miles north of Winterton Steeple, and the lifeboat made for Great Yarmouth, where she arrived at 10.15 a.m. It was then learned that *Meriones* had again been attacked from the air and this time set on fire, but that afterwards the aeroplane had been shot down by another ship in the area. After a meal, the lifeboat crew left for Cromer by motor bus, arriving at 2.15 p.m. on 26 January. The easterly swell, which made recovering the lifeboat impossible, continued for several days, and it was not until the afternoon of 30 January that she was back at her station. The flag officer in command at Great Yarmouth expressed his appreciation of the lifeboat's work during this service and the rescued crew made a collection among themselves, for each member of the lifeboat's crew. The Liverpool and London Underwriters, through the owners, made a donation to the RNLI. This service was particularly long and arduous, having been carried out in bad weather and bitterly cold conditions.

On 13 March 1941, *H.F. Bailey* was launched at 2.50 p.m. after reports had been received that a vessel was in difficulty, and appeared to be sinking but was under tow by another vessel. Twenty minutes after launching, the lifeboat found the steamship *Essex Lance*, of London, carrying wheat and flour, and bound from Hull to London. Coxswain Blogg went on board, found that she had been badly damaged by an enemy bomber the previous evening, and that her crew of forty-four had taken to the boats and spent the night on HMT *Coventry City*. Some had returned to the steamer and the Cromer lifeboatmen found nineteen on board. Although tugs were standing by, at about 4.35 p.m. HMT *Strathranrock* hailed the steamer and told her master that she was to be abandoned and that she would take the crew to Great Yarmouth. So the lifeboat transferred the nineteen men and their belongings from the steamer to the trawler, and then returned to station while the trawler made for Great Yarmouth. During the next three days, the lifeboat assisted the Admiralty salvage officer in attempting to salve *Essex Lance*, making several trips to and from the casualty. The steamer eventually refloated on 17 March and was towed away by tugs.

Convoy 559

On the night of 5 August 1941, a convoy of merchant ships, escorted by naval vessels, was making its way down the east coast through a north-north-westerly gale, accompanied by rough seas and rain squalls reducing visibility. During the early hours of 6 August, the convoy was off the Norfolk coast when six of the steamers, *Oxshott* of London, *Deerwood* of London, *Gallois* of Rouen, *Taara* of Parmu, Estonia, *Aberhill*, of Methil, Fife, and *Paddy Hendly** were driven onto the Haisborough Sands. News of the stranding did not reach the lifeboat station until 8 a.m., when reports suggested that several ships were aground at the southern end of the Middle Haisborough Sands. *H.F. Bailey* put out at once under the command of Coxswain Henry Blogg and an hour and forty minutes later reached the Haisborough Sands to find the seas breaking heavily over them. The six steamers were close together but were rapidly being smashed to pieces in the heavy seas. Naval ships were standing by in deeper water and an RAF patrol was overhead but they could do little to help. Twelve men from the six steamers had already drowned in rescue attempts, although most of the crew of *Taara* had been rescued by a whaler from one of the accompanying destroyers.

H.F. Bailey made first for *Oxshott*, which had only her masts, funnel and upper works amidships showing above water. As the lifeboat approached about sixteen men, roped together, were seen hanging behind the vessel's funnel in an extremely precarious situation. Coxswain Blogg immediately made to get alongside but nowhere on the steamer could a rope could be made fast. But Blogg could see in her cracking upper works a wedge-shaped opening and he steered for this, taking the lifeboat right over the submerged deck and onto the vessel. The sea kept washing the lifeboat out, but again and again he forced the boat's bow into this opening and held it there until all sixteen men had been hauled into the lifeboat. Throughout this extremely dangerous manoeuvre, heavy seas were breaking over the lifeboat and twice she bumped on the submerged deck.

The coxswain then took the lifeboat alongside the second steamer, *Gallois*, and by use of the lifeboat's engines held her alongside, head to wind, while some of the steamer's crew jumped aboard and others slid down ropes. One man fell into the sea but the lifeboatmen hauled him aboard unhurt. From *Gallois*, *H.F. Bailey* rescued thirty-one men and then left the sands to transfer the forty-seven rescued men to a destroyer. While she was transferring the men, the No.2 lifeboat *Harriot Dixon* arrived and came alongside *H.F. Bailey* so Second Coxswain J.J. Davies could board her. Having already taken part in two rescues, he was fully acquainted with the state of the seas.

H.F. Bailey then approached the third steamer, *Deerwood*, which had only her bridge above water, so it was there her crew had gathered. Coxswain Blogg drove the lifeboat right over the steamer's bulwarks and the submerged deck and, by skilful use of the engines, held the lifeboat against the bridge while the nineteen men of the steamer's crew – all that remained – jumped aboard. With three crews now rescued, Blogg and his crew made for a fourth ship, *Aberhill*, but found the Great Yarmouth and Gorleston lifeboat *Louise Stephens* had arrived and was already engaged in rescuing its crew. *Louise Stephens* had set out at 8.25 a.m. and reached the Haisborough Sands three hours later. She found that the crew of the first steamer which she had approached had already been rescued, so she made for another, *Aberhill*, which was lying in the surf with her back broken. With great difficulty, *Louise Stephens* went alongside on the steamer's lee side, amidships. Ropes were thrown enabling the lifeboat to be held close to the steamer until the steamer's entire crew of twenty-three had jumped to safety. Then the lifeboatmen cut the ropes and the lifeboat made for another steamer, but found that her crew had already been rescued by Blogg.

---

* The names of the steamers, as given by the lifeboatmen when they returned ashore, were checked by Lloyd's Register. All were found there except *Paddy Hendly*. No steamer with that name has been found in the register, and as all the rescued men were transferred at once by the lifeboats to naval vessels, and none was brought ashore, checking the vessels' names was not possible. It is most likely this vessel was in fact *Betty Hindley*.

H. F. Bailey had gone on to *Taara*, but *Harriot Dixon* was already alongside her. This steamer, too, had had her back broken, and both her bow and stern were under water. The coxswain of *Harriot Dixon* held the lifeboat against the steamer's bridge, with his engines working, head to wind and sea, and the eight remaining men of the steamer's crew jumped aboard her. Meanwhile, *H.F. Bailey* had gone on to the sixth of the steamers, *Paddy Hendly*, which had also had her back broken, with *Harriot Dixon* standing by having completed the rescue of the eight men from *Taara*. Coxswain Blogg took the lifeboat alongside and held her against the steamer, with his engines working, head to wind and sea, while the twenty-two men of the crew jumped aboard. The water was so shallow that twice the lifeboat bumped on the sands and ran aground as she was moving clear of the wreck, but fortunately refloated on the next sea.

Harriot Dixon transferred her rescued men to a destroyer and made for Cromer, while *Louise Stephens* was already on her way back to Gorleston, followed by *H.F. Bailey* with forty-one rescued men. On her way, she examined the wreck of a trawler which could be seen with only one mast and some of her upper works above water, but found no one on board, so the lifeboat continued until she met a destroyer. She transferred the forty-one men to her and then, at the destroyer's request, went to another trawler, HMT *Arkwright*. *Arkwright* transferred to her two dead bodies and the lifeboat continued to Gorleston, where she arrived just before 5 p.m., having completed an outstanding series of rescues. *H.F. Bailey* had rescued eighty-eight men, *Louise Stephens* twenty-three and *Harriot Dixon* eight. Two other lifeboats had also been called out, *Foresters Centenary* from Sheringham and *Michael Stephens* from Lowestoft, but had arrived too late.

When *H.F. Bailey* reached harbour, she was found to be severely damaged. She had twice been driven over sunken decks, had been bumped severely on the sands, and at one point had run aground, resulting in three holes in her port bow. About 20ft of her port fender had been torn off, her stem had been damaged and the bolts had been forced right through six or eight inches of the deadwood and punctured some of the air cases inside the hull. The lifeboat stations involved in this rescue received a message from the flag officer in charge at Great Yarmouth, congratulating the coxswains and crews of all the lifeboats, 'I have been instructed by the Commander-in-Chief, Nore, to convey his sincere admiration for the superb seamanship and courage displayed by them on the morning of Wednesday 6 August. The flag officer in Yarmouth Command wish to associate themselves in this highly deserved commendation.'

As a result of this series of outstanding rescues, which the official report described as 'a service of great difficulty and danger, carried out with splendid skill and courage', the RNLI awarded Coxswain Blogg a second service clasp to his Gold medal, with a copy of the Vote Inscribed on Vellum. He was also awarded the British Empire Medal. Silver medals went to Second Coxswain John J. Davies, who took command of *Harriot Dixon* when she reached the sands, and to Coxswain Charles Johnson of Great Yarmouth and Gorleston. The Bronze medal was awarded to three other Cromer lifeboatmen: Second Coxswain Leslie Harrison, in *Harriot Dixon*; Henry W. Davies, motor mechanic of *H.F. Bailey*, received a second clasp to his Bronze medal; and H.V. Linder, motor mechanic of *Harriot Dixon*. G.F. Morris, motor mechanic of the Great Yarmouth and Gorleston lifeboat, also received the Bronze medal. The other eighteen members of the three crews involved were accorded the Thanks of the Institution Inscribed on Vellum: William T. Davies, of Cromer, bowman; James W. Davies, assistant motor mechanic; Henry T. Davies, signalman; W. Allen, signalman; and J.R. Davies, R. Cox and S.C. Harrison, lifeboatmen; W. H. Davies, of Cromer, assistant motor mechanic of *Harriot Dixon*, and J. J. Davies jnr; R.C. Davies, G. Cox, C. Brakenbury, and L. Harrison, lifeboatmen; J. Wright, second coxswain of the Great Yarmouth and Gorleston lifeboat; T. Morley, bowman; A. Bush, assistant motor mechanic; W. Parker, signalman; and L. Symonds, lifeboatman. In addition, a number of gifts were received from the owners of some of the vessels which the lifeboat had helped.

The awards were presented to the lifeboatmen on 28 November 1941 by the Third Sea Lord, Vice Admiral Sir John Cunningham KCB, who visited Cromer and took the opportunity to boost moral on the home front. He said one of the ship's officers, in describing the Cromer lifeboat, stated: 'It was one of the finest feats of seamanship I have ever seen. It was a "do or die" attempt. They were 100 per cent men – every man of that lifeboat crew.' Sir John continued that nowhere was the team spirit more essential than in a ship, and even more essential in a lifeboat. 'If we pull together', said Sir John, 'we will see this foul thing, Nazism, crushed. If we criticise here and cavil there it is going to be a darned long time to finish it'. Concluding, Sir John sympathised with the family of the late signalman Allen, and said 'that was part of the sacrifice of admiralty; we pay and will pay, but by God, we will get value for it'. There was also a surprise presentation for the crew involved in the service when Signalman Allen lost his life: each received a wallet from Mrs V. A. Young, of Barry, wife of the steamer's chief officer, who wrote that the wallets were sent 'in appreciation of saving my husband and the crew'.

The next service after the Convoy 559 episode took place on 15 September 1941 and was less dramatic but still a test of the lifeboatmen's stamina. At 6.28 a.m. the Cromer Coastguard reported a vessel awash about five miles north-north-east of Cromer, so *H.F. Bailey* launched at 7.05 a.m. into a strong north-easterly wind and found the motor vessel *Pontfield*, of Newcastle, laden with petrol. She had struck a mine and broken into two. A destroyer had the aft part in tow, and was trying to keep it from drifting ashore while the survivors of the crew had been taken to Harwich. Coxswain Blogg went alongside the fore part, found no one was aboard and so stood by for over an hour, by

H.F. Bailey *at Robinson's Yard, Oulton Broad, for repairs following the service to Convoy 559 in August 1941.*

when it was clear that the fore part was rapidly sinking. The lifeboat was taken to the after part, as the attempts to tow it had been abandoned and it was now only about three-quarters of a mile from the shore. Some lifeboatmen boarded it and half an hour later two tugs arrived to take the aft part in tow. The lifeboat stood by until the tug had taken the after part into Yarmouth Roads, where they arrived at 2.30 p.m. the following day. The lifeboat then returned to her station at 7 p.m., having been out on service for thirty-six hours.

A day after returning from the *Pontfield* service, *H.F. Bailey* was again asked to help a casualty of war. The steamship *Teddington*, of London, with a valuable cargo on board, had been attacked by German aeroplanes and set on fire. Her crew had been taken off by a naval vessel and the steamer had stranded about three miles south-east of Cromer. On 17 September, the Admiralty salvage officer asked the No.1 lifeboat to take firemen and pumps to the vessel. Later in the day she took out acetylene plant, and on several subsequent days carried salvage men and stevedores between Cromer and the wreck. Working in relays, the lifeboatmen assisted with the work of salving cargo, and it was not until 6 November that the last lifeboat trip was made. On several occasions, the No.2 lifeboat *Harriot Dixon* went out in place of *H.F. Bailey*, and between them the two boats were engaged on twenty-eight days between 17 September and 6 November.

English Trader

In the middle of helping *Teddington*, Coxswain Blogg and the crew of the Cromer lifeboat were involved in one of the most outstanding rescues of the war. This service, to the steamer *English Trader*, has become one of the most famous of all the rescues performed by Blogg, despite the fact that he was not awarded the Gold medal for his efforts. War had been ongoing for just over two years and the Cromer lifeboat already had an outstanding service record to its credit. However, during this service, the lifeboatmen were tested to the limit when their boat was almost lost, and sadly one of their own did lose his life.

The steamship *English Trader* was built in 1934 as *Arctees* but renamed in 1936 after being purchased by the Trader Navigation Co. of London. In October 1941, she was part of the eastward-bound Convoy EC90, which consisted of about thirty ships with destroyer escort. They were to sail from the Thames north to the Firth of Forth before proceeding round the north of Scotland to Oban and then on to Africa. On 25 October the convoy formed in the Thames estuary and began its journey up the east coast, past Suffolk and into the North Sea. After a failed attack on it by German aircraft, the convoy was steaming slowly through the wide channel between the Hammond Knoll to starboard and the Haisborough Sands to port. Between 1 a.m. and 1.30 a.m. on 26 October, *English Trader* found herself in the grip of the strong ebb tide, unable to make progress against it. Unknown to the steamer's crew, the strength of the tide had in fact taken the ship and pushed her aground. The first that those on board knew about it was a sudden but slight jolt at about 1.45 a.m., quickly followed by another more severe jolt which threw them off their feet and left the vessel stranded with the crew powerless. By daybreak, the weather was rapidly worsening and the wind had reached gale force, while the waves had smashed one of the lifeboats and driving spray was continuously flying over the boat deck. The lifeboat on the port side, despite being in the lee of the weather, could not be got away in the turbulent seas on the sandbank, so the crew was stranded on their ship relying on others to save them.

Meanwhile, at 8 a.m. on 26 October, the Cromer Coastguard telephoned Coxswain Henry Blogg to inform him that the Yarmouth Naval Base had asked the lifeboat to go to the aid of the stricken steamer. At 8.15 a.m., *H.F. Bailey* was launched into the gale which was now blowing from the north-north-east, with heavy squalls of rain, hail and sleet making conditions extremely cold, accompanied by a very rough sea. When the lifeboat reached Hammond Knoll at 11.35 a.m., *English Trader* was seen aground on the sands with little more than her masts, funnel and chart-room above water and with forty-four men stranded on board. Five others had been swept overboard and drowned before the lifeboat arrived. With her hull nearly under water and the heavy seas crashing around her, Blogg was presented with the most appalling problem that he had ever had to face, as he said afterwards.

The difficulties were compounded by the seas which were not running true: one would run along the weather side from forward, and another from aft, and when they met they would go up nearly mast high and then crash down on the steamer. At times, the only visible parts of the casualty were the tops of the masts, the lee side of the chart room, where the crew was huddled, and the funnel. On the lee side the sea was not as bad as on the weather side, but it was still very heavy and confused. The fore derricks had broken loose and were swinging about with every sea, the hatch covers were off, and the sea was covered with cargo washed out of the hold. Getting alongside was impossible in such conditions, though the lifeboat was taken as close as possible, enabling the crew to signal that they would make an attempt at slack water about four hours later. However, at about 1.15 p.m., Blogg thought he saw an opportunity to get alongside and succeeded in getting the lifeboat fairly close to the lee side of the steamer, but very heavy seas, coming round both her bow and stern and bursting amidships, made it impossible to actually get close enough to help. The lifeboat fired a line, but it was aimed at a high angle to reach the crew on the bridge, and was blown back by the fierce gale. The lifeboat was forced to pull away, but an hour later made a second attempt. Blogg was forced to approach broadside to the sea, putting the lifeboat in considerable danger. What happened next is best described in the coxswain's own words:

> We were trying to approach about half speed, and when still about 100 yards away a huge wall of water suddenly rose up on our port side. There was a shout of 'Look out!' and before I could even give a half turn of the wheel to meet the oncoming sea I was lifted out of the boat just as though I had been a bit of cork. We were simply overwhelmed by the sheer weight of water. How the boat righted herself I shall never understand. It must indeed have been the hand of Providence. The boat must have been hit hardest abaft the fore cockpit. Had she been hit as hard along her whole length there would be no lifeboat crew in Cromer today.

The captain of *English Trader* said afterwards that he saw the lifeboat's keel come right out of the water. During the 'knock down', Blogg, Second Coxswain Jack Davies, and three other members of the crew were thrown overboard. Two other members of the crew were also thrown out but managed to grab the guard rails and haul themselves aboard again. The mechanics in the canopy fell against its side while the rest of the crew was flung about, knocked off their feet and thrown flat until the sea passed over them. As the boat came upright, the second coxswain's son sprang to the wheel, brought the boat under control, and steered to where his father and the coxswain were floating. They were hauled on board, and the coxswain at once took command again. The lifeboat then went to pick up the other three men, but it proved very difficult actually getting them on board as they were so waterlogged. The signalman, Edward Allen, the last to be rescued, had then been in the water for twenty-five minutes by the time he was picked up and was unconscious by the time the lifeboat reached him. Once aboard the lifeboat, he was revived and sat up, spoke a few words, but then suddenly and tragically collapsed and died.

It was now about 3 p.m., nearly seven hours since the lifeboat had left Cromer, and her crew was exhausted. Various small ropes had been washed overboard and became entangled round the propellers, reducing the boat's speed and making manoeuvring difficult. Blogg decided to make at once for Great Yarmouth. On the way, the lifeboat crew tried to contact Yarmouth Naval Base by radio telephone to ask for a doctor and an ambulance to be waiting when she arrived. She could not get through to the base, but her message was picked up by the Great Yarmouth and Gorleston lifeboat *Louise Stephens* (ON.820), which relayed it to Yarmouth.

Meanwhile, the Great Yarmouth and Gorleston lifeboat, which had been launched at noon under the command of Coxswain Charles Johnson, had a very difficult journey, travelling nineteen miles in the face of a strong northerly gale with a rough sea and flood tide. The journey took her more than three hours, and she reached Hammond Knoll about 3.30 p.m., just half an hour after the Cromer lifeboat had left on her way to Great Yarmouth. The two lifeboats had passed without seeing one another. While the water was slack, between 4 p.m. and 6 p.m., *Louise Stephens* made five separate attempts to go alongside *English Trader* and get under her lee, being very heavily buffeted and shipping a considerable amount of water in the process. She was faced with the same difficulties as the Cromer lifeboat: loose, swinging derricks and floating cargo. During one of the five attempts she succeeded in firing a line over the wreck and got a mooring rope secured between them. The lifeboatmen were able to haul their boat alongside, but the rope parted and the lifeboat was swept away. With the seas increasing and darkness setting in, the captain of *English Trader* blew a whistle and waved to the lifeboat to go away. It was now 6.15 p.m. and the coxswain decided to return to Gorleston for the night.

At about the same time, the Cromer lifeboat had arrived at Yarmouth, and the body of the signalman was landed ashore. Some of the crew was so exhausted that they had to be helped out of the boat, but they immediately refuelled her in readiness for a further attempt at rescue early next morning. The crew was taken to the Shipwrecked Sailors' Home where they were given hot baths, hot drinks, food and dry clothes. At the same time a telephone call was put through to Cromer for more dry clothing and oilskins, which came at once by road, and for another man to take the place of signalman Allen.

The Gorleston lifeboat was now on her way home. The terrible weather combined with the absence of lights made the journey a particularly difficult one, but Coxswain Johnson stayed inshore and followed the coast south until the lifeboat reached Gorleston at about 10.30 p.m. The crew was so wet and cold, and the night so dark, that the coxswain decided not to refuel the lifeboat until morning. He told the crew to assemble again at 5.30 a.m. Later that night, when Blogg heard that the Great Yarmouth and Gorleston lifeboat had returned, he telephoned Coxswain Johnson to discuss arrangements for the next morning. He said that he intended to go to sea again at 4 a.m., while the Gorleston coxswain decided to wait until daylight.

Next morning, between 3.30 a.m. and 4 a.m., Blogg was up to obtain weather reports both from the Yarmouth Naval Base and Cromer Coastguard. Both told the same. Wind and sea had gone down a little but the weather was much as it had been the previous day. At 4.15 a.m. he called at the Naval Base and asked that the boom defence might be opened and within half an hour *H.F. Bailey* had put to sea. She had three hours of darkness before her, the ropes were still round her propeller. and she had twenty-two miles to go against the gale. The journey took three hours and twenty minutes, and the lifeboat reached the sands at about 8 a.m., by which time the north-easterly wind changed, backing to the north-west, and both wind and sea were much lighter.

The fore part of *English Trader* was now under water, but with little difficulty the lifeboat was able to go alongside the steamer's lee rail, which was only about two feet above her. Within half an hour the forty-four survivors of the crew had been taken on board and the lifeboat was making again for Great Yarmouth, where she arrived at about 11.30 a.m. and landed the men. Although both wind and sea had gone down, it was still too rough for the Cromer lifeboat to be recovered up the slipway, so her crew left her at Gorleston and returned to Cromer by car. Meanwhile, the Great Yarmouth and Gorleston lifeboat had put out at 6.30 a.m., reaching Hammond Knoll two hours later to find that the Cromer lifeboat had rescued the crew, and so she returned to her station where she arrived at 11.30 a.m. Cyril Jolly, in *The Loss of the English Trader*, stated that:

> The service to the English Trader was his [Blogg's] supreme trial, and the sea almost beat him. As Henry Blogg himself said when the lifeboat was 'knocked down', the boat was hit hardest abaft the fore cockpit. Had she been hit as hard along her whole length there would be no lifeboat crew in Cromer today. But the boat did right herself and Henry Blogg finished the job.

For this truly remarkable rescue, one of the most famous in the history of the lifeboat service, the following awards were made by the RNLI: to Coxswain Blogg, a third clasp to the Silver medal for gallantry which he already held; to each of the crew, already holders of the Bronze medal for gallantry, with one or more clasps, another clasp: John J. Davies, snr, second coxswain, and Henry W. Davies, motor mechanic, third clasps; to James W. Davies, assistant motor mechanic, and the late Edward W. Allen, boat signalman, second clasps; to William T. Davies, bowman, and John J. Davies jnr and Sidney C. Harrison, lifeboatmen, clasps; the Bronze medal to crew members Henry T. Davies, boat signalman; William H. Davies, Robert C. Davies and James R. Davies. To the coxswain and each of the eleven members of the crew a copy of the Vote Inscribed on Vellum, except to the late Edward W. Allen, whose widow was awarded a relative's certificate recording the gallantry of his death. George R. Cox, who took the place of Edward Allen on the second service, the Thanks of the Institution Inscribed on Vellum and an additional monetary reward. A pension was granted to Allen's widow on the same

Edward Walter Allen, the signalman who lost his life during the epic service to the steamer English Trader *in October 1941. He was the only Cromer lifeboatman to lose his life on lifeboat service.*

scale as if he had been a sailor of the Royal Navy killed in action, and the funeral expenses were paid by the RNLI. The only Cromer lifeboatman to lose his life on service, Allen was a dedicated and well-respected member of the crew who had been out on numerous occasions, including all of the medal-winning services.

The Great Yarmouth and Gorleston crew was also recognised by the Institution: Coxswain Charles Johnson received a third clasp to the Bronze medal and each of the other six members of the crew were accorded the Thanks of the Institution Inscribed on Vellum: John Wright, second coxswain; Thomas C. Morley, bowman; George Mobbs, motor mechanic; Arthur G. Bush, assistant motor-mechanic; William Parker, signalman; and Lewis Symonds. Many messages of congratulations were received, including messages from the flag officer at Great Yarmouth, the inspector of Coastguard, and the owners of *English Trader*, the Trader Navigation Co., which also made a donation to the Institution. One of the rescued seamen from *English Trader*, who had stood on the wrecked vessel as it was being pounded by the seas, watched the efforts by the Cromer lifeboatmen to reach the casualty. The tribute Hyman Rothman, the ship's carpenter, broadcast to the rescuers is perhaps the most fitting way to end the story:

> Blogg's seamanship – well, he knew his job. In all my life I have never seen anything like, when they [almost] capsized, the way they saved one another's lives. It was marvellous, and, the second time, the wonderful way Blogg manoeuvred the lifeboat towards us. He knew every wave and how to get between them. I can't forget the man who died – trying to save us. I want his wife to know – I want all the people of England to know, that we will never forget how he gave his life to save others.

Other Wartime Services

The rescues performed by the Cromer lifeboat during the remaining years of the war were much less spectacular than that to *English Trader* but were no less necessary. During 1942, *H.F. Bailey* undertook several services to help casualties either from aircraft or injured as a result of aircraft action. At 9.45 a.m. on 29 January, she was launched in strong winds, with rough seas and snow squalls, to search for an airman who had been seen in a dinghy to the north-east, but nothing was found. After a couple of hours, at 12.13 p.m., a wireless message was received stating that a Spitfire was circling over the dinghy seven miles north of Cley. Another Spitfire circled the lifeboat and guided her to the airman's dinghy. The lifeboat found and rescued the airman, but the weather was too rough to get the lifeboat back on the slipway at Cromer so she made for Great Yarmouth, arriving at 6.20 p.m. For this service, a letter of thanks was received from the director-general of Aircraft Safety.

H.F. Bailey was called to another casualty of war on 15 March after a convoy had been attacked during the previous night by enemy E-boats, which in turn were attacked by destroyers and by HMS *Vortigern*. *Vortigern* had been hit by two torpedoes and sank, so the lifeboat was called out to search for survivors ten miles north-east of Cromer. The lifeboat put out at 7.57 a.m. and by 9.43 a.m. had reached the position, finding a number of other rescue boats there. The lifeboat found wreckage, picked up eleven bodies and continued to search until 1.25 p.m., but found no one alive so returned to her station at 3 p.m. Sheringham lifeboat *Foresters Centenary* also put out and found one body and a barrage balloon. The lifeboats transferred the bodies to a motor boat which took them to Lowestoft, and then returned to their stations.

During 1943, only two effective services were performed. The first, on 12 March, resulted in the salvaging of a partly submerged barrage balloon about six miles off the station. The second, on 26 July, proved to be the shortest service of the war. The coastguard reported that an aeroplane had crashed into the sea about a mile north of Cromer so, at 3 a.m., *H.F. Bailey* was launched into a moderate southerly breeze but smooth sea. Almost immediately after launching, the lifeboatmen heard cries and found a man in the water. The searchlight was used to pick out three more men found about a hundred yards further east. While they were being taken aboard the lifeboat, another man was heard shouting, and so he was rescued too. The five men were the crew of a Wellington bomber. The lifeboat was back at her station and had landed the men just twenty-two minutes after setting out.

On 7 December 1944, the naval base at Great Yarmouth asked, via the coastguard, that the lifeboat launch to the British-manned Liberty ship *Samnethy*, which had stranded on Hammond Knoll two days earlier. At 12.20 p.m. *H.F. Bailey* launched and reached the area, twenty-three miles from the station, three hours later to find four naval salvage tugs and a motor launch standing by the casualty. Coxswain Blogg boarded *Samnethy* and agreed with the captain and salvage officer that the lifeboat would stand by in case the ship had to be abandoned, and the captain agreed to provide food. Throughout the night and into 8 December, the lifeboat remained on scene. During the night of 8 December the wind and sea worsened, and throughout the day the wind increased, at times to gale force, with squalls of sleet, heavy seas and intense cold. At about 9 a.m. on 9 December, Coxswain Blogg warned the salvage officer that if the ship's crew was to be taken off, it must be done before dark. At 2.30 p.m., the lifeboat was secured alongside but heavy seas parted the rope which then fouled the lifeboat's port propeller. After this had been cleared the lifeboat was again secured alongside, and despite rising and falling 12-15ft, managed to take off the thirty-five men. She put them on board a tug and then at 7.30 p.m. again went alongside *Samnethy* to take off the thirteen remaining members of the crew and four salvage officers. This service, which had lasted sixty hours, had been particularly arduous, and the rescued men collected over £40 which was given to the lifeboatmen in gratitude. Each member of the crew was provided with an increase in the usual money reward by the RNLI.

Greatest of the Lifeboatmen

The name of Coxswain Henry Blogg dominated the accounts of Cromer rescues throughout the first half of the twentieth century and his extraordinary feats of lifesaving have made him one of the most famous lifeboatmen of all time. 'He was the very embodiment of the spirit of courage of the north Norfolk fishermen... A very gallant man of simple tastes, great courage and strong character,' according to Lord Templewood, former Home Secretary and Foreign Secretary, speaking during the memorial service for Henry Blogg at Cromer's Church of St Peter and St Paul in June 1954. At the same service, Reverend D.T. Dick, the town's vicar, described Blogg as 'Cromer's greatest son'. Indeed, much has been written about Henry Blogg, both during his life and since his death, and his significance to Cromer lifeboat history cannot be overstated.

Blogg was born in a small cottage in New Street, opposite the pier, on 6 February 1876, and lived all his life in the town. He joined the lifeboat crew in 1894 and was appointed second coxswain in 1902. Blogg's first two services in charge of the lifeboat took place over the winter of 1908-9. On 19 December 1908, as acting coxswain, he took *Louisa Heartwell* to the smack *Marcus*, of Lowestoft, on the Haisborough Sands, but the lifeboat's services were not needed as the crew of the smack had boarded the lightvessel and been taken from that by the Palling lifeboat. On 14 January 1909, the lifeboat launched under Blogg to the steamer *Selby*, of Stockton, which had gone ashore at Mundesley. The steamer's captain refused assistance, as he had gone close to the shore because of the weather, so the lifeboat returned to station having not been needed. In November 1909, Blogg was officially appointed coxswain,* and so began his long and distinguished career at the helm.

He was coxswain for the first time on 23 November 1909, when two lives were saved from the barque *Alf*, of Laurvig, but the first incident which brought wider public recognition to both the lifeboat station and its coxswain was the rescue of the *Fernebo*'s crew in 1917, for which he was awarded the first of three Gold medals. Further outstanding rescues performed during the 1920s, notably to the tanker *Georgia* in 1927, brought more media attention. When he was awarded the Gold medal for this service, it was the first time in more than seventy-five years that a man had twice won the RNLI's highest accolade for actual rescues. At the RNLI's Annual General Meeting held in London on 28 March 1928, HRH Prince of Wales, President of the Institution, remarked before presenting the award:

> Coxswain Blogg's achievement is one which confers honour not only on himself, not only on the splendid crew which he leads, not even only on the Norfolk stations, which have a magnificent record… but on the lifeboat service, whose spirit he so splendidly embodies and I am sure we shall all join in congratulating him on the unique distinction.

Left: *Coxswain Henry Blogg with the Prince of Wales at the presentation of the Gold medal for the* Georgia *rescue, 1928.*

Right: *Coxswain Henry Blogg with Second Coxswain Jack Davies, on the pier in front of the lifeboat house.* (MPL)

---

* His actual title was Superintendent Coxswain, a post that gave him overall charge of the whole station with responsibility for all aspects of its running. When a No.2 lifeboat was operated, the Superintendent Coxswain was in charge of both boats. After Blogg's retirement in 1947, the post reverted to Coxswain and the 'Superintendent' part of the title was dropped.

Two pictures of Coxswain Henry Blogg with his dog Monte, which was rescued from the steamship Monte Nevoso *in October 1932.*

The spotlight was again turned on the station after the dramatic rescue from the barge *Sepoy* in December 1933. Probably because of the series of extraordinary photographs taken during the rescue by local photographers, which have been published many times, both the dangers of lifesaving and the daring efforts of the Cromer lifeboatmen, in particular, were brought to the public's attention like never before. The images graphically depicted the lifeboat closing in on the casualty, and then being driven by Blogg on to the barge's deck so that the stranded men could be snatched from the rigging by the lifeboatmen. For this daring service, Blogg received a second service clasp to his Silver medal and the crew was all accorded the Thanks Inscribed on Vellum, but the photographs undoubtedly contributed towards the widespread publicity that this rescue brought to the Cromer station.

The wartime services of the Cromer lifeboatmen were performed under the command of Blogg, who had shown such courage, bravery and seamanship in the face of adversity that by the time war had begun he was already regarded as one of the greatest lifeboatmen; yet he was destined to undertake further medal-winning services before the war was over. Such an unlikely hero as Blogg was too good for the media to ignore and the wartime propaganda machine, in full swing to keep up morale on the home front, took full advantage, often exaggerating accounts of rescues but able to emphasise his bravery and courage in the face of hostile conditions as an example to all. His exploits and those of the lifeboatmen of Cromer, already well known throughout the country, were further highlighted when he was featured on the cover of the *Illustrated* magazine for 7 March 1940, which ran the headline 'The Lifeboat's Out'. Having sent its photographer to Cromer to capture the lifeboatmen at work, the magazine explained, 'Britain's courageous lifeboatmen have taken their place in the front line of this war.' The fact that the magazine did not need to explain who Blogg was shows how well known he had become.

Blogg's heroism and the extraordinary deeds he performed to save lives at sea against all odds undoubtedly marked him out as exceptional. But he seems to have been very private, despite his lifesaving exploits earning him national recognition. Apparently he was a man everyone knew, but who no one knew well. One man, acquainted with him for thirty years, Frank Smith, confessed that he had 'never succeeded in getting behind his strange reserve to the man himself'. He was, according to Smith, 'a man of long silences, few words and incisive speech'. When he was in London for the presentation of one of his medals, he was offered £100 just to walk onto the stage of one of the capital's theatres, but refused point-blank. He did make radio appearances, but only on condition that it was to boost public recognition of the RNLI, and not to talk about himself. This modesty was reflected in the first and only public speech he made, at the end of his career, during which he stated, 'Cromer always has had good boats and good crews. And it always will.'

He remained as coxswain until the end of September 1947, when he retired at the age of seventy-one having been given special dispensation to remain beyond the usual retirement age of sixty-five. During his time on the lifeboat, he went out on 387 occasions and helped to save 873 lives. The last service in which he was involved took place on 4 January 1948. The lifeboat went to the steam trawler *Balmoral*, which was aground on Haisborough Sands, with Blogg as an ordinary crew member under Coxswain Henry Davies.

Soon after Blogg had retired, the station's new lifeboat (described in the following chapter) was named after the famous coxswain, with the great man himself remarking it was 'the best boat I have ever handled or seen'. During the naming ceremony, at which the Admiral of the Fleet Sir John Cunningham christened the new lifeboat, Blogg was the centre of attention. The Admiral said, 'We in the Admiralty had a very lively appreciation of the consummate seamanship which Henry Blogg exhibited on so many occasions.' It was a proud day for Blogg, as not only did he receive a copy of his portrait painted by T.C. Dugdale RA and a certificate of service, but from friends and admirers he received a leather-bound volume which contained cameos of crabs, Cromer Church, his beach hut and a distress signal. The address inside read, 'In the seventy-two years that you have lived in Cromer and particularly during the fifty-three years that you have served for RNLI, you have by your deeds and example brought great credit upon the town, which is proud to call you a citizen, and upon the lifeboat service.'

Coxswain Henry Blogg and the lifeboat crew in 1939, left to right: G. Cox, R. Cox, J.R. Davies, J.J. Davies jnr, W.H. Davies, J.J. Davies snr, Henry Blogg, J.W Davies, H.T. 'Shrimp' Davies, F. Davies, R.C. Davies and H.W. Davies. (MPL)

H.BLOGG   L.HARRISON

Left: *Henry Blogg and Leslie Harrison, Stand-by Coxswain, on the pier.*

Right: *Coxswain Henry Blogg in oilskins.*

Henry Blogg died on 13 June 1954 after a short illness. His funeral was held four days later at the Church of St Peter and St Paul where he had been married fifty-two years earlier. In the church, 1,400 people gathered to pay homage to Blogg while another thousand waited in the churchyard and around the church's walls. During the funeral service, Lord Templewood spoke; 'Thanks to his leadership the Cromer lifeboat has become the most famous of all lifeboats.' The service ended with the hymn 'Eternal Father Strong to Save', after which the flag-draped coffin was lifted onto the shoulders of four Norfolk coxswains: Henry West of Sheringham, William Cox of Wells, James Brown of Caister and Bertie Beavers of Gorleston. A procession of mourners formed and followed the coffin along High Street and New Street, out through the town to the new cemetery where, on high ground overlooking the heath and wood with the sea distant, Henry Blogg was laid to rest.

Several memorials to Blogg and his lifesaving exploits exist. One of the first was unveiled on 11 August 1955, during the annual Lifeboat Day. A shelter in Church Square provided by the Henry Blogg Memorial Fund was opened and dedicated with a wooden plaque on the shelter unveiled by the chairman of Cromer Urban District Council. Present at this ceremony were John Smith of Ormesby, Yorkshire, who had been rescued from a ship aground on the Haisborough Sands in 1915 and whose subscription to the memorial fund was the first to be received, and Captain van der Hidde, a Dutchman who had also been rescued by Blogg. After the shelter had been dedicated by the vicar of Cromer, two maroons were fired into the overcast sky. The party then walked down to the No.1 Lifeboat House at the end of the pier, where Lord Templewood unveiled a commemorative tablet erected by the RNLI under the wreck chart on the south wall. This was dedicated by the vicar, after which the lifeboat was launched.

Perhaps the most notable monument to Blogg is the bronze bust and bronze inscription in a granite setting, set facing out towards the Haisborough Sands, at the East Gangway, above the lifeboat house (subsequently the lifeboat museum). This was unveiled at a special ceremony on 23 May 1962 by Earl Howe, chairman of the RNLI Committee of Management. The bust was made by James Woodford, RA, and the original plaster cast was shown at the Royal Academy's summer exhibition of 1962. It was provided by an anonymous female donor who, after the ceremony, sent a donation to the Cromer branch in recognition of what she described as 'a very beautiful and moving occasion.' Coxswain Henry Davies, Blogg's nephew and coxswain after him, laid a wreath, and the vicar of Cromer, Revd C.W.J. Searle-Barnes, conducted a short service. Anthony Gurney, a county councillor, formally presented the bust to the townspeople of Cromer on behalf of the donor and Councillor J.E. Webster, chairman of the Cromer Urban District Council, accepted it. In 1998 the bust was removed for renovation and so in May that year a replica was placed in the position of the original, facing seawards. Originally it was planned to make the replica out of fibreglass, but it has actually been made from metal. The original bronze bust had deteriorated due to the exposure to wind and weather on the cliff-top site, and so was removed to be cleaned up and subsequently placed in the new lifeboat house at the end of the pier.

Left: *Coxswain Henry 'Shrimp' Davies laying a wreath at the unveiling ceremony of the bust of Henry Blogg on the East Cliff, 23 May 1962.*

Right: *The bust of Henry Blogg on the East Cliff gazing seaward over the North Sea. (Nicholas Leach)*

Perhaps the best reminder of Blogg's daring exploits came in 1991 when the lifeboat in which Blogg carried out several daring rescues returned to Cromer to form the centrepiece of the permanent displays in the lifeboat museum. This lifeboat, *H.F. Bailey*, served the station from 1935 to 1945 and saved 518 lives during her time. Surrounding the lifeboat in her new home were photographs, artefacts and newspaper articles relating to the medal-winning rescues and, two years later, replicas of the medals that Blogg was awarded also went on display. The medals had been kept in a velvet-lined box by Henry 'Shrimp' Davies, who had them mounted for display at the museum only to find that the insurance costs were so high that they remained locked away in a bank vault. The security risks were overcome when copies were made by model-maker John Dowcra in 1993 and presented to the station. The originals have only been displayed once before, in 1976, the centenary of Blogg's birth. According to Davies, Blogg's nephew and successor as coxswain, 'Henry never flaunted the medals and I do not know if he would be very happy at what we are doing. I think he was very proud to have them but he never walked around wearing them.'

The combination of his lifesaving exploits with his great modesty made Henry Blogg 'the greatest of the lifeboatmen', according to his biographer Cyril Jolly. In looking back over his life and achievements, the words of a former chief inspector of lifeboats, Commander T.G. Michelmore, are perhaps the most fitting:

> He was a big man in every sense of the word, a kindly genial man of exemplary character and possessing a youthful spirit; a magnificent seaman of very few words with the courage of the lion; a man of quick decisions and resolute action, sparing neither himself, his crew, not the lifeboat, in taking grave risks to rescue unfortunate seamen faced with disaster. He always succeeded and always beat the fury of the gale.

Summary of Henry Blogg's Awards

1917, 9–10 January	Awarded the Gold medal for saving 11 from the steamship *Fernebo*, of Gothenburg.
1924, March	Awarded the Empire Gallantry medal, replaced by the George Cross in 1940.
1927, 21–22 November	Awarded Gold clasp for saving 15 from the steam tanker *Georgia*, of Rotterdam. Queen of Holland also sent a gold watch for Blogg.
1932, 14–16 October	Awarded Silver medal for saving 29 from the steamship *Monte Nevoso*, of Genoa. In 1935 the Italian Government sent a silver medal to Blogg. He was also awarded a Canine Defence Silver medal for saving the ship's dog.
1933, 13 December	Awarded the Silver clasp for saving two from the barge *Sepoy*, of Dover.
1939, 9 October	Awarded Silver clasp for saving 29 from the steamship *Mount Ida*, of Piraeus.
1941, 6 August	Awarded the Gold clasp and the British Empire Medal for assisting Convoy 559, which included the steamships *Oxshott*, *Gallois*, *Deerwood* and *Betty Hindley*.
1941, 26 October	Awarded Silver clasp for service to the steamship *English Trader*, of London, during which 44 lives were saved.
1953, June	Awarded the Coronation Medal.

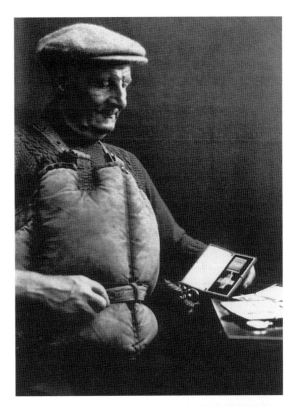

*A formal study of Henry Blogg, with his
George Cross. (By courtesy of Eastern
Counties Newspapers Ltd)*

*Henry 'Shrimp' Davies with Blogg's medals.
(By courtesy of David Gooch)*

7

Lifesaving in the Post-War Era

After almost six years of hostilities, the Second World War ended in the spring of 1945, and with the surrender of the German forces on 8 May 1945 the war in Europe ended. When Japan surrendered on 14 August, a new era of peace began. The wartime months of 1945 had been a relatively quiet time for the Cromer lifeboat, with only one effective service performed: on 4 February 1945, *H.F. Bailey* went to the fishing vessel *Valder*, of Hartlepool, which was towed to Yarmouth with a broken down engine. What proved to be the last service of the war took place on 4 March when *H.F. Bailey* searched for a crashed bomber, but she returned to station after failing to find anything. *H.F. Bailey* was launched for what proved to be the last time as Cromer lifeboat on the afternoon of 22 August 1945 but she only found a patrol vessel's marker buoy which resembled a canoe from a distance. Having searched until 6.20 p.m. without finding anything, the lifeboat returned to station.

By the time of this last service, the Cromer lifeboatmen were looking forward to the arrival of a new lifeboat. Named *Millie Walton*, the new boat arrived from her builder's via Gorleston on 20 December 1945 and, after a series of trials and practice runs, was hauled up the slipway and successfully housed. *H.F. Bailey* had been launched earlier in the day with Coxswain Blogg in charge and taken to Gorleston, leaving with the remarkable record of nearly 450 lives saved during the war and over 150 launches. This lifeboat can claim to be perhaps the most famous of all Cromer's lifeboats as she was involved in some of the most dramatic rescues in the history of not just the Cromer station but of the lifeboat service as a whole. From Gorleston, she went to Rowhedge for refit and then in August 1946 was placed on station at Helvick Head on Ireland's

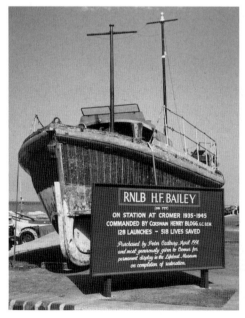

Left: *Perhaps Cromer's most famous lifeboat, H.F. Bailey, on the promenade outside the lifeboat museum during her restoration in the early 1990s prior to going on display inside the museum. (Paul Russell)*

Opposite above: *The 46ft Watson cabin motor lifeboat* Millie Walton *(ON.840) at Cromer before she became* Henry Blogg, *the name given to her in July 1946. Built in 1945, she was originally allocated to Douglas, Isle of Man, before coming to Cromer. (By courtesy of P.A. Vicary)*

Opposite below: *Coxswain Henry Blogg in front of the lifeboat sent to Cromer in December 1945, which was renamed in his honour. (By courtesy of P.A. Vicary)*

south coast. She has since returned to Cromer and is displayed in the town as the main exhibit in the lifeboat museum (see Appendix 7).

The new lifeboat was a 46ft 9in twin screw Watson class lifeboat, with a forward steering position, the first lifeboat to be so designed. Hitherto, motor lifeboats had carried auxiliary sails but as post-war lifeboats were built with twin engines and twin screws, it was no longer necessary to have the steering position aft where the coxswain could keep an eye on the sails. Two boats were built with the steering position forward, the first of which was *Millie Walton* (ON.840). These two boats also had a cockpit aft, similar to some 46ft Watsons, but the design in later 46ft 9in Watsons was changed so that the amidships cockpit was protected by a canopy and windscreen. Her twin Ferry VE.4 four-cylinder diesels, each of 40bhp, gave a maximum speed of 8.22 knots and a cruising speed of 7.5 knots. She carried 112 gallons of fuel, giving a radius of action of 115 nautical miles at full speed and 152 at cruising speed. *Millie Walton* was built by the Sussex Shipbuilding Company of Shoreham, one of only five lifeboats built by this firm. She was funded from the legacy of Mrs M.E. Walton, of Derby, after whom she was

Above: Henry Blogg *returning from exercise, November 1964. This excellent photograph gives a good indication of the deck and cabin layout of the design, which was the first to have a midship steering position. As the first with midship steering, she was sent to Cromer so that Blogg and his crew could test her out. (By courtesy of Eastern Counties Newspapers)*

Left: *Henry 'Shrimp' Davies, in front of the crab boat* Provider, *was coxswain from 1947 until 1976 serving on both* Henry Blogg *and* Ruby and Arthur Reed *lifeboats. He was involved in many outstanding rescues and in 1970 was awarded the British Empire Medal. (By courtesy of* Eastern Counties Newspapers*)*

named, and was originally sent to Cromer on a temporary basis. The new design was to be tried out by the Cromer crew, who were regarded as one of the most experienced in the country, but as Coxswain Blogg and the crew liked her so much they asked for her to be stationed permanently at Cromer. The Institution acceded to this request and allocated its general funds to pay for the boat so that she could be renamed.

The first service performed by the new lifeboat (and the only one under the name *Millie Walton*) took place on 7 March 1946 when she went to the motor collier *Corcrest*, of London, one of the fleet of Cory Brothers, which had gone aground on the Haisborough Sands and needed help. At 5.05 p.m. the lifeboat was launched and began the twenty-mile journey to the casualty. She fought her way through a strong easterly breeze and rolling heavy seas, but still had some way to go when at 7 p.m. a radio message was received that *Corcrest* was breaking up. When the lifeboatmen reached the collier, her crew of twenty-two was waiting on deck wearing lifebelts. They had rigged rope ladders down the ship's side so they could climb down as the lifeboat came alongside. Despite being seventy years old, Coxswain Blogg handled the lifeboat as skilfully as ever, enabling the shipwrecked men to climb down the ladders to safety. It took half an hour to transfer the men to the lifeboat and as soon as they were aboard course was set for Great Yarmouth. Once the rescued men had been landed ashore safely, it was learned that *Corcrest* floated off the sands. The collier was subsequently towed into Yarmouth Roads and anchored before being brought into harbour by the Cromer lifeboatmen.

The naming ceremony of the new lifeboat was delayed until 1948 because, firstly, the pier was not considered safe for a large number of people as it was undergoing renovation, and secondly, major repairs to the slipway during summer 1947 put it out of action. Because the naming had to be held during the summer it was postponed until 7 August 1948. The events of the day were described by the *Eastern Daily Press*:

> With a record of fifty-three years as a lifeboatman, during thirty-eight of which he was coxswain at Cromer, Mr Henry George Blogg was the chief figure in the naming after him of Cromer's No.1 lifeboat by Admiral of the Fleet Sir John Cunningham. Mr Blogg, who retired last September, received from the Royal National Lifeboat Institution a portrait of himself, the work of Mr. T.C. Dugdale, RA, and a framed certificate of service. He also received a cheque and an illuminated address in a green morocco-covered album from many of his friends and admirers.

At sea, two motor launches dressed overall had anchored off the West beach, and the lifeboat, dressed overall, was on the slipway. The ceremony was presided over by Viscount Templewood, president of the Cromer branch, who said Blogg had become a national figure and the lifeboat station a great national institution. In receiving the lifeboat on behalf of the branch, Blogg made what was the first public speech of his career, 'Thank you all very much. I am very pleased to accept this boat for the station, because I know it is the best boat that has ever been on it.' The service of dedication was conducted by Reverend D.T. Dick, vicar of Cromer, and Revd W. Hughes, the Methodist minister. Commander H.L. Wheeler, RN, Eastern district inspector of lifeboats, described the lifeboat, and Brigadier R.J.P. Wyatt, MC, organising secretary of the RNLI for the South-Eastern England district, presented the boat to the branch. Coxswain Henry Davies presented his crew to Sir John, who said he was proud to name the boat after a very gallant man. 'I have much pleasure in naming her *Henry Blogg* and wish all who sail in her good luck on errands of mercy', he declared. He then broke a bottle of wine on the lifeboat's stern and her launch was accompanied by cheers from the thousands ashore.

The *Henry Blogg* lifeboat gave more than two decades of service at Cromer, during which time she saved almost 150 lives. During 1947 she was not called upon at all, but in 1948 undertook a number of notable services. The first took place on 4 January when she went to a vessel on the North Middle Haisborough Sands. At 9.45 a.m., two hours after launching, she reached the casualty, the steam trawler *Balmoral*, of Grimsby, which had been abandoned by her crew. As the trawler was drifting into deep water, five of the lifeboat's crew went aboard while the lifeboat went in search of the trawler's crew. They were found about three miles away in a small ship's boat and all eleven were taken on board the lifeboat, which then returned to the trawler with the small boat in tow. The crew reboarded their vessel, which had been anchored by the lifeboatmen, and finding her undamaged made for Grimsby. The lifeboat escorted her as far as the Haisborough lightvessel and then returned to station.

What proved to be the most testing rescue for Coxswain Henry Davies since he had succeeded his uncle Henry Blogg as coxswain took place on 8 July 1948. The 650-ton Dunkirk steamer *François Tixier*, bound from Goole to Rouen with 500 tons of coal, capsized in heavy seas about four miles off Sheringham and was seen in difficulties by Cley lookout. With the Sheringham lifeboat undergoing refit at Oulton Broad, *Henry Blogg* was launched to the steamer's aid and made a dramatic sight as she went through the heavy seas with many people watching her go. Once on scene, she stood by the steamer which

Presentation on 13 September 1949 of French awards for the François Tixier *service. Pictured left to right, front row: R.C. Davies, H.W. Davies and Henry Davies; middle row: G. Rook, L.B. Harrison, L.J. Harrison, S.C. Harrison; and back row: J.R. Davies, J.J. Davies, George Cox, Tom Jonas and Frank Davies.*

The steamship Monte Nuria, *of Bilbao, which went aground off Sheringham and her fore hold filled with water in August 1948.* Henry Blogg *launched on 25 August, under the command of ex-Second Coxswain J.J. Davies, with a scratch crew to the steamer. Subsequently, when they had returned from fishing, Coxswain Henry Davies and several other regular crew members were transferred to the lifeboat via Sheringham fishing boats, with Coxswain Davies assuming command. Apart from refuelling on 28 August and charging her R/T batteries on 29 August the lifeboat remained standing by until 31 August. (By courtesy of P.A. Vicary)*

was dragging her anchors in a worsening gale with a heavy list to port. The lifeboat went alongside to speak to the captain, but as he would not leave Coxswain Davies took the lifeboat round the ship trying to persuade the crew, but they also refused. While this was happening the cargo was shifting further to port, so when the ship's crew failed in their attempt to steady the vessel with the anchors, they agreed to leave.

One man jumped into the water and was picked up, while the next reached the lifeboat via a rope passed from the ship. Then, using the beeches buoy, eight more men were taken off the steamer which, by this time, was rolling on her beam ends. After an eleventh man was taken off via the beeches buoy, five men remained on board. At this point, the steamer rolled over and settled under the water with the last five men standing on the stern. As they went into the water, fortuitously a raft came floating away from the ship, into which they climbed to be picked up by the lifeboat soon afterwards.

After saving the steamer's crew, the lifeboat battled through heavy seas to reach Great Yarmouth, where the sixteen rescued French seamen were landed at the Lower Ferry and then taken to the Shipwrecked Sailors' Home where they were given coffee and hot baths, followed by a meal. According to the *Eastern Daily Press*, they 'huddled round a fire… [and] talked volubly in their own tongue of the gallant Cromer lifeboatmen who had rescued them from the North Sea'. The youngest member of the crew was seventeen-year-old Hubert Joseph, of Cancale. 'It was my sixth trip between Goole and Rouen with coal', he said. 'I think the cargo started slipping and we were lucky that the lifeboat was close at hand when we turned off. No one was hurt, but we were lucky, for although we were only in the water for a few minutes swimming was almost impossible in terrible seas.' The Cromer lifeboatmen went to a quayside café at Gorleston for hot drinks and then returned home by motor coach, leaving the lifeboat until the weather was calm enough for rehousing. Coxswain Davies commented with a degree of modesty, 'It was a nice job perhaps, but we have done bigger ones. Please don't make too much fuss about it.'

In recognition of their efforts during this rescue, the crew was presented with awards by the French Government. On 13 September 1949, Capitaine de Corvette de la Loge d'Ausson, Commanding Officer of the French fishery protection vessel, *Ailette*, made the presentations during a special ceremony held in the town. Coxswain Davies received the French Maritime Cross and Diploma and each of the other eleven members of the crew a French lifesaving medal inscribed with the name of the recipient and containing the words 'Courage and Devotion'. The recipients were Second Coxswain Lewis Harrison; R.C. Davies, bowman; H.W. Davies, mechanic; L.J. Harrison, assistant mechanic; F. Davies, signaller; and Messrs. S.C. Harrison, J.J. Davies, J.R. Davies. G. Cox, G. Rook and T. Jonas.

After a number of routine services during the next few months, the last service of 1948 proved to be a long and arduous one. At 6.40 p.m. on 20 December 1948, *Henry Blogg* was launched to the motor vessel *Bosphorus*, of Oslo, a 2,111-ton vessel with a cargo of oranges and thirty-seven people on board. The lifeboat found the vessel aground in rough seas on the Haisborough Sands, two miles north-west of South Middle Buoy. Her captain requested that the lifeboat stand by, and so *Henry Blogg* anchored off the west side of the bank until 7.45 a.m. the following morning. Two tugs then arrived and, with the help of the lifeboat, a tow rope was attached. For more than six hours the tugs tried to refloat the motor vessel but without success, so the lifeboat and tugs anchored for the night. At 10 a.m. on 22 December, the lifeboat again passed a rope to one of the tugs and for three hours the tug tried to pull *Bosphorus* clear, but the rope parted and fouled her propeller. A further unsuccessful attempt was made by another tug, after which the captain of the motor vessel asked the lifeboat to land the only passenger. In going alongside, the lifeboat grounded and was damaged, but refloated, took off the passenger and landed him at Great Yarmouth.

Coxswain Davies sent to Cromer for dry clothes and food and decided to remain at Yarmouth for the night. At 5.30 a.m. the following day, 23 December, the lifeboat returned to the Sands and again assisted as tugs, one from Holland and another from Hull, attempted to refloat *Bosphorus*, but she remained fast on the Sands. On 24 December more tugs arrived, making seven in total, and at 2 p.m. the lifeboat left to get stores for the casualty, returning at midnight in time for a fresh attempt at towing. This time the casualty moved a few yards. Next day, Christmas Day, the weather was better and the lifeboat was able to lie alongside to transfer stores. The captain thanked the lifeboatmen and said that, as the weather was fine, she should return to station and he would send for her if needed again. So the lifeboat returned to Cromer at 5.45 p.m., having been away for nearly five days. Three days later, however, with the weather worsening, *Henry Blogg* again set out to the motor vessel, reaching her at about 4 p.m. By 9 p.m. the wind had increased to gale force, but at 3 a.m. on 29 December the tugs began another tow and, just over two hours later, *Bosphorus* was at last refloated. The lifeboat stood by until daybreak and, once the captain had signalled that all was well, returned to her station, having spent a total of 142 hours at sea over nine days.

On 21 November 1950, *Henry Blogg* performed another good service when she launched at 6.24 a.m. to the auxiliary barge *Thyra*, of Rochester, bound for London with a cargo of wheat. The barge was making heavy weather, leaking, and the two crews were both exhausted. Once the lifeboat was on scene, three lifeboatmen boarded the casualty and the lifeboat took her in tow, but in the strong south-south-easterly wind the tow parted, and so with the weather worsening the lifeboat acted as an escort as the barge made way under her own power. *Henry Blogg* remained in attendance until *Thyra* reached Kings Lynn Roads, and then the three lifeboatmen reboarded the lifeboat, which was taken to Wells and berthed by 3 p.m. She returned to Cromer the following day.

During 1952, *Henry Blogg* undertook a number of routine rescues, including two towards the end of the year. On 26 October she went to the steamship *Ask*, of Bergen, bound for Sunderland in ballast with a crew of twenty-two, which was ashore on the Haisborough Sands eighteen miles off Cromer. Once on scene, the lifeboatmen took soundings round the vessel so that when she went astern at slack tide she refloated. On 23 November, the lifeboat went to the steamship *Grove Hill*, of Middlesbrough, which had broken down and was dragging her anchor in a strong and bitterly cold north-north-westerly wind. The lifeboat stood by until a tug arrived and began towing the vessel during the early hours of the following morning. The lifeboat escorted both vessels to Great Yarmouth, where they arrived at 11.15 a.m. Due to the bad weather rehousing at Cromer was impossible, so the lifeboat remained in port until 29 November.

The dangers of the sea were brought home to the townsfolk of Cromer in June 1953 when tragedy struck, affecting the town as a whole and the lifeboat station in particular. On 5 June, just after 10 a.m., Jimmy Davies' crab boat, *The Boy Jimmy*, was returning to land its catch when it was caught by a big wave which filled and sank it about 100 yards from the beach, in full view of the promenade. The three fishermen on board failed to get out and, before any help could arrive, had drowned. Jimmy Davies, a Cromer councillor and coxswain of the No.2 lifeboat, his brother Frank, and twenty-one-year-old Ted Bussey all lost their lives. Although the waves hitting the shore were quite big, the men would have often encountered similar ones. Every effort was made to save the three men using other crab boats and one boat was launched at great risk to its occupants in the attempts to help, but by then *The Boy Jimmy* had sunk. Henry Blogg helped launch the one crab boat on the beach and, in doing so, collapsed and lay within a few feet of the water's edge.

Fishermen searched the beach but found nothing while a large crowd, including Sheringham fishermen who had hurried to Cromer when the tragedy became known, watched as the No.2 lifeboat was launched to shepherd in two crab boats which were still at sea and which both landed safely. The body of Jimmy Davies was later found about 200 yards west of the Overstrand promenade. In response to the tragedy, Cromer went into mourning. Coronation bunting was removed and flags were flown at half-mast.

Less than a week after the tragedy, on 11 June 1953, the lifeboat was in action again. At about 6.30 p.m., Coxswain Henry Davies saw a vessel approaching from the north-west and thought she was in a dangerous position. When he was informed by the Coastguard that she had nearly capsized east of Cromer pier and had requested assistance,

Henry Blogg *on the slipway in 1956, probably after a launch for Lifeboat Day, with holiday makers on board. (By courtesy of Eastern Counties Newspapers)*

An excellent photograph of No.2 lifeboat Harriot Dixon *and tractor T49 at the East Gangway during the 1950s. The tractor made the launching and recovery procedure faster and much easier for the shore helpers. (By courtesy of Eastern Counties Newspapers)*

the lifeboat was launched at 6.50 p.m. into the fresh breeze and rough sea and found the small motor vessel *Norok*, of Goole, with the commanding officer of a Sea Cadet Unit and nine cadets on board. The casualty had lost her small boat and was experiencing engine problems. The lifeboat began to escort her to Great Yarmouth, but off Caister her engines failed so the lifeboat had to tow her to port. Both boats arrived at 10.15 p.m. but as the weather would not allow the lifeboat to be rehoused at Cromer she remained at Yarmouth for the night, returning to station the following day.

During October 1954, *Henry Blogg* performed two routine services. On 2 October she took a sick man off the Cromer lightship and landed him at Cromer, from where he was immediately transferred to Cromer hospital. He was found to be suffering from a perforated duodenal ulcer which was successfully operated on. On 13 October, *Henry Blogg* launched to the crab boat *Why Worry*, which was being blown out to sea by a strong south-westerly wind and an ebb tide. When the lifeboat arrived at the scene, *Why Worry* was found with her engines broken down and nearly half full of water. The boat's crab pots were transferred to the lifeboat to lighten her and make room for baling. She was taken in tow by the lifeboat and brought to Cromer beach.

In August 1956, the No.1 lifeboat *Henry Blogg* became the first British lifeboat to be fitted with a VHF radio transmitter and receiver. The installation of the equipment was necessary because of the increasing part played in sea rescue by aircraft and helicopters. The new equipment enabled the lifeboat to communicate with an aircraft at 3,000ft and within a radius of about thirty miles. The new transmitter replaced radio-telephone equipment which was retained for other purposes but which could not be used to communicate directly with aircraft. Messages had to be channelled via the aircraft operational base and over telephone land lines to Cromer Coastguard and thence by RT to the lifeboat.

During 1958, *Henry Blogg* went for overhaul and in her place came the 45ft 6in Watson motor lifeboat *Cunard* (ON.728), built in 1930 for the St Mary's (Isles of Scilly) station, which undertook two services while at Cromer. The first was performed on 2 February 1958 when she landed an injured man from the steamship *Hudson Bank*, of London. The second occurred a month later, on 2 March, when news was received that the German motor vessel *Continental* and the ship *Wansbeck*, of Newcastle, had been in collision ten miles north-west of the Haisborough lightvessel. The German vessel had sunk but five of her crew had been rescued by *Wansbeck*, though another man was missing. The reserve lifeboat was launched at 5.50 a.m. and within half an hour had reached the vessel. She then carried out a search together with *Wansbeck* and other ships. The missing man could not be found, so the lifeboat went alongside *Wansbeck* to take off the five survivors. As *Wansbeck* was taking in water forward, though was not in immediate danger, her captain made for the Humber. The men were transferred to the lifeboat, which continued searching until 8 a.m., and then returned to station.

On 31 May 1958, *Henry Blogg*, back on station after overhaul, had to assist the Sheringham lifeboat after what started as a routine service when the Trinity House superintendent at Great Yarmouth requested the lifeboat take a sick man off the Dudgeon lightvessel. The Sheringham lifeboat *Foresters Centenary* launched with a doctor on board and reached the lightvessel at 1.10 p.m. The doctor gave the sick man a sedative, after which he was strapped to a stretcher and transferred to the lifeboat. The lifeboat then set off for her station but, at about 4.40 p.m., when she was nine miles

Henry Blogg *towing the Sheringham lifeboat* Foresters' Centenary *on 31 May 1958 after the latter's engine had broken down.*

Above: Henry Blogg *towing the ex-former Hunstanton lifeboat* Mayfly (ON.440) *into Great Yarmouth on 29 May 1962. The former lifeboat, named* Licensed Victualler *when in service, was stationed at Hunstanton from 1900 until 1931 and was then sold out of service to become the yacht* Mayfly. *(By courtesy of* Eastern Counties Newspapers*)*

Right: *Reserve lifeboat* Cunard *with rescue helicopter and No.2 lifeboat* Harriot Dixon *during Lifeboat Day, 10 August 1961. (By courtesy of P.A. Vicary)*

north-east of Sheringham, the gear which drives the oil and water pumps broke down. The Cromer lifeboat was therefore called out and at 4.58 p.m. *Henry Blogg* was launched. She towed the Sheringham lifeboat to her station, and then returned to Cromer at 7.40 p.m. while the sick man was taken to hospital.

On 16 February 1961, an unusual call for help was received at 8.23 a.m. when the honorary secretary was informed that a vessel, the tanker *Wave Chief*, had collided with the Haisborough lightvessel, which was sinking. Ten minutes later *Henry Blogg* was launched and reached the lightvessel at 9.50 a.m. On arriving at the scene, the lifeboatmen found crew from the tanker on the lightvessel to help stop the water and so some of the lifeboat's crew joined them. About an hour later, the Trinity House vessel *Mermaid* reached the scene and some of her crew boarded the damaged lightvessel. The lifeboat transferred a pump from the tanker to the lightvessel and escorted *Wave Chief's* boat back to her. By 11.30 a.m. the lightvessel was deemed to be sufficiently seaworthy for towing, so a line was rigged from *Mermaid,* and the lifeboat returned to station.

During the afternoon of 29 May 1962, the lifeboat was called to a cabin cruiser in difficulty off Sheringham and signalling for assistance by flying a flag and blowing her

Above: Henry Blogg *and No.2 lifeboat*
Harriot Dixon *on exercise, April 1964. (By
courtesy of P.A. Vicary)*

Left: Henry Blogg *alongside the motor vessel*
Joika, *of Oslo, on 11 March 1964, during
what was a routine service.*

horn. On arrival off Cromer, the cruiser, an old lifeboat named *Mayfly*, approached the
beach and her crew appeared to be looking for a place to land, but found a heavy swell
breaking on the beach. As the vessel was still flying distress signals, *Henry Blogg* was
launched and the lifeboat crew found most of her crew of five very seasick. The vessel
had a fuel leak and her owner expected the engine to fail imminently. Coxswain Henry
Davies advised him to steer south towards Great Yarmouth, where the calmer water
would help those who were seasick. Just after passing Haisborough, *Mayfly's* engine
stopped and so the lifeboat took her in tow. After passing into smoother water off
Hemsby Hole, the sick members of the cabin cruiser's crew began to feel better and by
the time they reached Gorleston had fully recovered. Because of strong north-westerly
winds preventing recovery, the lifeboat had to remain at Gorleston until 3 June.

On 29 September 1963, the Coastguards notified the Honorary Secretary that a small
dinghy was in difficulty trying to get to the beach. The Overstrand fishermen, owing to
big seas breaking on the shore, advised the dinghy to wait until the lifeboat arrived. The No.2
lifeboat *Harriot Dixon* was launched at 4.54 p.m. but, in the meantime, the dinghy had made
its own way towards Bacton and, after the lifeboat had travelled six miles in the direction of
the casualty, the Coastguard informed the lifeboat crew that the dinghy was ashore at Bacton.
Although the dinghy had turned over as it reached the beach, the sole occupant was safe.

This proved to be the last service launch by *Harriot Dixon*. During 1964, she suffered
engine problems and due to her unreliability was replaced by a reserve lifeboat which served
as the No.2 lifeboat until a 37ft Oakley, then under construction at East Cowes, was ready.

On 15 June 1964, *Harriot Dixon* left Cromer for the last time, launching in front of a crowd of holiday-makers, and was taken by No.2 coxswain, Lewis Harrison, to Great Yarmouth where the reserve 35ft 6in Liverpool *Jose Neville* (ON.834), formerly at Caister, was picked up. *Jose Neville* stayed at Cromer until September 1964, when the boathouse floor was lowered to accommodate the new lifeboat, but performed only one service during this time.

The last No.2 lifeboat to serve at Cromer was of the 37ft Oakley class, designed by and named after Richard Oakley, the RNLI's Consulting Naval Architect. The Oakley lifeboats were self-righting by virtue of a process which involved the transfer of 1.54 tons of water ballast into a righting tank built on the port side. She was the first self-righting lifeboat to serve at Cromer in the twentieth century. The first 37ft Oakley entered service at Scarborough in 1958 and the boat allocated to Cromer was the thirteenth of the class. Built by J.S. White at East Cowes, she was fitted with a twin 52hp Parsons Porbeagle four-cylinder diesel engine. The new boat was funded from the legacy of Miss Jane Graham King, of Surrey, in memory of her father and mother, and was named *William Henry and Mary King* (ON.980). She was placed on station in October 1964 and during her time at Cromer as the No.2 lifeboat launched on service twelve times and is credited with saving one life.

Her passage to her new station was described in detail in *The Lifeboat* for March 1965. In his article 'On passage with the RNLI', the station's honorary secretary, Dr P.S. Barclay, described bringing *William Henry and Mary King* from Cowes to Cromer. The

Right: Harriot Dixon *leaves the boathouse at the East Gangway for the last time, 15 June 1964. She served the station for thirty years making her the longest-serving lifeboat at Cromer. (By courtesy of Eastern Counties Newspapers)*

Below: Harriot Dixon *launches from Cromer for the last time, 15 June 1964. She left the station before the new No.2 lifeboat had been completed because her engines were considered unreliable. Six months after leaving Cromer, she had been sold out of service. (By courtesy of Eastern Counties Newspapers)*

The reserve 35ft 6in Liverpool motor lifeboat Jose Neville (ON.834) on the East Beach in June 1964. Built in 1941 for Caister, she served at Cromer temporarily before the new No.2 lifeboat William Henry and Mary King *had been completed. (By courtesy of Eastern Counties Newspapers)*

Reserve lifeboat Jose Neville *outside the lifeboat house during her brief time at Cromer from June to September 1964. During twenty-two years at Caister, she is credited with saving seventy-five lives. (By courtesy of P.A. Vicary)*

boat left in the early morning and called overnight at Newhaven, Ramsgate, Orfordness and Lowestoft on her way to Norfolk. She left her last port of call at 7 a.m. and turned for home, with 'Palling church, Happisburgh lighthouse and all the familiar landmarks blinking between the waves until Cromer church and pier hove up ahead to tell her that she had reached home at last', as Barclay recalled. He concluded his account by describing the new lifeboat as 'A rugged boat for a splendid station. She will continue to maintain a history and tradition that is second to none round the coasts of the British Isles.'

The new lifeboat was formally named on 8 July 1965 by HRH Princess Marina, Duchess of Kent, who arrived at Cromer by helicopter which landed on the playing field of the Secondary Modern School to be met by the Lord Lieutenant of Norfolk, Colonel Sir Edmund Bacon. Large crowds had gathered at the slipway, which was decorated with bunting and flags, as the RNLI's Public Relations Officer, Patrick Howarth, met Princess Marina at the stand and presented Dr D. Vaughan, president of the Cromer branch, to Her Royal Highness. Mr J.H. Rounce, chairman of the branch, opened the proceedings. Mr T.H. Sutton, on behalf of the executors and members of the family of the late Miss J.G. King, donor of the lifeboat, presented the boat to the RNLI and it was formally accepted by Commander H.F.P. Grenfell, RN, a vice president of the Institution and member of the Committee of Management, who in turn handed it into the care of the Cromer branch. The service of dedication was conducted by the bishop of Norwich, the Rt

Revd W.L.S. Fleming, assisted by Revd C.W.J. Searle-Barnes, vicar of Cromer. After a vote of thanks proposed by Mr J.E. Webster, Mr Rounce asked Princess Marina to name the lifeboat *William Henry and Mary King*.

The first service by *William Henry and Mary King* took place on 2 November 1964, although on this occasion she was not, in the end, needed. Cromer Coastguards reported to the honorary secretary that they thought they had seen the crew of a trimaran, which was rolling in heavy seas half a mile off Cromer pier, attempting to light a flare. *William Henry and Mary King* was launched into heavy seas at 4.15 p.m., but by the time she got to within hailing distance of the trimaran *Nimble 1 Key* she was off Sheringham, and reported that no flares had been fired and that no assistance was required.

During the 1960s, the lifeboats were being called with increasing frequency to pleasure craft. The demand on lifeboats made by yachts and dinghies was typified by the service on 5 July 1964 when *Henry Blogg* went to a yacht in difficulties close inshore near Mundesley Church. A rope had fouled the yacht's propeller and, while trying to clear it from a dinghy, one of the yacht's crew had fallen overboard. He had appeared ill as he climbed aboard again and the woman on board had raised a flag requesting medical help. *Henry Blogg* was launched at 4.20 p.m. and a helicopter's help was also requested. When the lifeboat reached the yacht, *Sally Brown*, three members of the lifeboat crew boarded

Right: *37ft Oakley* William Henry and Mary King *beaches after her first service. (By courtesy of Eastern Counties Newspapers)*

Below: *At the Annual Lifeboat Service, August 1966,* William Henry and Mary King *is blessed, with a large crowd of supporters in attendance. (By courtesy of Eastern Counties Newspapers)*

Top: William Henry and Mary King *landing a sick man from the trawler* St Lucia, *8 December 1966. (By courtesy of Eastern Counties Newspapers)*

Middle: *A sick crew member from the fishing vessel* Karin Keogh *is brought ashore from* William Henry and Mary King, *29 May 1967. During her short spell at Cromer,* William Henry and Mary King *performed twelve services and saved one life. (By courtesy of Eastern Counties Newspapers)*

Left: *One of three crab boats helped by* William Henry and Mary King *on 5 August 1966. Owing to deteriorating sea conditions, concern was felt for the safety of three crab boats still at sea so the No.2 lifeboat was launched at 8.30 a.m. in a moderate to fresh west-north-westerly wind and rough sea. She reached the crab boats* My Beauty, Autumn Rose *and* Lewis James, *distributed lifebelts to their crews, and stood by until the three boats were safely beached. (By courtesy of Eastern Counties Newspapers)*

Opposite: Henry Blogg *exercising with an RAF Rescue helicopter off the pier, April 1964. (By courtesy of P.A. Vicary)*

to try to clear the fouled propeller and get her under way. With this successfully achieved, the lifeboat returned to station after what had been a routine call.

On 27 November 1965, *William Henry and Mary King* was involved in assisting a series of local fishing boats caught out in bad weather. By noon, the weather had deteriorated considerably and as five local fishing boats were at sea, the No.2 lifeboat was launched to stand by at 1.15 p.m. The boats were making for Cromer in the moderate north-westerly breeze and very rough sea. The first boat, *Charles Perkins*, was met about a mile south of Cromer and escorted safely to shore by the lifeboat, which then proceeded south for about three miles to the fishing boat *George Robert*. After escorting her to Overstrand, about a mile further south three more boats were found. One of these, *Young Fisherman*, had broken down and was in danger of driving ashore, so was taken in tow to Overstrand where she was beached. The lifeboat then escorted *Black Beauty* and *Lewis James* to Cromer and returned to her station at 3 p.m. after a busy few hours.

During the last days of 1965, the No.1 lifeboat, together with lifeboats from neighbouring stations, was involved in the search for survivors from the oil rig *Sea Gem* which collapsed and sank in the North Sea on 27 December with thirty-two crew on board. Five of the crew died in the disaster, nineteen were saved by the steamship *Baltrover* and eight were still not accounted for. The oil rig, which belonged to the British Petroleum Co, had been the first to find natural gas in the North Sea and was positioned forty-seven miles north-west of Cromer and thirty-six miles north-east of Spurn Point. Lifeboats from Humber, Cromer No.1, Skegness and Wells were called out to search for the survivors and spent a total of 113 hours at sea, but were unable to find anyone. The first lifeboat to be launched was the Humber boat *City of Bradford III* (ON.911), which put out at 2.40 p.m. and arrived at the scene five hours later. She carried out an extensive search of the area in conjunction with aircraft and other vessels and returned to her station at 4.25 a.m. on 29 December after being at sea for nearly thirty-eight hours.

Skegness lifeboat *Charles Fred Grantham* (ON.977) launched at 6.30 a.m. on 28 December and carried out a thorough search. She returned past the Humber lightvessel down the coast to Skegness and returned to her station after fourteen hours on service. Cromer lifeboat *Henry Blogg* launched at 10.40 a.m. on 28 December and searched the area of the casualty as well as standing by while salvage operations were attempted. After twenty-seven hours at sea, she returned to her station to be relieved by Wells lifeboat *Ernest Tom Neathercoat* (ON.982), which also stood by during salvage operations and remained on service for twenty-one hours. On 30 December, Humber lifeboat again launched to take a party of skin divers to the wreck and helped with salvage operations. These combined searches were carried out in northerly gale force winds and a very heavy swell with sleet and rain falling intermittently throughout. In recognition of the lifeboats' assistance, the British Petroleum Co. made a donation to the crews.

One of the final services performed by *Henry Blogg* took place during the early hours of 16 January 1966. At 1.10 a.m., the coastguard informed the honorary secretary that they had received a message from the North Haisborough lightvessel that red flares had been sighted six miles south-east of her. *Henry Blogg* was launched at 1.35 a.m. in a gentle north-easterly breeze and a moderate sea. The lifeboat, after receiving a message from the vessel *Brittenburgh* that she would stand by until the lifeboat arrived, found the casualty, the motor vessel *Start*, half a mile north-east of the Middle Haisborough Buoy. The vessel's radio and rudder were out of action so the lifeboat stood by until the tug *The Octopus* arrived at 8.30 a.m., and took *Start* in tow. The lifeboat escorted both vessels to Great Yarmouth, arriving at 3 p.m., and returned to her station on 18 January.

Less than three months later, on 3 April 1966, *Henry Blogg* was launched for what proved to be her last service at Cromer. She put out at 5.15 a.m. to stand by the oil rig *Constellation* which had been reported adrift. However, although later acknowledged that the rig's tow was under control, the initial anxiety that the rig might go aground prompted the request for the lifeboat, which reached the casualty and stood by while thirty-eight of the rig's crew were evacuated by helicopter. *Henry Blogg* then returned to Cromer, but the heavy seas prevented her being rehoused so she went to Gorleston. When she had launched down the slipway to go to the oil rig, a sea had broken on the port side slewing the bow to starboard, broadside to the sea and damaging the rudder. As a result, she was taken away from station for repairs and never returned.

With a new lifeboat allocated to the station, and the beach-launched No.2 lifeboat able to provide adequate cover, no reserve No.1 lifeboat was sent and the opportunity was taken to repair the slipway and enlarge the boathouse in readiness for the new lifeboat. The boathouse was therefore empty from April 1966 until March 1967, with *William Henry and Mary King* covering. The improvements to the boathouse involved the replacing of a section of wooden slipway with steel at a cost of approximately £20,000. Apparently, the old slipway was slightly twisted and this had damaged the lifeboat's steering gear on her last launch.

The No.2 lifeboat was involved in a number of rescues during this period when no slipway-launched lifeboat was on station, starting on 2 June 1966 when she performed a routine but lengthy service after the Coastguard informed the honorary secretary that the cabin cruiser *Shell Duck* had been seen by a helicopter apparently broken down surrounded by oil three miles south-west of Newarp lightvessel. *William Henry and Mary King* launched at 10.05 a.m. into a light breeze from the south-west and a calm sea. At 1.15 p.m. she reached the cabin cruiser, made fast a line and then towed *Shell Duck* to Great Yarmouth. After securing the casualty, she returned to Cromer, reaching her station at 9.10 p.m.

Just after midnight on 29 May 1967, *William Henry and Mary King* was launched with a doctor aboard on what proved to be her last service at Cromer. She went to the aid of an injured man on board the cutter *Karin Hoegh*, of Denmark, but had difficulty locating the casualty. After launching, she made a direct passage for Haisborough lightvessel, intending to rendezvous with the cutter. She steamed for eighteen miles with the crew keeping a lookout. At about 3 a.m. a faint light was spotted, but proved to be a false alarm so the lifeboat went back towards the lightvessel. She remained in communication with Humber Radio, but language problems with the casualty made establishing the vessel's precise position difficult. After investigating two trawlers, the lifeboat reached the Haisborough lightvessel at 5.40 a.m. and the lifeboatmen were at last able to locate the casualty, which was seen on the horizon steaming towards the lightvessel. The lifeboat went alongside the cutter at 6.30 a.m. and the skipper was transferred on board. The lifeboat then set course for Cromer, where she beached at 8.20 a.m., and the casualty was taken to an ambulance and then to Cromer hospital, where he underwent an operation on a perforated duodenal ulcer. In his report of the incident, the honorary secretary noted, 'If this is to be the last service of ON.980 at this station, a proud conclusion.'

Less than a month after this service, *William Henry and Mary King* was removed from Cromer and the No.2 station was officially closed, although in effect the inshore lifeboat took its place. *William Henry and Mary King* was sent to Bridlington where she was placed on station on 2 October 1967. She went on to serve the Yorkshire station with distinction for more than twenty years, and when she was replaced in December 1988 had performed almost 300 services and saved eighty-three lives. She can now be found at the Children's Culture Centre, Park School, Avron Road, London, where she is used as a climbing frame by local children.

The Inshore Lifeboat

Before the No.2 lifeboat was withdrawn, discussions had been held about placing an inshore rescue boat (IRB) at Cromer. This new type of rescue craft was better suited to answer the type of calls that were increasingly being made on lifeboats, not just at Cromer but at many stations throughout the British Isles. As a result of increasing numbers of people using the sea for recreational activities during the 1960s, the number of inshore incidents to which lifeboats were called increased, as exemplified by some of the services above. Conventional offshore lifeboats, such as *Henry Blogg*, were not well suited to such work and a simple, fast rescue craft was required for dealing with these casualties.

Inshore rescue boats, later known as inshore lifeboats (ILB), were introduced into Britain in 1963, since which time the design has been refined and developed as the boats have become ever more efficient and effective lifesaving tools. The 16ft inflatable lifeboats, made from tough nylon coated with hypalon, are usually crewed by two or three, powered by a 40hp outboard engine, and can be launched quickly and easily. They carry a variety of equipment, including VHF radio, GPS, flexible fuel tanks, flares, an anchor, a spare propeller, a compass, first-aid kit and knife. The ILB's advantage over the conventional lifeboat was its speed which, at 20 knots, was considerably faster than any lifeboat in service during the 1960s. The ILB also has the advantage of being able to go alongside other craft easily, or pick up persons in the water, without causing or suffering damage.

On 15 February 1967, a meeting was held to discuss the placing of an ILB at Cromer, with the result that ten volunteers put their names forward as potential crew members. The first boat, No.101, arrived on 15 March and two days later was exercised in heavy surf conditions under divisional inspector Dag Pike. The boat was subsequently placed on station, thus maintaining the tradition of two lifeboats at Cromer, but had to wait until 6 June for its first call. The new ILB was formally dedicated at a ceremony held on 6 August 1967 in front of the No.2 lifeboat house during the annual lifeboat service. The vicar of Cromer, Revd C.W.J. Searle-Barnes, conducted the service and dedicated the inflatable craft, and Dr Paul Barclay, honorary secretary, pointed out that the service was being held at a place where boats had been launched on rescue missions for well over a century, so the ILB was continuing a long tradition. By this time, ninety-five inshore rescue boats were in service with the RNLI and up to 1966 had been called out 729 times, saving 328 lives.

The ILB was initially based at the East Gangway boathouse and housed in the 1902 lifeboat house, from where the No.2 lifeboat had operated. However, on 6 August 1970 it was moved to a new boathouse located at the foot of the Melbourne slope, west of the pier. This house was built from glass fibre and soon became known as the 'igloo' because of its appearance. Moving the ILB to this location was intended to overcome the recurring problem of the launchway being blocked by fishing boats drawn up on the slipway in front of the East Gangway boathouse.

Almost as soon as it entered service, the new rescue craft was in action and proving herself in situations for which an inflatable lifeboat was specifically intended. The ILB was the ideal craft when, on 22 June 1968, a young girl got into in difficulties about 300 yards from the beach. She was launched at 1.42 p.m. in a light south-westerly breeze, picked up the stranded swimmer, took her back to the beach and returned to station just over twenty minutes after launching. During the afternoon of 2 July 1968 the ILB was launched to two boys clinging to the struts below the end of the pier and shouting for help. They had been swimming in the area and had found the ebb tide too strong, so were brought ashore by the ILB. These two services were typical of the kind of work performed by the inshore lifeboat, and the following summary and service descriptions are included to show the kind of work carried out during the 1970s.

1970 Four launches, one life saved: The ILB responded in quick time to a bather in difficulties and shouting for help off the West Beach during the early evening of 30 June. She reached the swimmer and pulled him aboard, and also brought to safety another swimmer who had gone to the assistance of the first. At about 11.15 a.m. on 18 October, the ILB was returning to station from exercise when the crew was asked to advise several small boats which were line fishing just over a mile off the beach that a gale had been forecast as imminent. The boats were escorted to the shore safely, but during this operation, carried out in rising winds, choppy seas and increasing breakers, two small fishing dinghies were seen off Runton about two miles to the north-west. The ILB

The second ILB to serve at the station, D-26, outside the unusual ILB house, known as the 'igloo', to the west of the pier, August 1970, with Donny Abbs (left) and E. Love. (By courtesy of P.A. Vicary)

D-26 lands four survivors from a capsized cabin cruiser, 19 July 1971. (By courtesy of Eastern Counties Newspapers Ltd)

therefore proceeded to the scene and made contact with one of them, *Lucy Jane*, taking off three persons. This and another dinghy were then escorted back to Sheringham where all were landed safely, by which time the weather had deteriorated with a westerly wind reaching force four to five.

1971 Fourteen launches, five lives saved: After the ILB launched on a routine exercise at 9.30 p.m. on 13 June, the crew found a yacht with a man requesting assistance to free a rope from the propeller. Two lifeboatmen boarded the yacht, but were unable to clear the propeller so, with a sick man also on board who was incapable of leaving his bunk and would not leave the yacht for medical attention, the offshore lifeboat launched and towed the yacht to Blakeney.

1972 Three launches, one life saved: During the afternoon of 24 July, the ILB launched to a canoeist who had capsized beneath the pier. A portion of the canoe's bow sticking was out of the water with its occupant nearby. The ILB proceeded to the pier and rescued the youth who had cuts to his hands. He was subsequently taken to hospital for treatment.

1973 Seven launches, five lives saved: In March, a new inshore lifeboat, D–197, was placed on station, having been funded by the RNLI's Gravesend branch. On 8 August, the new ILB went to a motor boat which was drifting towards the pier as its outboard motor would not start. By the time the casualty was reached, it had drifted through the pier as far as the next groyne, but the ILB was able to tow the drifting dinghy to the beach where its occupants were safely brought ashore.

1974 Ten launches, two lives saved: On 4 June, the Coastguard requested the lifeboat bring an injured seaman ashore from the dredger *Marinex V*. A decision was made to use the ILB, which launched at 4.07 p.m. and was alongside the dredger within fifteen minutes. The patient was quickly transferred to the ILB, which landed him on the beach, from where he was taken to Cromer hospital by ambulance.

1975 Ten launches, five lives saved: On 10 August, whilst at sea on exercise, the ILB's crew was informed that a small inflatable dinghy had capsized about a mile from the station and its two occupants seemed to have disappeared. The ILB arrived at the scene at 11.22 a.m. to find one lad clinging to the dinghy and the other under the upturned craft. The two survivors were taken aboard the ILB and, together with the dinghy, were landed on the beach none the worse for the experience. The ILB left the scene, but returned later to get the survivors' names and addresses.

1976 Thirteen launches, five lives saved: On 11 July, the ILB launched at 2.26 p.m. to two yachts in difficulties off the pier. Both yachts had capsized, but one was righted by its occupants and reached the beach without further help while the other was towed ashore by the ILB. The ILB did not rehouse, but put out again to another capsized yacht, this one in difficulties off West Runton, which was reached at 3.42 p.m. and, with the help of the ILB crew, was righted and towed to Sheringham. Four days later, the ILB again assisted a capsized dinghy off Sheringham. Because it was low water, the ILB was able to reach the casualty faster than the Sheringham offshore lifeboat. The ILB crew found the sailing dinghy *Gurgle,* took off the two crew and took it in tow. The dinghy was beached at Weybourne, two miles west of Sheringham, where its crew was put ashore and the ILB returned to station.

1977 Thirteen launches, ten lives saved: On 23 July, ILB helmsman Donny Abbs was informed that an inflatable with one occupant paddling and one person trying to swim was being carried by wind and tide towards the east side of the lifeboat slipway. Two minutes later, the ILB was launched and rounded the pier to reach the casualty at 4.08 p.m. The casualties were picked out of the water and landed on the beach.

1978 Nine launches, two lives saved: Occasionally, the ILB was called to a large vessel, as on 9 July 1978 when she went to the aid of two motor vessels which had been in a collision. *Camilla Weston* was in collision with the German motor vessel *Koralle* four miles east of the Happisburgh lighthouse. Although neither vessel was badly damaged, a

Relief inshore lifeboat D-96 assisting the 43ft motor launch Enterprise, *11 June 1979. (By courtesy of Eastern Counties Newspapers Ltd).*

D class inflatable D-197 on her trolley outside the lifeboat museum with, from left to right: D. Harvey, Donny Abbs, and the honorary secretary, Jim Smith. (By courtesy of Eastern Counties Newspapers Ltd)

crew member from *Camilla Weston* was injured in the collision and, after obtaining medical advice from Hull Infirmary, the master of *Camilla Weston* requested that the injured man be evacuated to Cromer hospital. So a rendezvous was arranged and the Cromer ILB took the injured man off his vessel at the Foulness Buoy. He was landed at Cromer and taken to the local hospital.

1979 Thirteen launches, four lives saved: After the motor launch *Enterprise* was seen in difficulty off Sheringham on 11 June, the ILB was launched and proceeded to the scene. She reached the casualty at 3.12 p.m. and towed the motor launch into deeper water to the west of the pier. A speedy launch was essential on 16 September after a sailing dinghy capsized off West Runton. The ILB crew found that the dinghy's two crew had lost their baler and were unable to right the craft, having already capsized twice. Both were exhausted, while one was in the water and the other on one side of the dinghy, which was drifting with the tide towards Cromer. The yacht was righted and then towed to Cromer where it was beached.

1980 Ten launches, six lives saved: On 30 August, the ILB launched in a freshening wind to a skiff containing divers a mile and a half from the beach at Overstrand. Once out of the shelter of the cliffs, the ILB faced winds gusting to force six. She reached the skiff *Boy Jimmy* to find that one diver was still under water. The lifeboat crew advised that the diver be recalled to the boat and then escorted the skiff back to the beach. The crew of the skiff had been unaware of the impending weather conditions.

Ruby and Arthur Reed

Following the departure of *Henry Blogg* and the alterations to the pier boathouse, the station's new lifeboat was completed by William Osborne's yard at Littlehampton, Sussex, in 1966. She was of the 48ft 6in Oakley class, a wooden-hulled self-righting design which employed a similar method of self-righting to that used in the smaller 37ft Oakley, of which the No.2 boat was an example. Her displacement of thirty tons included almost three tons of water ballast. The wheelhouse was positioned amidships and was fully enclosed to provide crew protection, with an aft cabin serving as a chartroom and housing for the electronic equipment. She was fitted with twin 110hp Gardner 6LX six-cylinder diesel engines, which gave a speed of approximately 9 knots.

Unusually, she had two self-righting trials, both at Portsmouth in June 1966. The trials involved turning the boat through 180 degrees, after which she righted herself in six seconds. The first took place on 22 June, with the second the following day for the benefit of the media and her donor, Mrs R.M. Reed, Eastbourne, whose gift was made in memory of her husband, Mr A.E. Reed, of Stamford. The new lifeboat was ready for service by March 1967 and, after extended sea trials, set off for her station. Before she reached Cromer, the new lifeboat had performed her first service. As she sailed past Overstrand, the passage crew on board spotted one of the Cox brothers broken down offshore in his fishing boat. Although he was in no danger, the lifeboat gave him a helping tow along to Cromer where he rowed ashore.

Ruby and Arthur Reed reached Cromer Pier at noon on 14 March 1967 and was housed for the first time with great care and accuracy. Although a rough sea and freshening wind suggested that a practice launch would not be possible, the weather improved and a launch was undertaken. At some point during this first exercise, either when the lifeboat ran down the slipway or when she was being rehoused, the port propeller was damaged and about six feet of the oak bilge keel on the port side was splintered. Although the damage was not as bad as at first feared, the boat was taken away to Lowestoft for repairs, while modifications were effected to the slipway. Once these were finished, she returned to station to begin her service career. During the temporary absence of the new boat, the No.2 lifeboat *William Henry and Mary King*, due for withdrawal when the slipway lifeboat was placed on station, covered the area.

Ruby and Arthur Reed was formally christened and dedicated at a ceremony on 21 June 1967 at the Pier Pavilion. The proceedings were opened by Mr J.H. Rounce, chairman of the branch, and the boat was presented to the RNLI by the donor, Mrs R.M. Reed. The lifeboat was delivered into the care of the branch by Commander H.F.P. Grenfel, DSC, RN, a vice president of the RNLI. The service of dedication was conducted by the Rt Revd the Lord Bishop of Lynn, the Rt Revd W.S. Llewellyn, MA, assisted by Revd C.W.J. Searle-Barnes, MA, vicar of Cromer, and the Revd J.R. Sharp, minister of Cromer Methodist Church. Following a vote of thanks by Mr H.F. Smallpiece, JP, chairman of the Cromer Urban District Council, Mrs Reed named the lifeboat.

Opposite above left: Ruby and Arthur Reed *undergoing her self-righting trials.*

Opposite above right*: The propeller damage sustained by* Ruby and Arthur Reed *when she was launched for the first time down the slipway on 14 March 1967. (By courtesy of Eastern Counties Newspapers Ltd)*

Opposite below: Ruby and Arthur Reed *arriving at Gorleston on passage to her station, 13 March 1967. She had been built at Littlehampton by William Osborne Ltd. (By courtesy of Eastern Counties Newspapers Ltd)*

Right: *John Allen, mechanic from 1961-1972, who served on* Henry Blogg *and then 48ft 6in Oakley* Ruby and Arthur Reed. *(By courtesy of Eastern Counties Newspapers)*

During the seventeen years she served at Cromer, *Ruby and Arthur Reed* launched on service 125 times and saved fifty-eight lives. The following descriptions cover the main rescues she performed. Her first service took place on 4 July 1967, only a few days after her naming ceremony, when she put out at 9.33 p.m. to investigate red flares about two miles east of Haisborough lookout. On arrival at the scene, the motor fishing vessel *Renovate* was found at anchor with engine failure. Two engineers from the fishery cruiser HMS *Belton*, which was standing by, were on board. The lifeboat was asked to stand by whilst attempts were made to effect repairs, and did so until 3.55 a.m. when the repairs were completed. *Renovate* proceeded on passage and the lifeboat returned to her station at 6 a.m. The vessel was later taken in tow by the Lowestoft lifeboat.

At 1.15am on 19 December 1967, the coastguard informed the honorary secretary that a sick man was on board the trawler *Rotha*, ten miles north-east of the Haisborough lightvessel. As fog would make contact difficult, *Rotha* was advised to make for Cromer and the lifeboat would launch to meet her when she was about four miles out. So *Ruby and Arthur Reed*, with a doctor aboard, launched at 3.20 a.m. and ten minutes later the trawler fired a flare which enabled the lifeboat to confirm her radar course. When the lifeboat came alongside the trawler, the doctor went aboard and examined the patient who was found to have a strangulated hernia, so was taken aboard the lifeboat and given a pain killer. The lifeboat returned to station, and the patient was transferred to an ambulance.

At 5.27 p.m. on 2 March 1968, the coxswain and mechanic saw distress flares from a small vessel two miles north-west of the lifeboat house and within ten minutes *Ruby and Arthur Reed* had launched. The casualty, a small pinnace, was found bumping on rocks and being driven towards the shore by a light north-easterly breeze, so the lifeboat towed it to deeper water. One of the crew of two had an injured finger, so was taken aboard the lifeboat while three of the lifeboat's crew went aboard the pinnace to help anchor her. The injured man was taken to Cromer for hospital treatment, after which the lifeboat returned to the pinnace and, with another lifeboatman aboard it, towed it to Blakeney. Owing to poor visibility and a freshening wind the coxswain decided to leave the lifeboat at Blakeney overnight, and she returned to station at 10.58 a.m. on 3 March.

At 6 p.m. on 30 June 1968, a small boat was reported to be in difficulties off Sheringham beach. *Ruby and Arthur Reed* was launched just over ten minutes later, soon followed

Opposite: *The naming ceremony of* Ruby and Arthur Reed *took place on 21 June 1967, when the donor Mrs Ruby Reed was on hand to christen the boat in memory of her husband, Mr A.E. Reed, of Stamford in Lincolnshire. She was presented to the crew by Coxswain Henry 'Shrimp' Davies before the formal dedication. (By courtesy of Eastern Counties Newspapers Ltd)*

Right: Ruby and Arthur Reed *returning from service to a dinghy on 4 February 1968, from which she saved three people. (By courtesy of Eastern Counties Newspapers Ltd)*

by the Sheringham lifeboat *Manchester Unity of Odd Fellows* (ON.960). She carried on board a member of the crew of the cabin cruiser *She's A Lady*, who had rowed ashore to obtain help after his boat had struck a rock at speed and started leaking. The Sheringham lifeboat reached the cruiser at 6.36 p.m. and the Cromer lifeboat ten minutes later. Members of the lifeboats' crews went aboard to bale out the cruiser as it was taking in a considerable amount of water. She was then taken in tow by both lifeboats to Blakeney, where she was moored safely, and the lifeboats returned to their respective stations.

During the latter half of the twentieth century, launches to merchant ships were few and far between, and usually involved a medical evacuation, as on 20 May 1972. At 9 p.m., the Coastguard received a message that the trawler *Boston Viscount* had a badly injured man on board and asked that the lifeboat land him at Cromer. The Coastguard made arrangements for the lifeboat to rendezvous with the trawler at the Foulness Buoy, and also contacted Cromer hospital to warn them of the casualty's arrival. The lifeboat crew assembled at about 11.30 p.m. and *Ruby and Arthur Reed* launched ten minutes later with a doctor on board. She reached *Boston Viscount* at the Foulness Buoy as agreed at about midnight. As the man was walking wounded, he was easily transferred to the lifeboat. When the lifeboat reached Cromer, the man was met at the pier by the ambulance and conveyed to Cromer hospital. He was detained overnight and discharged the following day, having had the laceration on his forehead stitched.

During much of 1973 and 1974, the reserve lifeboat *The Good Hope* (ON.821), a 46ft Watson motor type built in 1939 which served at Montrose for much of her career, was on station. She performed a number of services, the first of which involved escorting in a crab boat on 5 November 1973. Her next service proved to be one of the most outstanding of this era. On 15 November 1973, an explosion aboard the 300-ton deep-sea trawler *Boston Jaguar* left the ship without steering gear, with her mate killed and a crew member hurt with suspected internal injuries, thirty-seven miles from Cromer. The trawler received medical advice via Humber Radio Station recommending that the injured man be taken ashore as soon as possible, but the skipper of *Boston Jaguar* thought it unwise to transfer the injured man before he had been examined by a doctor. On receiving this information from the Coastguard, honorary secretary Dr Paul Barclay decided that, although liable to seasickness, he must go out with the lifeboat himself as, of the other four local doctors, he was the one most suitable for the task. Professional medical help, beyond the knowledge of the qualified first-aider, crew member Richard Davies, was clearly needed. With Dr Barclay on board, *The Good Hope* launched at 11.10 p.m. under the command of Coxswain Henry Davies into a north-westerly, gale force eight wind, with 20ft seas running against a northerly ebbing tide.

Gorleston Coastguard directed *The Good Hope* to Dudgeon lightvessel, as the trawler *Boston Wasp* reported having *Boston Jaguar* in tow at 11.11 p.m. and heading for the lightvessel. The lifeboat established radio contact with both trawlers soon after launching and relative positions were exchanged at frequent intervals. Despite heavy head seas, the lifeboat reached the lightvessel at 1.30 a.m., travelling twenty-one miles in two hours and twenty minutes. The trawlers were now eight miles east-north-east of the Dudgeon, so Coxswain Davies altered course to intercept them, reasoning that in the prevailing weather it would not be safe to have the two trawlers stopped close to the lightvessel. Visual contact was made at 2.15 a.m. and the lifeboat approached the casualty ten minutes later. The wind had now decreased to force six, but rough seas and a heavy north-west swell were running, and the weather remained cloudy with rain.

Coxswain Davies took the lifeboat alongside *Boston Jaguar* and passed a securing line. Dr Barclay and Richard Davies stood by at the starboard rail, but the first attempt to sheer alongside the trawler's starboard side resulted in the lifeboat being knocked away. At the second attempt the impact threw both men from the rail onto the lifeboat deck, but at the third approach the coxswain held the lifeboat alongside long enough to allow the two to jump on to the trawler's deck. In the heavy seas and swell, the lifeboat then stood off from the casualty to await the doctor's report. Dr Barclay first established that the mate of the trawler was dead, having sustained severe head injuries and a severed arm when gas containers exploded. Then, with help from Richard Davies, he attended to the injured deckhand who had facial lacerations and was severely shocked. At 3.02 a.m., Dr Barclay instructed that the deckhand should be taken off the trawler by helicopter at first light and taken to Cromer hospital for further examination.

With this course of action decided, the helicopter from RAF Coltishall agreed to depart at 6.30 a.m. and the tow then altered course for Cromer with the lifeboat escorting. Coxswain Davies decided it imprudent to attempt to go alongside *Boston Jaguar* a second time and so the doctor agreed that he and Richard Davies should remain aboard; throughout the passage from Cromer, Dr Barclay had suffered from severe seasickness, but not until he had attended his patient did he rest. During the tow towards Cromer, Richard Davies realised that the skipper and crew of *Boston Jaguar* were still too shocked to give a rational appraisal of the situation, so organised the covering of the mate's body and removal of the severed limb from view. He then helped in maintaining the vessel's course during the tow by *Boston Wasp*. At 6 a.m. the lifeboat and tow arrived off Cromer with the trawler piloted through the shallows by Richard Davies. The RAF helicopter arrived at 6.50 a.m. and at 7.05 a.m. the injured deckhand and Dr Barclay were lifted off and taken to Cromer hospital. Due to the rough sea conditions rehousing was impossible, so the lifeboat, after Richard Davies had been transferred back on board, made for Great Yarmouth in company with the tow, arriving at 10.30 a.m. The tow continued to Lowestoft and the lifeboat crew returned by road to Cromer.

For this long and difficult service, Dr Paul Barclay was awarded the Bronze medal; the Thanks of the Institution Inscribed on Vellum was accorded to Coxswain Henry Davies and crew member Richard Davies. Medal service certificates were presented to the remainder of the crew, Second Coxswain L.B. Harrison; mechanic R. Amey; assistant mechanic L.J. Harrison; and crew members J. Lee, and W.H. Davies.

1 *The lifeboat house built in 1902 at the East Gangway and used for the No.2 lifeboat until 1967. Later converted into the lifeboat museum, it housed H.F. Bailey (ON.777) as the main exhibit, the bow of which can be seen through the main doors. (Nicholas Leach)*

2 *The lifeboat house and its slipway, completed in 1923, had an operational life of more than seventy years. (Nicholas Leach)*

3 *48ft 6in Oakley* Ruby and Arthur Reed, *on station 1967 to 1984, in her original colours of white superstructure, off Cromer pier. (From an old photograph supplied by Paul Russell)*

4 Ruby and Arthur Reed *being hauled up the slipway during the recovery procedure. The protective tunnel for the starboard propeller can clearly be seen. (From an old postcard supplied by Paul Russell)*

5 Ruby and Arthur Reed *off Cromer pier with her superstructure orange, the standard RNLI livery since the 1970s. (Paul Russell)*

6 *Relief 46ft 9in Watson lifeboat* Guy and Clare Hunter *greets the new 47ft Tyne* Ruby and Arthur Reed II *arriving at Cromer for the first time, December 1985. (By courtesy of Eastern Daily Press)*

7 Cromer lifeboat crew, June 1986. Back row, left to right: P. Everitt, D. Pope, P. Jeffries, T. Garwood, John Davies, R. Brownsell, J. Balls, P. Abbs, A. Muirhead; front row, left to right: J. Jonas, Donny Abbs, Coxswain Richard Davies, W. Davies, and J. Howard. (Poppyland Photographs)

8 The lifeboat house and slipway at the end of the pier with 47ft Tyne Ruby and Arthur Reed II about to launch. This photograph clearly shows the boathouse and its neighbour, the famous Pavilion Theatre at the end of the pier. (Frank Muirhead)

9 Ruby and Arthur Reed II *on exercise with an RAF Westland Wessex helicopter during Lifeboat Day, 6 August 1992. (Paul Russell)*

10 Ruby and Arthur Reed II *leaving Gorleston on 24 July 1996, having attended the Naming Ceremony of the new Gorleston lifeboat* Samarbeta *after the service to the yacht* Giselle. *(Paul Russell)*

11 *Relief 12m* Mersey Her Majesty The Queen *on the East Beach during the launch and recovery trials, 22 November 1995. (Paul Durrant)*

12 *Relief 12m Mersey* Her Majesty The Queen *on her carriage at the head of the East Gangway, where she was kept during her time on station. (Nicholas Leach)*

13 *12m Mersey* Her Majesty The Queen *with D class inflatable D-436* Chloe *off the pier, June 1998. (Nicholas Leach)*

14 *Recovery of 12m Mersey* Her Majesty The Queen *using Talus MB-H tractor T98 during National Lifeboat Stations Open Day, June 1998. (Paul Russell)*

15 *12m Mersey* Her Majesty The Queen *launching on service to the yacht* It's Only Me, *12 August 1998. (Paul Russell)*

16 *The impressive new lifeboat house and slipway at the end of the pier, completed in 1999. (Nicholas Leach)*

17 *Recovery of* Ruby and Arthur Reed II *up the slipway of the new lifeboat house, 6 August 2000. (Paul Russell)*

18 Ruby and Arthur Reed II *launching for Lifeboat Day, 5 August 2001. (Paul Russell)*

19 Opposite above: Ruby and Arthur Reed II *at sea during Lifeboat Day, 5 August 2001. (Paul Russell)*

20 Opposite below: *The spectacular sight of relief 47ft Tyne* St Cybi II (Civil Service No.40) *(ON.1095) launching on exercise, August 2003. (Paul Russell)*

21 *D class inflatable D-197, on station from 1972 to 1984. (Paul Russell)*

22 *Recovery of D class inflatable D-307* Spirit of Round Table *on the West Beach, August 1984.*
(Nicholas Leach)

23 *D class inflatable D-436* Chloe, *on station from 1992 to 2001. (Paul Russell)*

24 *D-436* Chloe *on exercise with Sheringham Atlantic 75 lifeboat B-702* Manchester Unity of Oddfellows, *May 1999. (Paul Russell)*

25 *Relief D class inflatable D-439* Phyllis Mary *during the Lifeboat Open Day, June 2000. (Paul Russell)*

26 *ILB crew with D class inflatable D-568* Seahorse III *after her Naming Ceremony, 20 October 2002. (Paul Russell)*

27 *D class inflatable D-568* Seahorse III *on exercise, August 2001. (Paul Russell)*

28 *D class inflatable D-568* Seahorse III *beaching after exercise, August 2003. (Paul Russell)*

29 *Two of Cromer's most famous lifeboats,* H.F. Bailey *(fourth) and* Harriot Dixon, *at sea off the pier. (From a painting by Phil Weeks)*

Above: *Presentation on 8 August 1974 of the RNLI's Thanks Inscribed on Vellum for the service to the trawler* Boston Jaguar. *Pictured, left to right, are: Ralph H. Amey, William H. Davies, Richard Davies, L.B. Harrison, Coxswain Henry T. 'Shrimp' Davies, John Lee, L.J. Harrison, Dr Paul S. Barclay and Wing Commander C. Sinton. (By courtesy of Eastern Counties Newspapers Ltd)*

Right: *Reserve lifeboat* The Good Hope *(ON.821) arriving at Gorleston on 30 November 1973 following the service to the fishing vessel* Katrina Ann R.91, *during which she saved the lives of the four crew. (By courtesy of Eastern Counties Newspapers Ltd)*

A little more than two weeks after the *Boston Jaguar* service, *The Good Hope* was involved in another long service. At 11.27 p.m. on 30 November 1973, Coxswain Davies was informed that red flares had been sighted, and the lifeboat launched at 11.53 p.m. She found the fishing vessel *Katrina Ann* about three quarters of an hour later in complete darkness, drifting, leaking badly aft having just taken two heavy seas, and in danger of sinking. A rope was passed to her port side and the lifeboat went alongside to enable four of the crew to jump on board the lifeboat. An attempt was made to tow the casualty but in the heavy swell the rope parted. The rig tender *Arctic Shore* managed to secure a rope to *Katrina Ann* and started towing, but after about fifteen minutes the casualty sank. Conditions were too bad to rehouse at Cromer, so the lifeboat proceeded to Gorleston, where she arrived at 6.26 a.m. on 1 December and was forced to stay until 10 December, until conditions off the slipway had improved sufficiently to allow her to be recovered.

During the early hours of 6 February 1974, the German vessel *Leila* went aground on the Haisborough Sands and requested assistance. In view of the ship's position, and the fact that she had lost power, the lifeboat was launched. *The Good Hope* reached the casualty at 3.52 a.m. to find the Trinity House vessel *Patricia* already on scene and passing a rope. So the lifeboat stood off and escorted the casualty under tow by *Patricia* to a safe anchorage off Happisburgh lighthouse. As no further assistance was required, the lifeboat set course for Cromer at 7.26 p.m., arriving an hour and a half later to be rehoused. After the *Leila* service, *The Good Hope* performed one further service before leaving the station.

Ruby and Arthur Reed's first call after returning from refit took place on 31 August 1974 when the master of Lightvessel 22 was taken ill with a nervous breakdown. The lightvessel was being towed by the Trinity House vessel *Patricia*, the master of which requested immediate assistance. A doctor was lifted onto the lightvessel by helicopter and the lifeboat was launched to bring the doctor and patient ashore. When the doctor arrived aboard Lightvessel 22, the ill man was physically restrained and given sedation. In the meantime, *Ruby and Arthur Reed*, which had launched at 7.07 a.m., rendezvoused with the casualty at 8.58 a.m., and the patient and doctor were transferred on board and landed at Cromer at about 10.30 a.m., after which the lifeboat was rehoused.

During the latter half of 1975, *Ruby and Arthur Reed* performed a number of difficult services. On 8 September 1975, she towed the 37ft yacht *Irishman* with ten German students aboard clear of the Haisborough Sands and safely into Great Yarmouth. The Germans, eight men and two women, had chartered the yacht from a Dutch owner for a holiday cruise and went aground during the night while bound from Grimsby to Yarmouth, intending to go on to Lowestoft and across the North Sea to Den Helder. 'She was pounding heavily on the sands and we could not go alongside, so we fired a line', explained Coxswain Davies. On 12 December 1975, the lifeboat was called to the 9,670-ton freighter *Alexandria*, with fifty-two people on board, which grounded on the Haisborough Sands in 50mph gale force winds. *Ruby and Arthur Reed* took turns with the Gorleston lifeboat to stand by the vessel until three Dutch tugs, *Poolzee*, *Smit Enterprise* and *Smithbank*, towed it free on 14 December. The lifeboat spent nearly forty-eight hours away from station in conditions described by Coxswain Davies as 'a bit rough'.

This was one of the last services performed by Henry 'Shrimp' Davies, who retired in February 1976 to be replaced as coxswain by Richard Davies, a member of the crew since 1960. 'Shrimp', who joined the crew in 1931 and was one of Cromer's best-known coxswains, appeared on *This Is Your Life* with Eamonn Andrews the night before he retired. From the generation of men whose lifeboat careers began during the era of oars, he served for many years under Coxswain Henry Blogg and was involved in some of the most dramatic rescues in the station's history. He had the unenviable task of succeeding Blogg, his uncle, as coxswain just after the Second World War, but served the post for

Left: *Henry 'Shrimp' Davies, in oilskins and life jacket, was one of Cromer's longest-serving coxswains and part of the famous Davies family of lifeboatmen. (By courtesy of P.A. Vicary)*

Opposite: Ruby and Arthur Reed *towing the catamaran* Katabatic *back to Cromer pier after it had capsized, 22 February 1977. The lifeboat towed the casualty to the mooring buoy, from where it was recovered by the owner while the survivors were landed at the boathouse.*

twenty-nine years, combining his skilled seamanship, learned through two decades as a crab-boat crewman under Blogg, with a quiet assertiveness which brought the best from his lifeboatmen. His bravery earned him a number of medals and certificates, and in 1970 he was awarded the British Empire Medal at a ceremony in London for 'maintaining the highest traditions of the lifeboat service'. He stepped down from lifeboat service in 1976 but remained a familiar figure, running the family deckchair business on Cromer's west beach. When he died in June 2002, lifeboat operations manager Chris Barnes described him as 'a true gentle man, from the days when men of steel rowed boats of wood'.

The work of lifesaving continued under Coxswain Richard Davies, and on 15 September 1976, *Ruby and Arthur Reed* was launched to the aid of the yacht *Mr Micawber*, which was being driven by a northerly wind and flood tide towards Cromer. The yacht was in danger of being driven ashore to the west of the pier and slipway. As the lifeboat approached, the casualty grounded, its two crew jumped overboard and the vessel's masts were carried away. Coxswain Davies took the lifeboat into the broken water and picked up the two men, then went as close as possible to the casualty and Second Coxswain Billy Davies jumped onto the yacht to secure a line so that it could be towed into deep water. The casualty was then towed to Great Yarmouth, which was reached at 4 p.m. As conditions were not suitable for rehousing, the lifeboat remained at Great Yarmouth until 17 September.

During February 1977, the lifeboat was called upon to perform three services in the space of less than a week. The first was to the cargo vessel *Atlantic Duke*, which was aground near the South Middle Haisborough Buoy. Another cargo vessel, *American Moon*, was standing by as *Ruby and Arthur Reed* launched at 9.27 a.m. on 19 February. She reached the casualty an hour and a half later to relieve the Gorleston lifeboat, which had been on the scene during the night. The casualty was eventually refloated on 20 February, and the lifeboat left the scene at 11.50 a.m. that day. Two days later, *Ruby and Arthur Reed* launched to a catamaran that had capsized half a mile east of the station. She reached the casualty at 11.07 a.m. and took aboard the three youths who had been on the craft. The catamaran had turned over with the sails still set, so righting it proved to be a difficult task, but it was eventually completed so the lifeboat could tow it to a mooring buoy. The final service of a hectic week came on 24 February, when the lifeboat was called to stand by the chemical carrier *Thorodland*, aground near the South Middle Haisborough Buoy. She stood by until the casualty freed herself from the sands unaided during the mid-afternoon.

Left: Ruby and Arthur Reed *approaching the quayside at Gorleston, with the rescued captain from the cargo vessel,* Nimrod. *(By courtesy of Eastern Counties Newspapers Ltd)*

Opposite: Ruby and Arthur Reed *during overhaul at J.E. Fletcher's boatyard, Oulton Broad, April 1979. (Poppyland Photographs)*

Later in the year, on 14 November 1977, the lifeboat was called upon after the cargo vessel *Nimrod*, on passage from Whitstable to Leith with a cargo of stone chippings, reported she was listing to starboard and required urgent assistance. Her position was given as two miles west of Dudgeon lightvessel. With a near gale force seven wind blowing, *Ruby and Arthur Reed* launched at 4.26 a.m. and set off at full speed. While en route it was learned that *Nimrod* had capsized and sunk within three minutes. At this time it was thought that her five crew members had taken to life rafts, but in fact they were in the water. Three ships in the vicinity, *Dutch Mate*, the ferry *Norwave* and *Haico Holwerda* searched for survivors. The men in the water could be heard shouting but, even when located, could not be picked up by the high-sided vessels in the 8-12ft waves. A helicopter managed to winch one to safety and, because of his condition, immediately took him back to shore.

The lifeboat arrived on scene at 6.20 a.m. and began to search. With the help of *Norwave's* searchlight, one man was found. but picking out of the water was not straightforward. Coxswain Richard Davies started to approach, but found, with the high seas lifting the lifeboat, it was too dangerous with a risk of the boat coming down on top of the man. So he decided to go upwind and let the lifeboat blow down on the casualty. This approach proved successful. Suffering badly from exposure and in great pain, the man was unable to help himself. With two crew members lying on the deck and hanging through the guardrail he was pulled alongside; then other crewmen leaning over the guardrail pulled him clear of the water and on board. He was taken below where members of the crew worked to revive him. Another survivor was picked up by *Haico Holwerda* and the last two men were successfully winched to safety by a second helicopter. Having made certain that *Nimrod's* crew of five were all accounted for, the lifeboat began the passage back to station, but was unable to rehouse because of the heavy swell, so went to Great Yarmouth, where the survivor was landed at 12.09 p.m. For this service a letter signed by Captain Nigel Dixon, the RNLI's director, was sent to Dr Paul Barclay, chairman of Cromer branch, thanking Coxswain Davies, his crew and honorary secretary D.L. Snelling.

The lifeboat performed two services to fishing craft during 1978, the second of which took place on 4 September 1978. *Ruby and Arthur Reed* was launched to the aid of the crab boat, *Charles Perkins*, which was being rowed towards the lifeboat station with three crew on board, only one of whom was an experienced fisherman. Due to the waves near

the beach, it was decided to launch the lifeboat and either tow the boat, or put experienced crew members aboard. On arrival alongside, it was discovered that the crab boat was half full of water, its engine had broken down and the crew was exhausted. One man was taken on board the lifeboat and two of the lifeboat crew were put on the crab boat. The lifeboat then stood by whilst the crab boat was rowed ashore. This routine service was typical of the kind of assistance the lifeboat often provides to the local crab boats.

While *Ruby and Arthur Reed* went for refit during 1978 to 1979, the relief lifeboat *William Gammon – Manchester and District XXX* (ON.849), built in 1947 and originally stationed at The Mumbles, was on station temporarily. She performed only one effective service during her time at Cromer, on 6 March 1979, to a crewman on board the Haisborough lightvessel, who had fallen down a ladder and injured his back and legs and so required medical assistance. The lifeboat launched at 1.35 p.m. with the station's honorary medical adviser on board, and reached the lightvessel at 3.10 p.m. The doctor, coxswain and three crew then went aboard, and first aid and morphine were administered by the doctor. Due to the man's injured back considerable care had to be exercised in moving him, but he was taken onto the lifeboat which left the lightvessel at 4 p.m. and arrived at station just over an hour later. The lifeboat was rehoused and the casualty passed to waiting ambulance men, who took him to the Norfolk and Norwich hospital.

Ruby and Arthur Reed returned to station in 1979 and on 3 May 1980 was involved in a long, difficult service to the Danish motor fishing vessel *Bess*. She launched at 10.15 a.m. into very rough seas and north-easterly gale force winds of eight to nine to the fishing vessel, which had broken down and had no electric power. Arriving on scene within an hour, Coxswain Richard Davies attempted to get a line aboard the vessel, but the vessel's towing positions were found to be rotten so two crew, Clive Rayment and W.H. Davies, went on board and a holding line was attached to the bottom of the mast to keep the vessel's head to sea, with another vessel providing a lee. Fortunately, after five minutes the engines were restarted and the fishing vessel was able to make headway. A third lifeboatman went aboard as the pumps had to be worked manually and the four men on the vessel were exhausted. As the engine was working Coxswain Davies decided his only choice was to escort the vessel to Wells and they reached the Foulness Buoy at 2.44 p.m. At 6 p.m. the three fishermen were transferred to the lifeboat and the Wells lifeboat launched to escort

Top: Ruby and Arthur Reed *landing a life raft from the cargo vessel* Ems *on 30 January 1981. (By courtesy of Eastern Counties Newspapers Ltd)*

Middle: *The lifeboat crew after the service to the cargo vessel* Ems, *January 1981, from left to right: Coxswain Richard Davies, Clive Rayment, Dick West, Billy Davies, Mac MacKinnon, Donny Abbs and John Jonas. (By courtesy of Eastern Counties Newspapers Ltd)*

Left: Ruby and Arthur Reed *returning from service to the oil rig supply vessel* The Cuttlefish *on 30 November 1981. (By courtesy of Eastern Counties Newspapers Ltd)*

both vessels into Wells. Once alongside Wells Quay, it became apparent that the fishing vessel was in a very poor condition and the skipper had no idea of his position. The lifeboat was unable to return to station until 7 May due to the adverse sea conditions.

The first service of 1981 took place in the early hours of 30 January. *Ruby and Arthur Reed* launched after reports of a collision between two ships near the Middle Haisborough Buoy. The lifeboat arrived on the scene at 2.20 a.m. to find the cargo vessel *Ems* had sunk after being in collision with a smaller vessel, *Udine*, which with other ships in the area had rescued twenty-one people, although two were still missing. *Udine* was acting as on-scene commander, while the area was combed for the missing men, with both Cromer and Gorleston lifeboats assisting in the search through the debris of containers and upturned life rafts. At daybreak, Cromer lifeboat found two upturned life rafts still attached to the sunken vessel, so these were checked then left to mark the wreck. The search was abandoned at 9.35 a.m. and *Ruby and Arthur Reed* returned to station with a life raft.

The most outstanding rescue of 1981 was performed by the inshore lifeboat. At lunchtime on 1 May 1981 the ILB launched to the crab boat *George William*, which had been swamped and sunk off East Runton, her crew of two thrown into the water. Within six minutes of the call the ILB was at sea, manned by helmsman Clive Rayment and crew members Frank Muirhead and Chris Craske. The weather was fine with good visibility but a fresh to strong breeze – force five to six – was blowing, creating a moderate to rough onshore sea. As the ILB went through the surf, although the outboard engine was tilted to clear the ground, the propeller still touched bottom in the troughs. Once clear of the surf, a course was set for the casualty, a mile and a half to the west. Maximum speed was maintained as far as possible, but the engine had to be eased back to get the craft through the bigger seas.

As she neared the casualty, the ILB was informed that the two fishermen were in the water 150 yards north–east of East Runton beach. An approach was made from the north through seas breaking in shallows over an offshore bank. The lifeboat then had to round the capsized crab boat and her floating debris before heading back north to reach the men in the water. One fisherman was hanging on to a lifebuoy, the other to a crab pot marker buoy and, by 12.30 p.m., the two men had been brought safely aboard. Both survivors were suffering from hypothermia, so, rather than try to put the two men ashore at East Runton, Rayment headed as fast as possible for Cromer's Fishermen's Beach, while crew members Muirhead and Craske tended the survivors. At 12.37 p.m. the inflatable lifeboat beached

Chris Craske, the helmsman Clive Rayment, and Frank Muirhead following the award of a Bronze medal for the service to the crab boat George William *in May 1981. (By courtesy of Eastern Counties Newspapers Ltd)*

Left: *Presentation of certificates following the Bronze medal service in May 1981. Left to right: Chris Craske, Dr D. Vaughan (president of the Cromer branch), helmsman Clive Rayment, and Frank Muirhead. (Poppyland Photographs)*

Below: *Recovery of D class inflatable D-307, at the west beach in August 1984. (Nicholas Leach)*

at Cromer, where the two survivors were carried to a waiting ambulance, while the ILB was refuelled and made ready for service. For this difficult service, the Bronze medal was awarded to Clive Rayment and medal service certificates were presented to crew members Frank Muirhead and Christopher Craske.

The last service of 1981 was undertaken in rough weather on 30 November after a mayday was received from the oil rig supply vessel *Cuttlefish* that she had grounded on the Haisborough Sands and her engine room was being flooded. *Ruby and Arthur Reed* launched at 4.05 p.m. in rough seas and north-westerly force seven to eight winds, making full speed to the scene. Four men were taken off by helicopter but a further two men remained on board. On arrival at the scene, the lifeboatmen found the vessel was very low in the water and taking heavy seas. The two men remaining on board had to be forcibly pulled from the vessel, and in doing so one received a slight hand injury. The lifeboat touched bottom going across the sandbank, but got clear safely. She left the casualty at 6.30 p.m. and arrived at Great Yarmouth two hours later, where she was forced to remain until 3 December when the weather abated.

Ruby and Arthur Reed undertook three routine services in 1982 but the ILB had a busy year, and was involved in fifteen. On 18 July the ILB was covering the annual Sheringham to Cromer Raft Race, when it was called to a small inflatable which was drifting three miles off Overstrand. The RAF helicopter which was in the area was also sent to the scene. The ILB arrived at 3.57 p.m. and found that the inflatable's 2hp outboard was not working. After discussing the situation with the owner, the lifeboat crew persuaded the occupants to board the ILB which then took the inflatable in tow and landed all at Overstrand beach at 4.12 p.m., after which the ILB returned to station.

During the evening of 10 August 1983, Great Yarmouth Coastguard requested the ILB launch to an exhausted swimmer stranded on the seaward end of a groyne at Overstrand. The force three to four wind and rough sea, combined with the water swirling back from the promenade wall, made it impossible for the swimmer to reach the beach. The ILB launched at 8.53 p.m. and arrived on the scene but, due to the considerable backwash from the groyne and promenade, a line had to be thrown to the swimmer so he could be pulled into the ILB. Landing at Overstrand would have been difficult, so the casualty was brought back to Cromer, wrapped in a plastic sheet for

Ruby and Arthur Reed *involved in a winching exercise demonstration with the RAF Wessex rescue helicopter for Lifeboat Day on 12 August 1982, with Sheringham lifeboat* Manchester Unity of Oddfellows *(ON.960) also on hand. (By courtesy of Eastern Counties Newspapers Ltd)*

Donny Abbs, mechanic from 1979 to 1987. (By courtesy of Eastern Counties Newspapers Ltd)

warmth during the return journey, made in near darkness, and then taken to Cromer hospital for a check-up.

During 1983 plans were put forward to build a new boathouse for the ILB on the east side of the pier because launching from the 'igloo' building, situated to the west of the pier, was proving rather difficult, as it involved taking the ILB over a rocky section of beach. After plans for the new Marley-type house near the East Gangway had been approved, the building was ready in 1984. In June 1984, a new inshore lifeboat was sent to the station, D-307, funded by the Sheringham and Cromer Round Table. The new house was ready by the end of the summer and it was formally opened at a ceremony on 19 August 1984, when the new D class inflatable was also dedicated.

One of the first services performed by the new ILB took place on 8 July 1984 to the yacht *Karelia*, which was disabled off Cromer pier about half a mile to the north. The ILB crew found the yacht, bound from Dundee to France, with its generator and wiring burnt out. The yacht had been off Cromer for about twelve hours but had been unable to request assistance by radio as the batteries were flat. The ILB crew checked the persons on board were alright, and arranged to land the batteries to be recharged to provide navigation lights at night. Winchman Ted Luckin was taken out from the lifeboat station to check the yacht's engines and advised the owners to sail to Great Yarmouth the following day for engine repairs. After an hour on scene, the ILB left the casualty and returned to station.

ILB service summary 1981-90

	Launches	Lives saved
1981	14	5
1982	15	2
1983	7	1
1984	8	0
1985	17	24
1986	10	3
1987	9	1
1988	6	0
1989	18	0
1990	8	2

What proved to be the last service performed by *Ruby and Arthur Reed* at Cromer took place on 4 September 1984, when she launched to escort two crab boats, *Provider* and *Star*, which had been working between Mundesley and Bacton. Three Cromer fishermen jumped to safety in roaring surf at Trimingham shortly before their boat, *Provider*, was smashed against a breakwater and totally wrecked as North Norfolk was hit by a sudden squall at around 9 a.m. *Provider* was one of several crab boats caught in the storm, but most of the others managed to get to safety. *Star* was beached at Bacton and the lifeboat, with second coxswain Billy Davies at the helm and former coxswain Henry 'Shrimp' Davies among the crew, continued to Great Yarmouth, unable to rehouse because of the conditions. Coxswain Richard Davies was ashore at Trimingham from where he had been working in his own crab boat and he stood by to maintain radio contact with the lifeboat, while the three from *Provider* struggled to safety. Cromer Coastguards patrolled the coast from Weybourne to Bacton in a mobile unit, checking the safety of crab boats, and helped to salvage personal belongings from *Provider* before she broke up against Trimingham breakwater.

By the time of this service, *Ruby and Arthur Reed* was ready for a refit and so, on 4 September 1984, left Cromer for what turned out to be the last time. She never returned, although the new lifeboat then allocated to the station was not ready. After a major

D class inflatable D-307 exercising with an RAF Wessex search and rescue helicopter, June 1985. (Paul Russell)

overhaul at J.E. Fletcher's Boatyard, Oulton Broad, she was placed on station at St David's in December 1985. In her place at Cromer came the relief 46ft 9in Watson lifeboat, *Guy and Clare Hunter*, built in 1955 and stationed at the Scilly Isles station of St Mary's for more than twenty-five years, until transferred to the Relief Fleet in 1981. *Guy and Clare Hunter* remained on station for more than a year while the station's new lifeboat was being completed and performed a number of services during this time. The first took place on 4 April 1985 after reports had been received that a vessel was aground on the Middle Haisborough Sands. She launched at 1.45 a.m. and found the small motor vessel *Klass I* with four on board. The lifeboat, which had to cross the sands as the vessel was on the north-east side, stood by until the tide had risen sufficiently for the vessel to float off. After the lifeboatmen had checked the vessel could proceed to the Humber, the lifeboat left the scene at 4.40 a.m. and reached her station just over an hour later.

On 28 July 1985, *Guy and Clare Hunter* assisted the yacht *Helm Spray III* which had reported a steering problem and whose crew was unsure of their position. With the weather worsening, the lifeboat launched at 3.15 p.m. and proceeded to the casualty, about forty miles north-east of Cromer. After a search and liaison with the various gas platforms in the area, the casualty was located at 10 p.m. and a tow was rigged. At 11 p.m. the tow began, but as the casualty had no rudder the lifeboat had to use her drogue on the casualty to keep it on course, so the tow had to proceed at half speed. The long passage took more than seven hours, and both vessels arrived off Wells harbour entrance at 6.15 a.m., where the tow was handed over to the Wells ILB.

The annual Sheringham to Cromer Raft Race on 11 August 1985 turned into something of a disaster when the sixty-two rafts, which had assembled off Sheringham, were caught out by bad weather. Sheringham lifeboat and both Cromer lifeboats were on hand to act as safety boats and escort the rafts, but at 1.45 p.m., fifteen minutes after the race had started, Coxswain Davies requested that the race be abandoned as the conditions were deteriorating with strong south-easterly winds and rain. Some of the rafts were breaking up and their crews were suffering from cold and cramp. The various support vessels were kept busy plucking people from broken or damaged rafts and escorting some ashore, with *Guy and Clare Hunter* picking up thirty persons who were transferred to the ILB and taken ashore. No loss of life was reported, although twenty-eight persons attended hospital suffering from mild exposure. During September 1985, *Guy and Clare Hunter* performed two further services, both routine in nature, and three months later was replaced by a new Tyne class lifeboat.

8

The Modern Era

The introduction of the inshore lifeboat in the 1960s took place at the same time as significant developments in offshore lifeboat design, all intended to meet the changing demands on the lifeboat service and the need for lifeboats to reach casualties more quickly. The first of the faster offshore boats, the Waveney, was based on a United States Coast Guard (USCG) design for a 44ft steel-hulled lifeboat. The RNLI purchased one of these boats from the USCG in 1963 and took it on a tour of lifeboat stations in Britain and Ireland to assess its suitability and ascertain crew opinions at first hand. As the first design of 'fast' lifeboat it was a radical departure from the traditional designs then used by the RNLI, but crews were very positive about the boat and it was soon accepted into service. The Waveney and the larger 52ft Arun, introduced soon afterwards, were designed for operations from an afloat berth, so stations where slipway or carriage launching was employed needed other designs. Therefore, in the late 1970s, the RNLI began designing a fast lifeboat type to be launched from a slipway to replace the traditional Watson and Barnett lifeboats and, as at Cromer, the larger 48ft 6in Oakley and Solent types. Slipway launching requires a special hull design which gives protection to the propellers and rudders, while the hull itself has to be sufficiently strong to withstand the stresses of being hauled up a slipway.

The basic lines plan for the hull of the 'fast slipway boat' (FSB), as it was originally known, was provided by the National Maritime Institute and featured a semi-planing hull, constructed from steel, with a shallow draught, long straight keel and flared bow above the waterline. Protection for the propellers was given by partial tunnels, substantial bilge keels, and a straight wide keel ending in a hauling shoe for winching the boat back

into its house, all necessary for slipway launching and working in shoal waters. The wheelhouse had a low profile to fit into existing boathouses, with a flying bridge amidships and a separate cabin aft of the upper steering position. The hull shape of the new design enabled a top speed of approximately 18 knots to be achieved by the twin propellers, which were each driven by a 425hp General Motors 6V-92-TI diesel engine. The two main tanks carried 510 gallons of diesel between them, with a reserve tank of 102 gallons, giving a range at full speed of 238 nautical miles.

The design was given the class name Tyne, in line with the RNLI's policy of using names of rivers for lifeboat classes, and the prototype ON.1074 was taken on a tour of the country during 1982 under the command of the district inspector, Tom Nutman, and Staff Coxswain A. Hunter. On 1 September 1982, the new boat, while on her way from the Humber to Lowestoft, visited Cromer, enabling Coxswain Richard Davies, Second Coxswain Billy Davies and Donny Abbs, mechanic, together with former Coxswain Henry 'Shrimp' Davies, to go on board and give the new design their approval. Soon after ON.1074 had ended her tour, the RNLI ordered a further four Tynes from the Fairey Marine boatyard at Cowes, and these were allocated to Padstow, Holyhead, The Mumbles and Cromer. Meanwhile, the prototype boat was named *City of London* and in November 1983 went on station at Selsey, while the second prototype, ON.1075, was allocated to the Relief Fleet and named *Sam and Joan Woods*.

Once a new lifeboat had been allocated to the station, a local appeal was organised to raise the necessary money. Headed by Tony Webster, chairman of the Cromer branch and also chairman of the town council, the appeal got off to a good start when the remainder of the bequest from Mrs Ruby Reed, amounting to just over £100,000, was donated to the fund. Mrs Reed's bequest, part of which was first used to buy the station's lifeboat in 1967, made up the largest donation to the appeal, so it was decided that the new boat would be named *Ruby and Arthur Reed II*. £430,000 was needed to fund the new lifeboat, but the appeal was so successful that it exceeded this amount. Before the new boat was ready, one of the two Tynes already built, *Sam and Joan Woods* (ON.1075), came to the station for launching trials to determine what alterations, if any, would be

Opposite: *The prototype 47ft Tyne* City of London *(ON.1074) visiting Cromer on 1 September 1982 during trials round Britain. After these were completed, she went to Selsey as station lifeboat. (By courtesy of Eastern Counties Newspapers Ltd)*

Right: *47ft Tyne* Sam and Joan Woods *with* Ruby and Arthur Reed, *August 1984. The Tyne class was completely different to all previous lifeboats operated from Cromer. The class had a steel, semi-planing hull and was driven by powerful engines which enabled the boats to reach twice the speed of the Oakley and Watson motor lifeboats. (By courtesy of Eastern Counties Newspapers Ltd)*

47ft Tyne Ruby and Arthur Reed II *with* Guy and Clare Hunter *on 15 December 1985 as the Tyne arrived on station for the first time. (By courtesy of Eastern Counties Newspapers Ltd)*

needed to the boathouse. She arrived from the RNLI Depot at Poole in July 1984, after the RNLI's public open days. Coxswain Richard Davies was in command, with Jim Smith, honorary secretary, and a couple of the crew. The launching trials held on 23 July showed that very few alterations were needed to either boathouse or slipway.

The new lifeboat, *Ruby and Arthur Reed II* (ON.1097), was completed during 1985 and arrived at the station on 15 December, having been brought from the RNLI headquarters at Poole by Coxswain Davies and his crew via overnight stops at Ramsgate and Lowestoft. *Guy and Clare Hunter* was launched so that the new lifeboat could be recovered for the first time after a few minor adjustments had been made to the boathouse. Two launches and two further rehousing exercises were completed, after which Commander George Cooper, the RNLI's deputy chief of operations, who was supervising the boat's arrival, was satisfied that the boat could become operational.

Ruby and Arthur Reed II was formally named at a ceremony held at Cromer on 20 June 1986. She was christened by the Duke of Kent, president of the RNLI, with many Cromer townspeople in attendance, along with numerous well-wishers, supporters and holidaymakers, many of whom had donated generously towards the new boat. Tony Webster, chairman of the Cromer Lifeboat Appeal Committee, opened the proceedings and handed the lifeboat over to the RNLI. The Duke of Atholl, RNLI chairman, received the lifeboat on behalf of the Institution and delivered her into the care of the Cromer station with Jim Smith, BEM, honorary secretary, formally accepting her. After the service of dedication, The Duke of Kent addressed the audience, saying that the new lifeboat was a tribute to both the RNLI's designers and to the local people who had raised money to pay for her. The Duke then walked to the lifeboat house and named the lifeboat *Ruby and Arthur Reed II*. As the champagne broke across her bows, a helicopter from RAF Coltishall flew past flying the RNLI flag.

Ruby and Arthur Reed II performed many notable services, the most significant of which are described below. Her first service, which took place just over a month after her arrival, turned out to be a testing baptism. At 8.15 a.m. on 24 January 1986, news was received of a collision between the 76,000-ton Greek tanker *Orleans* and the 295-ton Dutch fishing vessel *Jan Van Toon*. The tanker, about sixty-five miles north-east of Cromer, had been struck on her starboard side in storm force ten north-westerly winds and fire had broken out along half her length. An RAF helicopter was first on the scene and had begun to lift off some of the tanker's crew and land them on a nearby gas rig. However, a second helicopter had to be sent when the first was forced to land on the gas rig after the winch wire had hit the rotor blades. Although some ships were on standby in the area, it was not known how many and so at 8.30 a.m. the new 47ft Tyne lifeboat was launched under the command of Coxswain Richard Davies.

The sea was very rough and at the station the wind was gusting to gale force eight. As the lifeboat neared the tanker three and a half hours after launching, winds had reached storm force ten gusting to hurricane force twelve. Once on scene, the lifeboat checked the tanker for leaks and the state of the fire which, fortunately, was confined to one tank and had been brought under control. For a while one of the tanker's crew was unaccounted for, but when he was found safe the lifeboat began standby duty, until the tug *Smit-Lloyd 123* was able to take *Orleans* in tow. Throughout an hour and a half standing by, the lifeboat and her crew endured winds up to 80mph, waves between 20ft and 25ft, snow, sleet, rain and very low temperatures. At 1.35 p.m. the tow was safely under way, so the lifeboat was able to leave the scene and escort a vessel, which had thirteen survivors from the tanker aboard, back to Great Yarmouth, where she arrived at 6.30 p.m., ten hours after launching. The weather had damaged the lifeboat's VHF aerials, MF radio and radar, and various repairs had to be carried out before she could return to station, but she and her crew had survived this difficult ordeal. Following this demanding service a letter of appreciation, signed by Commander Bruce Cairns, chief of operations, was sent to Coxswain Davies and his crew.

On 29 August 1986, the Wells lifeboat *Ernest Tom Neathercoat* (ON.982) launched to the London-registered fishing vessel *Nicholaus*, off Blakeney. The Wells Coxswain then requested additional help and a pump to keep the water level down as the casualty's own pumps were out of action. So, with a pump aboard, *Ruby and Arthur Reed II* launched at 5.30 p.m. and arrived on the scene an hour later. The pump and two crew were

HRH The Duke of Kent, President of the RNLI, addressed the crowd during the naming ceremony of Ruby and Arthur Reed II *on 20 June 1986. (By courtesy of Eastern Counties Newspapers Ltd)*

The 27ft yacht Phaedra *is brought into Great Yarmouth by* Ruby and Arthur Reed II *on 29 September 1988, after a nine-hour tow in severe weather. (By courtesy of Eastern Counties Newspapers Ltd)*

transferred to the stricken vessel, which was continually taking in water, and a tow was rigged as the vessel had run out of fuel. Great Yarmouth was the only port into which the vessel could be taken safely, so the vessel was towed there. The harbour was reached at 1 a.m. on 30 August and the casualty was berthed safely an hour later. The Cromer crew left by road at 2.45 a.m., leaving the lifeboat until 1 September, when weather and sea conditions had improved enough to allow rehousing.

On 4 June 1987, with the relief lifeboat *Sam and Joan Woods* on station, Great Yarmouth Coastguard requested assistance to the fishing vessel *Sonjan*, eleven miles north-north-east of Cromer. The vessel's engine was disabled and she was taking in water in heavy seas, with the crew concerned for their safety. The lifeboat launched at 8.14 p.m. and arrived on scene an hour later. In difficult sea conditions, an attempt was made to tow the vessel, but when this failed the lifeboat stood by as the rig supply tender, *Hector Read*, which arrived at 9.18 p.m., took over the tow. The lifeboat returned to station to collect a lightweight pump as it was too rough to pass a heavier pump from the rig supply tender. Once the pump had been got on board, the fishing vessel was successfully pumped out and the lifeboat escorted the vessels to Great Yarmouth. The lifeboat left Yarmouth at 1.58 a.m. and returned to station at 3.29 a.m., but as the swell was too great to safely rehouse, she was anchored off until 12.10 p.m. on 5 June.

On 29 August 1988, several lifeboats were involved in helping a group of divers about two miles north of Overstrand when three of them discovered the line had broken from their marker buoy. When they drifted away from their standby vessel, those on board the vessel fired a red flare and the Coastguard alerted the ILB and a Wessex SAR helicopter that was on exercise in the area. *Ruby and Arthur Reed II* launched at 2.42 p.m. and, along with the Sheringham lifeboat *Manchester Unity of Oddfellows* (ON.960) and Mundesley's private ILB, searched the area. The helicopter located the three divers and guided the lifeboat to the area to recover them from the water. Another two divers were also collected from the support boat and all five were landed at the boathouse. The support boat was escorted to the beach by the ILB after a well-executed combined rescue.

A month later, Cromer lifeboat was involved in a very long and testing service. In the early hours of 29 September 1988, Great Yarmouth Coastguard was contacted by the husband and wife crew of the 27ft yacht *Phaedra*, which was in difficulty in force eight to nine winds, and the two on board had no idea of their position. Although electrical power had been lost, the skipper managed to connect a car battery to the VHF radio to contact the coastguard, who obtained a bearing and located the yacht near the Vulcan and Leman gas field. The casualty was thirty miles north-east of Cromer, and *Ruby and Arthur Reed II* was under way just seven minutes after the coastguard's call. To reach the yacht, the lifeboat was forced to cut across the sandbanks, taking her into broken water. Coxswain Richard Davies reported later that the lifeboat 'handled well' in the atrocious conditions, with 20ft to 25ft waves coming aboard the lifeboat. At 2.30 a.m. the yacht was found, going round in circles with all sails set. At the coxswain's request the crew lowered the sails and a tow was successfully passed to the casualty. The extreme weather and height of the waves made it impossible for a lifeboat crew member to go aboard *Phaedra*, or for those on the casualty to be taken off.

Because of the conditions Coxswain Davies decided the only possible course was southerly, towards Bacton. In the heavy seas the tow was very slow, with the lifeboat managing only a knot or so and the casualty making heavy weather of the conditions. Towing began at 3 a.m. and for seven hours the lifeboat crew battled slowly south through the gale until at 10 a.m. they were under the lee of the land and conditions began to improve. A crew member was then put aboard *Phaedra* and the speed of the tow was increased. After a further two and a half hours at increased speed the lifeboat and casualty finally reached the shelter of Great Yarmouth, and the yacht was berthed alongside at 12.30 p.m. The crew of *Phaedra* was unhurt, although the skipper, Graham Wood, told a local newspaper, 'I knew that if we hadn't called the coastguard we wouldn't have seen the morning. The lifeboat boys were brilliant, really superb.' The rescue had involved the Tyne lifeboat and her crew being at sea in winds of up to force nine for twelve hours, nine of which were spent towing the casualty to safety in very severe weather, and for this exceptional and difficult service the Thanks of the Institution on Vellum was accorded to Coxswain Davies.

On 14 February 1989, *Ruby and Arthur Reed II* performed another long service after the 5,000-ton roll-on roll-off ferry *Tor Gothia* went aground in bad weather. The lifeboat launched at 11 p.m. to the ferry, which was aground on the Middle Haisborough Sands and needed immediate assistance. Extra crew members were taken aboard the lifeboat in view of the size of the casualty and the weather, with the south-westerly wind blowing force six to seven accompanied by rain and 20ft to 30ft seas. The eighteen-mile passage to the casualty took thirty-five minutes and, on arrival, the lifeboat found confused and boiling seas around the ferry which drew 15ft of water but was in only 10ft. The lifeboat stood by until a tug arrived at 4.45 a.m. when, despite a broken throttle cable on his boat, Coxswain Davies transferred an officer from the tug to the ferry in very difficult conditions – earning the praise of the tug's master for his expertise – and waited for the Sheringham lifeboat to arrive before setting course for Great Yarmouth to repair the cable and refuel. With repairs complete, *Ruby and Arthur Reed II* was back on the scene by 11.30 a.m., shortly after the ferry had been refloated. After checking for damage, *Tor Gothia* continued on her passage to Immingham at 12.30 p.m. and at 2 p.m., more than thirteen hours after launching, the Cromer lifeboat was back on station and ready for service. As a result of his efforts during this service, Coxswain Davies was sent a letter of appreciation from the RNLI's chief of operations.

On 21 November 1990, *Ruby and Arthur Reed II* was involved in another excellent service. At 5 p.m., Great Yarmouth Coastguard informed the station that the 1,300-ton ro-ro ferry *Stavroula* was aground on the Middle Haisborough Sand, but in no immediate danger. It was hoped to refloat her on the next high water at 9.20 p.m. but the Greek master had requested lifeboat assistance. So, at 6.07 p.m., *Ruby and Arthur Reed II* launched with Coxswain Richard Davies in command and set course at full speed to the Middle Haisborough Buoy, thirteen miles distant. At 6.30 p.m. the casualty called the Coastguard as the crew wanted to abandon ship and a few minutes later the lifeboat crew saw red flares dead ahead and saw the casualty aground on the Middle Haisborough Sand, lifting slightly in the swell. The wind had increased to east-north-east force four to five with a moderate sea, and a heavy swell of 15ft was running from the north-east.

At 7.10 p.m. Coxswain Davies approached the casualty on her port side, working the helm and engines continually, and asked the casualty's crew to take the lifeboat's lines forward and aft. However, as soon as the crew saw the lifeboat they hurried along the deck with their suitcases and immediately scrambled over the side onto the lifeboat. With no one left to take the lines, Second Coxswain Billy Davies and the assistant mechanic, John Jonas, went aboard and secured the lifeboat, but before the stern line could be attached a heavy swell rolled the lifeboat's starboard quarter against the vessel's side, bending the quarter rails. With nine survivors on board, the lifeboat moved off into deeper water and the two lifeboatmen checked the vessel. Assistant mechanic Jonas put out a chip pan on fire in the galley, which could have caused serious problems for the salvage attempt by the tug which was on the way from Lowestoft. The casualty was not found to be taking in water, but the rudder was jammed to starboard. At 7.20 p.m. two helicopters arrived and the master and engineer were returned to the vessel ready to refloat her, while the two lifeboatmen stayed on board to assist. The survivors were then transferred to one of the helicopters and before the tug arrived the lifeboat attempted to refloat the casualty by using a bow line and turning her to starboard, using her own engine and the jammed rudder. However, the line parted when the vessel grounded again.

The casualty was now heading south-west and the swell, which had built up to 20ft, began to run over the main deck, forcing the crew aft to shelter in the accommodation. The lifeboat was still standing by when a large swell came around the casualty's stern and rolled her heavily to starboard. Ten gallons of water entered the engine room through an air intake, but both engines continued to run normally. The lifeboat then lay off waiting for the tug. At 10 p.m. the casualty refloated herself under her own power but, as the rudder was jammed, the lifeboat came in again to secure a towline which kept the casualty off the sand. After some difficulty in passing the towline to the tug, the lifeboat crew on board the casualty secured the wire at 12.15 a.m. and the tow to Lowestoft began, with the master and engineer aboard. The lifeboat retrieved her hard-working crew, returned to station, and was rehoused at 1.45 a.m. and ready for service half an hour later. In recognition of their efforts during this long and arduous service, a collective Framed Letter of Appreciation signed by the chairman of the Institution was presented to Coxswain Davies; Second Coxswain W.T. Davies; R.J. Hannah, mechanic; John Jonas, assistant mechanic; and crew members P. Jefferies, P. Everitt, J. Balls and J. Howard.

In August 1992, a new D class inflatable was placed on station. D-436 *Chloe*, the fifth ILB at Cromer, was funded from the gift of Miss Iris Buckle, of Cockfosters, Hertfordshire, in memory of her mother, Chloe Long, of Hemsby. She was named and dedicated on 11 July 1993 at a ceremony held on the seafront outside the ILB house, during which the boat was blessed by the vicar of Cromer, Revd David Hayden, and officially accepted by John Leeds, one of the station's deputy launching authorities. Senior helmsman David Pope, who read the lesson, and two crew members, then took the boat to sea for a demonstration with the all-weather lifeboat and an RAF rescue helicopter.

ILB service summary 1991-2000

	Launches	Lives saved
1991	6	0
1992	6	1
1993	4	0
1994	6	0
1995	12	1
1996	6	0
1997	11	0
1998	8	0
1999	6	1
2000	10	0

Another notable service was performed by the Cromer lifeboatmen in *Ruby and Arthur Reed II* on 13 October 1993. During the afternoon one of the lifeboat crew picked up on his radio scanner a call from the 30ft yacht *Happy Bear* requesting help. He telephoned the coastguard, who requested an immediate launch, and by 3.20 p.m. the lifeboat crew was aboard *Ruby and Arthur Reed II* with Coxswain Richard Davies in command. In the poor conditions, Coxswain Davies had to choose precisely the right moment to launch and even then the lifeboat was completely buried by the seas, frequently disappearing from view as she clawed her way seaward from the slipway. An east-north-easterly force ten onshore wind, gusting to 55 knots, was creating a sea so rough that it reached up to the lifeboat station doors, while overcast conditions reduced visibility. The lifeboat headed straight into the bad weather, which was so rough that it was some time before the crew could go on deck, raise the aerials and try to contact the yacht. It proved impossible for the lifeboat to run at full speed, and at times she became airborne over the waves before crashing heavily into the troughs. Radio contact was established with the yacht at 3.45 p.m. and the lifeboat altered course to the south-east towards her.

The casualty was spotted at 3.57 p.m., about a mile off the lee shore at Trimingham, heading south-east with only a storm jib set. The engine was running, although the gearbox would not engage properly in forward gear, and she was being tossed around violently by heavy breaking seas. The skipper, in foul-weather gear and life jacket, was hanging on as best he could with his four-man crew below deck. The wind was still at gale force, with poor visibility and huge breaking seas. Coxswain Davies considered it dangerous to approach the casualty without causing serious damage, so manoeuvred the lifeboat off the casualty's weather beam and passed across a tow line. The skipper went forward and secured it while another of the yacht's crew took the helm. The tow got under way at 5.07 p.m. and the lifeboat set course for Cockle Gateway off Winterton aiming for Great Yarmouth, the only sheltered harbour within reach but more than twenty miles to the south.

Conditions during the long tow were very difficult. Heading downwind and downstream the casualty was making 6-7 knots over the ground, but by 5 p.m. daylight was fading and her gearbox problem was getting worse. On one occasion the yacht broached completely, ending up stern-to-stern with the lifeboat and on another a large sea broke over the yacht, leaving just the skipper's head visible above the water. By 6 p.m. the weather had begun to ease slightly, although it was still gusting to force nine with 20ft seas and the yacht's skipper was worried about taking the casualty into Great Yarmouth. So Coxswain Davies shortened the tow and went astern, bringing the yacht close enough to the lifeboat for Second Coxswain Billy Davies, in complete darkness, to jump across and take the yacht's helm. Just before 7 p.m., with only a slight sea off Yarmouth, the lifeboat entered port

Ruby and Arthur Reed II *still at Great Yarmouth on 17 October 1993, after the service to the yacht* Happy Bear *four days earlier. (Paul Russell)*

and made fast alongside the Town Quay at 7.38 p.m. Due to the severe weather, the lifeboat was unable to return to Cromer until 18 October, five days later, for rehousing.

For this outstanding service, the Bronze medal was awarded to Coxswain Davies. In his official report Tim Harrison, the deputy inspector for the Eastern Division, said, 'The launch was the roughest the station had experienced in the thirty years the coxswain had been involved.' For their part in the rescue, Second Coxswain Billy Davies, mechanic Paul Wegg, crew members Robert Brownsell, Gary Humphrey, and Paul Jeffries, and head launcher John Lee received Bronze medal service certificates.

During 1994, a series of routine rescues was performed. On 28 July 1994, *Ruby and Arthur Reed II* launched to the 34ft cruiser *Heather Down*, in difficulties seven-teen miles off Sheringham. A distress signal was sent when the boat, on her way to Hull carrying a couple and their son, became caught in heavy weather. Once on scene, the lifeboatmen escorted the casualty to Wells harbour, where it was handed to a local fishing boat. Two days later, the lifeboat was involved in saving two divers who got stranded and were hanging to a buoy when their dive boat went missing. They were rescued less than half an hour after the lifeboat had launched. On 22 September, the motor vessel *Nesico* requested the evacuation of her master who was suffering severe stomach pains. The vessel, then eight miles east of Cromer, was contacted and medical advice was given via the radio. The lifeboat was launched with Dr William Norman on board, who supervised treatment of the master, his transfer from the vessel to the lifeboat, and then from the lifeboat to the waiting ambulance.

On 27 June 1995, the Cromer lifeboatmen were involved in a routine but long service after the lifeboat launched to assist an ill man who had twice tried to commit suicide on board a rig standby boat. *Ruby and Arthur Reed II* rendezvoused with the supply vessel *Putford Puffin* thirty miles off Cromer at 12.00 noon. Dr William Norman, a local doctor who had been taken out by the lifeboat, and Coxswain Richard Davies went on board the vessel, and the twenty-four-year-old crewman was sedated for transfer to the lifeboat, with Dr Norman supervising the operation and treatment. As the lifeboat was unable to recover up the slipway, she went to Yarmouth, reaching the port just after 3 p.m. The sedated crewman was taken by ambulance to hospital at Gorleston and the lifeboat was moored up. She was rehoused at Cromer two days later.

Lifeboat Day 1996: Ruby and Arthur Reed II *performs a joint exercise with the RAF rescue helicopter for the benefit of holiday makers ashore. (Paul Russell)*

During 1996, *Ruby and Arthur Reed II* was called out on service five times before she left the station, while the new lifeboat house at the end of the pier was constructed, described below. The first call came on 2 April when she went to the aid of the Boston fishing boat *Juliet* after it started to ship water. The boat was four miles off Cromer at about 2.30 p.m., and the lifeboat towed the one-man vessel along the coast, handing over the tow to the new Gorleston lifeboat, the 14m Trent *Samerbeta* (ON.1208), which brought the casualty into Great Yarmouth. Unintentionally, *Ruby and Arthur Reed II* was at Gorleston for the naming of the new Trent lifeboat on 24 July, having just completed a service before the ceremony. She launched on 24 July to the 22ft sloop *Giselle*, following a Mayday message broadcast by the vessel after its steering failed when about a mile off Walcott. In the strong winds the crew had been unable to raise the sails, so the lifeboat went to their aid in difficult conditions with poor visibility, rough seas and winds of 25 knots. After getting a line to the yacht, the lifeboatmen towed the casualty and its two occupants to Gorleston. The crew was then on hand for the Gorleston naming ceremony, which was also attended by the Lowestoft lifeboat *Spirit of Lowestoft* (ON.1132), the Caister Volunteer Rescue Service lifeboat *Bernard Matthews*, and the Dutch lifeboat *Donateur* from the Wijk-aan-Zee station in Netherlands, as well as the Gorleston Atlantic 21 *Joseph B. Press*.

The last service of the year by *Ruby and Arthur Reed II*, and the last she performed as Cromer lifeboat for almost three years, took place on 15 August when she was launched to assist a pleasure cruiser with water in its engine room fourteen miles off the coast. Although the three people on board *Ocean Diver* managed to solve the problem before the lifeboat arrived, lifeboatmen went aboard to check the former RAF launch before it continued on passage to Grimsby on one engine.

A Twenty-First-Century Lifeboat Station

During the 1990s, the existing lifeboat house and slipway at the end of the pier, which had been built in 1923 and had given fine service over the years, started showing their age and needed ever increasing amounts of maintenance work to maintain an operational condition. After more than seventy years of exposure to the severe conditions of the North Sea, the supporting reinforced concrete structure was becoming more difficult and costly

Looking up the slipway into the boathouse, with 47ft Tyne Ruby and Arthur Reed II at the head of the slipway. The house was much altered internally throughout its life, including modifications in 1984 to accommodate a Tyne class lifeboat. (Nicholas Leach)

A fine photograph showing the lifeboat house and slipway at the end of the pier used from 1923 until 1996. It overcame the problems of launching across the beach and enabled a larger motor lifeboat to be operated from the station. (Frank Muirhead)

to repair despite the regular maintenance programme carried out by the RNLI. Sections of the structure had been coated in spray concrete in the 1950s and the outer end of the slipway had been reconstructed in steel in 1966. Emergency work on the submerged toe of the slipway, involving divers operating in difficult and potentially dangerous conditions, had to be undertaken in the early 1990s, but all these were short-term measures.

What was needed was a new building and, as a result of a comprehensive survey of the structure and a review of the future requirements for lifeboat cover from Cromer, in 1995 the Institution decided the entire boathouse and slipway would be replaced. Two major factors were taken into account in reaching this decision: firstly, the considerable cost and difficulty of carrying out repairs to the main supporting structure; and secondly, the need for a larger boathouse to accommodate the next generation of fast slipway lifeboat then in the early stages of development. As Cromer was regarded as a key lifeboat station, the RNLI saw slipway launching at this location as the most effective method of launching. Because the station's next lifeboat would be larger in all respects than the Tyne, already a tight fit in the boathouse, a new boathouse was the only realistic option.

Design studies were undertaken during 1995 by Bondesign Associates, and the construction work took place in 1997-98. The project, which represented a major investment for the RNLI, required careful planning in order for the building to blend in with the character of the historic pier. The Institution worked closely with the necessary local authorities and endeavoured to keep local people informed. The very exposed conditions at Cromer meant that no compromises could be made and the new lifeboat house was built with the intention that it would see operations for at least as many years as the building it replaced. The new house was more than twice the size of that which it replaced. Incorporated in the building was a tipping launching platform for the boat, together with offices, a mechanic's workshop, a good-sized crew room, changing room, toilets and shower, as well as a souvenir shop and visitor viewing area. The RNLI's shoreworks manager, Howard Richings, said that designing the new house had been 'challenging', adding, 'we have a lot of difficult sites, but this is the most exposed – open to the full force of the North Sea'.

Work on the new house began in 1997, after the removal of the 1923 boathouse. A team of twenty builders centred their work on a barge anchored at the end of the Victorian pier, while a former American wartime amphibious landing craft was used to bring equipment and materials from nearby Overstrand. The first task was to drill piles into the seabed to support the building platform, and then the piles to support the lifeboat house were put into place. Although the work went on for six days a week, between 7 a.m. and 7 p.m., it was stopped during performances at the Pavilion Theatre to minimise disruptions to the town's tourist trade. The work of piling continued throughout the whole of the 1997 holiday season and by the autumn the site was ready

After removal from Cromer, the 1923 lifeboat house ended up at Southwold and was subsequently converted into a lifeboat museum housing the former Southwold lifeboat Alfred Corry. *(Roger Swanston)*

With piling work complete, the framework of the boathouse together with the floor were put in place and the building begins to take shape. (Paul Russell)

Looking from the jack-up barge, which was used throughout almost the whole construction period, towards the lifeboat house, with the slipway largely complete. (Paul Russell)

The finishing touches are applied to the outside of the boathouse. (Paul Russell)

Almost ready: interior fitting-out work is undertaken in August 1998 to make the house ready for service. (Paul Russell)

for the concrete floor to be installed. Concrete was piped along the pier to the site in the early months of 1998 and in March and April the steel skeleton was placed onto the piles that had been driven into the sand. By May 1998 builders had covered the skeleton with the steel structure of the boathouse.

The hydraulic cradle for the lifeboat, which tipped the boat into position for launching, was tested in August 1998 when the electricity supply had been connected. The tilt-cradle mechanism kept the lifeboat horizontal rather than at an angle, as in the previous house, making routine maintenance work easier. Once the winch had been installed, the first slipway trials took place on 17 October 1998 when relief 47ft Tyne *Sam and Joan Woods* (ON.1075), which successfully completed three launches, had the honour of being the first lifeboat to use the new boathouse. After several weeks of further trials, during which a few minor problems were ironed out, the boathouse was declared operational on 4 March 1999, coinciding with the 175th anniversary of the RNLI's founding.

While the new lifeboat house was being constructed, the all-weather lifeboat operated from the beach and was launched by tractor and carriage, reviving a system that had not been practiced at Cromer for more than a quarter of a century. Because the Tyne was not designed for beach launching, the relief 12m Mersey *Her Majesty the Queen* (ON.1189) was sent to the station on 12 November 1995 for launching and recovery trials. A number of practice launches took place, the first at 9.30 a.m. when all went smoothly under the supervision of the district inspector. With more practice, the shore crew speeded up the recovery procedure, although at high tide it proved more difficult because little beach was available on which to work. The boat launched for the last time that day at 6 p.m. and then headed for Lowestoft. She returned a year later and, after further practice launches over the weekend of 16–17 November 1996. *Her Majesty the Queen* was placed on temporary station duty on 17 November 1996. She was kept in the open at the foot of the town's gangway near the lifeboat museum, with portable offices and temporary crew facilities located on the promenade.

Top: *Relief 12m Mersey* Her
Majesty The Queen *(ON.1189)
at Cromer on 16 November
1996, four days after she
arrived, approaching the beach
with the 1923 lifeboat house at
the end of the pier still intact in
the background. (Paul Russell)*

Middle: *Relief 12m Mersey* Her
Majesty The Queen *at the East
Gangway during her period of
Temporary Station Duty at
Cromer. (Nicholas Leach)*

Left: *Relief 47ft Tyne* Sam and
Joan Woods *leaving Cromer on
24 March 1999, after the station boat had returned from
refit. (Paul Russell)*

During 1997, improvements to the operation of the inshore lifeboat were implemented when a new launching tractor was supplied. The New Holland Ford 1920 diesel 4WD vehicle, with twelve forward and four reverse gears, fitted with Turf field tyres as an experiment for use on the sand, arrived on 7 October. The vehicle proved to be capable of handling the sometimes difficult terrain on the East Beach, and while intended primarily to launch the ILB, was also used to assist with the beach recovery of the 12m Mersey, towing the trailer containing the recovery skids.

The Mersey stayed at Cromer for more than two years, during which time she performed a number of services as the work of lifesaving continued throughout the boathouse construction. Her first service launch took place on 25 February 1997, when she assisted the cargo vessel *Inowroclaw*. On 9 July, she assisted in the search for three missing divers nine miles north-north-east of the station. After locating the diving support craft *Crusader*, she commenced to search the area assisted by the Sheringham Atlantic 75 B-702 *Manchester Unity of Oddfellows* and another fishing vessel. Despite poor

Above: *Launching tractor TA34 (registration number R814 YGV), sent to Cromer in 1997, was supplied to assist with launching the ILB as well as moving the skids needed for the carriage-launched lifeboat. (Nicholas Leach)*

Right: *Richard Davies, crew member since 1960 and coxswain from 1976 until retirement from the post in December 1999. (Paul Russell)*

visibility, the Sheringham lifeboat located the three divers, who were taken to Mundesley Beach escorted by *Her Majesty the Queen*. The lifeboat then returned to the scene in reduced visibility to locate the diving support craft, which was also escorted safely back to the shore. On 17 April 1998, the Mersey went to the oil rig support vessel *Laurids Skomager*, which had gearbox failure and was at anchor twelve miles north of the station. Although a tug had been requested and was proceeding, the lifeboat launched at 10 a.m. in a light north-westerly wind and was alongside the casualty within an hour. A tow was passed and the vessel was towed twenty-four miles to the tug. At 2.30 p.m. the tow was transferred to the tug, so the lifeboat returned to station.

Perhaps the most notable service performed by the relief Mersey took place in the early hours of 6 November 1998. At 12.30 a.m., Great Yarmouth Coastguard requested that the lifeboat launch to the 11m auxiliary yacht *Tange*, of Whitby, on passage from Whitby to Calais and drifting out of control towards shoal water and oil rigs sixteen miles off Cromer, after her crew had been overwhelmed by the conditions. The yacht was without power and in the force eight winds and rough seas, the crew of three were finding it impossible to make progress under sail. *Her Majesty The Queen* launched from the beach twenty minutes after the call, with Second Coxswain Billy Davies in command. He had taken additional crew members because of the likelihood that two of his crew would have to be put aboard the casualty. It was a bitterly cold night and as the lifeboat cleared the lee of the land the sea became very rough, making conditions for the rescuers very unpleasant.

Two of the merchant vessels which responded to the Mayday relay were asked to provide a lee for the casualty and monitor her situation until the lifeboat arrived. The lifeboat arrived on scene within an hour of launching to find the casualty rolling violently. Communication had been established with the yacht, and it became clear that the three on board were not in a position to help themselves. Second Coxswain Davies decided the safest option would be to put two lifeboatmen aboard and establish a tow, but the erratic movement of the casualty made getting anyone aboard very difficult. But with the ferry *Norbay* maintaining a lee, the lifeboat manoeuvred from leeward of the casualty to her starboard quarter. From here, she was edged close enough for crew members John Davies and John Balls to jump across. Once on board the casualty, the lifeboatmen found the yacht's crew frightened and cold but otherwise unharmed. They began to prepare the yacht for a difficult tow, spending twenty minutes preparing a

Launch of 12m Mersey Her Majesty The Queen, 14 September 1997, with the piling for the new lifeboat house and slipway in the background. (Paul Russell)

12m Mersey Her Majesty The Queen *upright on the beach during the recovery procedure, 14 September 1997. (Paul Russell)*

towing bridle which ran from the bow down both sides of the yacht and was made fast to strong points on the deck. Once the towline had been passed to the lifeboat and made fast, the tow began at 2.19 a.m. with the lifeboat set on course for Great Yarmouth, forty miles away. The ferry *Norbay* agreed to escort the lifeboat to provide a lee until more sheltered conditions were reached, while the second cargo vessel *Stefan K* was released.

The initial stages of the tow were difficult as the lifeboat was beam on and the sea was breaking over her on occasions, but despite this the yacht towed well. The two lifeboatmen on board took turns to steer and by 4.20 a.m. the tow was within four miles of the coast at Cromer, so Second Coxswain Davies was happy to release *Norbay*. Keeping close to the coast, the lifeboat continued to Great Yarmouth, arriving at the harbour entrance at 7.30 a.m., just over five hours after the tow began. After they had been safely landed, the three crew on board the yacht were taken to the town's Seamen's Mission to recover from their ordeal. The local coastguard praised the lifeboat crew, summed up by Yarmouth Coastguard watch manager, who said, 'The lifeboat crew managed to attach the tow in horrendous and dangerous conditions, and we are grateful to them.' With the yacht secure, at 9.17 a.m. the lifeboat left Yarmouth and sailed for Cromer; she was recovered, refuelled and ready for service at 12.01 p.m., eleven hours after launching.

In assessing this service, Martyn Smith, divisional inspector of lifeboats for the East, commented: 'This was an eleven-hour service to a yacht in danger of foundering off the exposed coast of North Norfolk. Second Coxswain Davies exhibited a high standard of seamanship and considerable initiative. All the crew demonstrated the necessary skills required to achieve a successful outcome in poor weather conditions.' Second Coxswain Davies was accorded the Thanks of the Institution Inscribed on Vellum, and Vellum service certificates went to the seven crew members involved: John Jonas, assistant mechanic; Gary Humphrey, second assistant mechanic; John Davies; John Balls; Adrian Woods; Paul Jeffries and Giovanni Vanzino. For crewmen Jeffries and Vanzino, it was their first night-time service on the all-weather lifeboat. A letter of appreciation from the director of the RNLI was sent to the masters and crew of the two merchant ships involved.

On 24 March 1999, the 47ft Tyne *Ruby and Arthur Reed II* returned to station after having been away for over two years while the new boathouse and slipway were built. She had departed in November 1996, and after a refit at Langney Marine, Eastbourne, was used as a Relief lifeboat, serving at Selsey from 14 August 1997 to 5 September 1997,

Shoreham Harbour from 5 September 1997 to 13 September 1997, and Padstow from 15 September 1997 to 14 November 1997. She was then taken to Falmouth Boat Co. to have her hull anti-fouled before going to St Helier on 25 November 1997, and moving to Appledore on 13 December 1997, where she stayed until 17 November 1998. Once the new boathouse was nearing completion, she was taken for overhaul at Denton's Shipyard at Strood, where she arrived on 26 November 1998. When this was complete, she returned to her station to be hauled up the new slipway for the first time.

The new lifeboat house and slipway were formally opened and dedicated at a ceremony on 20 May 1999 at 2.30 p.m., overseen by Cromer branch chairman, Tony Webster. The keys to the new house were handed over by Alan Korn, chairman of May Gurney Construction, which built the new house. The service of dedication was conducted by the Rt Revd Peter Nott, bishop of Norwich, assisted by Canon David Hayden, vicar of Cromer and honorary chaplain. A plaque in the boathouse was unveiled to mark the occasion. The lifeboat, which was also re-dedicated during the proceedings, should have been launched at the end of the ceremony, but this was cancelled as the weather was too rough to rehouse safely. The new house was funded from the bequests of Kenneth Brian Shaw, Howard and Margot Backhouse, a gift from Brenda Green together with donations in memory of Michael Victor Harman and Herbert James Raven.

On the evening of 2 October 1999, two men were reported to be in difficulties 150 yards from the beach, to the east of the pier. When Coxswain Richard Davies arrived at the scene one man was ashore, but one was still struggling in the water. Coxswain Davies dived into the sea and swam to the man, supporting him until the ILB arrived. For his bravery, he was awarded the Thanks of the Institution Inscribed on Vellum, and Vellum certificates were awarded to ILB Senior Helmsman Adrian Woods, and crew members Martin Steward and Adam Lincoln.

Ruby and Arthur Reed II continued the work of lifesaving from her new base and in the early hours of 11 March 2000 was one of five lifeboats involved in assisting the P&O North Sea ferry *Norstar* after a blaze had broken out in the funnel of the ship's main

Ruby and Arthur Reed II *launching to the yacht* Lady Patience, *which was in difficulties within site of the pier, 3 October 1999.* Lady Patience *had sail and engine problems, and her two crew were incapacitated, one needing the attention of a doctor who was taken out by the ILB. The yacht was towed to Bacton by the offshore lifeboat, where the Great Yarmouth and Gorleston lifeboat took over. (Paul Russell)*

Three Cromer lifeboat personalities: Billy Davies (coxswain 1999-2003), Jim Smith (honorary secretary 1978-1999) and Richard Davies (coxswain 1976-1999), 5 August 1999. (Paul Russell)

engine room. The ferry had sailed from Hull and alerted the Coastguard to the fire when she was eight miles off the Norfolk coast, just past Cromer. on board, the 721 passengers were ordered to muster stations on deck as crewmen tackled the fire in the funnel. The captain was forced to shut down one engine on the 173m-long vessel in case the fire spread, while other ships in the area were called to assist. Eight specialist fire officers from Suffolk were winched aboard by the search and rescue helicopter from RAF Wattisham to help contain the fire. The speed with which they reached the casualty ensured the situation was quickly controlled. At different times, Wells, Cromer, Gorleston, Lowestoft and Aldeburgh lifeboats all stood by as the ferry slowly moved south.

Another noteworthy service was performed on 10 July 2000 when *Ruby and Arthur Reed II* launched with Coxswain Billy Davies in command at 10.32 p.m. into a north-westerly force nine gale and rough seas to go to the aid of the 77ft ex-trawler *Excelsior*, with a crew of nine on board, whose skipper had reported steering failure several miles off north-east Norfolk. The lifeboat was two miles offshore before the crew was able to leave the shelter of the wheelhouse to put up radio and radar aerials. Finding nothing in the area upon arrival and learning that *Excelsior* was now on a south-easterly course, the lifeboat set off to intercept the vessel, taking heavy seas in the process. As sea conditions worsened, the lifeboat was hit by a huge wave from astern, causing her to broach heavily to port and stalling the port engine. Quick thinking and superb boat handling by Coxswain Davies prevented a full capsize as he put the starboard engine full astern, bringing the boat back onto an even keel. After restarting the port engine, passage was resumed and the casualty was reached at 12.16 a.m. on 11 July.

To attempt to transfer lifeboat crew with both boats rolling and plunging in the heavy sea was too dangerous, so Coxswain Davies manoeuvred abeam of the casualty where a line was successfully passed and secured to a bridle, enabling the vessel to be turned into the wind. The casualty's sails were then lowered and the main boom secured. Meanwhile, the Caister independent lifeboat *Bernard Matthews*, which had launched to assist at

Above: Ruby and Arthur Reed II *out of the water at Goodchild Marine, Burgh Castle, near Great Yarmouth, on 29 October 2000 awaiting maintenance work involving the removal of her engines. She has been taken to Goodchild Marine on a number of occasions for maintenance and repair work.* (Paul Russell)

Left: *An unusual photograph showing relief 47ft Tyne* City of Sheffield *(ON.1131), with Hartlepool Lfeboat still across her stern, launching on exercise on 3 December 2000. This lifeboat served at Hartlepool from 1997 to 2000, having been originally been built for Whitby in 1988. She came to Cromer directly from Hartlepool, after being replaced there by a larger lifeboat.* (Paul Russell)

10.52 p.m., arrived and took station ahead to guide the tow to the approaches of Lowestoft harbour, with those at the helm of the Cromer lifeboat displaying exceptional seamanship in towing the vessel through the narrow channels to Corton Roads, and finally, with the tow shortened, to a berth in Lowestoft. The lifeboat then stood down at the end of a long and difficult service in appalling conditions but was unable to return to Cromer for two days due to the poor weather. A Letter of Appreciation signed by the operations director was sent commending Coxswain Davies and the crew for their skill, seamanship and determination during this difficult service.

During 2001, the lifeboat was called upon to perform a number of long services. The first took place on 14 January 2001 when *Ruby and Arthur Reed II* launched at 11.15 p.m. in rough seas, good visibility and a north-easterly force six wind to the 86ft tug *Golden Cross*, which was acting as official escort to HM Yacht *Britannia*. The tug was reported to be losing power four miles north-east of Cromer. Arriving on the scene just before midnight and finding the casualty drifting having lost all power, Coxswain Billy Davies manoeuvred the lifeboat into position for a line to be passed to the four crew members on the tug, who secured it. A long tow to Great Yarmouth, thirty miles down the coast, then commenced. At 1.03 a.m., Gorleston lifeboat *Samarbeta* arrived on scene to escort the tow and provide assistance if required. The tug was towed without incident into Great Yarmouth and safely berthed at 9 a.m., but since weather conditions were unfavourable *Ruby and Arthur Reed II* remained in port until 16 January.

Two relatively routine services were performed in February 2001. On 16 February 2001, *Ruby and Arthur Reed II* assisted the occupant of a 16ft sailing dinghy in trouble eleven miles north of Cromer. The lifeboat reached the casualty at 11.03 a.m. and, after assessing the health of the occupant, escorted the craft to safety. Less than ten days later, on 25 February, *Ruby and Arthur Reed II* launched at 8.20 a.m. to assist the 2,400-ton tanker *Zanita*, which had lost power in a heavy swell and a force seven near gale accompanied by squally snow showers. The lifeboat arrived on scene within half an hour to find the vessel drifting at 4–5 knots, and stood by whilst attempts were made to restart the ship's engine. When these succeeded she soon got underway and headed for Yarmouth Roads at reduced speed. Requested by the tanker's master to remain in attendance, the lifeboat continued to escort the vessel which made good progress under her own power. Both craft arrived safely at an anchorage in Yarmouth Roads, so with no further assistance required, the lifeboat carried on to Lowestoft where she remained until weather conditions moderated to allow a return to Cromer.

On 20 June 2001, a new inshore lifeboat, *Seahorse III* (D-568), was placed on station. Funded by the Surrey-based Seahorse charity, the new ILB was officially named and dedicated at the station on 20 October 2002 on the town's seafront, having already been in service for more than a year and undertaken a number of rescues. At the naming ceremony, opened by Tony Webster, chairman of the station branch, dozens of local representatives and guests were in attendance. Richard Leeds, acting station honorary secretary, expressed gratitude to the donors on behalf of the whole station for the new boat: 'They have given something in the region of £15,000 to £18,000 for this boat, which is extremely generous. We are privileged to have been chosen for this amount of money.' James Woodhouse, a member of the RNLI's Committee of Management, accepted the lifeboat on behalf of the RNLI, and handed it over to the station branch. The service of dedication was overseen by Peter Paine, Great Yarmouth's port chaplain, after which the new boat was formally named by Mrs Barbara New. The D class inflatable was then launched for a short demonstration.

D-568 Seahorse III *being put through her paces in the surf off the Pier, 5 August 2001. (Paul Russell)*

The scene outside the lifeboat museum on 20 October 2002 during the naming and dedication ceremony of D-568 Seahorse III. *(Paul Russell)*

During 2002, the relief 47ft Tyne *Lord Saltoun* (ON.1138) spent some time on station in place of *Ruby and Arthur Reed II* and performed a number of services. On 13 February she launched into a heavy sea to assist the converted tug *Jack Rose*, which had lost all power and was drifting approximately a mile and a half off Bacton, unable to anchor because of gas pipes in the area, while the Dutch coaster *Star Borneo* was standing off. The lifeboat was on scene at 9.30 a.m. A tow was rigged and ten minutes later the tow proceeded towards Great Yarmouth, from where a commercial tug was organised to take over the tow from the lifeboat. On 20 June, *Lord Saltoun* was again out on service, this time assisting the 43ft motor cruiser *One Chance* five miles east of the lifeboat station. On reaching the casualty, the lifeboat took it in tow and proceeded to Great Yarmouth. Whilst on passage back to station, she was asked by the Coastguard to assist the RSPCA in rescuing a whale marooned at high tide at Walcott.

May 2003 proved to be a busy month for both Cromer lifeboats. On 7 May, *Ruby and Arthur Reed II* launched to help a yacht without power and becalmed about twenty miles north-east of the station. The vessel, on passage from IJmuiden to Grimsby, was towed into Great Yarmouth harbour. Four days later, the ILB towed in a fishing skiff which was taking water and had lost power off Overstrand. On 24 May, *Ruby and Arthur Reed II* went to the aid of the yacht *Rambling Rose*, about four miles off Cromer, and towed it towards Wells before handing over to the Wells lifeboat. And on the last day of the month a fine rescue occurred, this one demonstrating the dangers of bathing in the sea. A group of children swimming off the east beach went out too far to sea and two girls were carried by the tide and north-easterly breeze past the end of a groyne, under another groyne and beneath the pier. Seeing that they were in difficulty, a member of the public threw a lifebuoy down to them from the pier. When this landed short, Alan Herbert was lowered down to them on a buoy and a rope at considerable personal danger. He was joined by one of two North Norfolk District Council lifeguards, who had swum under the pier. They managed to grab hold of the girls, but one was face down in the water. Finding no signs of breathing, Mr Herbert applied mouth-to-mouth resuscitation.

By this time, the inshore lifeboat had launched and, approaching the pier, the ILB crew saw one of the lifeguards holding up a child. The ILB went under the pier and one crewman entered the water to go between the pier legs. Another lifeguard and Mr Herbert brought a girl to the ILB, onto which she was lifted. She appeared unconscious but was breathing and so was placed in the recovery position. The two adults were also taken on board the ILB and all three taken to the beach, where they were passed to paramedics. The girl was taken to hospital in critical condition, and later recovered. The ILB returned to the pier and picked up the other lifeguard and child. A second crew member entered the water to assist, and although the second child was disoriented she was otherwise okay. She was also taken back to the beach and handed over to paramedics. The first child was evacuated from the scene by the Norfolk Air Ambulance helicopter. Following this rescue, fifty-three-year-old Mr Herbert, of Norwich, whose efforts had saved the two girls, was awarded the Royal Humane Resuscitation Certificate. Major General Christopher Tyler, secretary of the Royal Humane Society, said, 'If it wasn't for the swift and efficient action of Mr Herbert, this incident could easily have ended in tragedy. He was the first to spot the emergency and was quick to take action, even though he risked being caught up in the strong currents himself.'

During 2003, improvements for the lifeboat station and museum were announced. As part of the £5 million Seafront Enhancement Project implemented by the North Norfolk District Council, a new lifeboat museum was to be built to the east of the East Gangway boathouse on the site of the Rocket House café and ILB house, both of which will be demolished. The initial plans for the new museum incorporated a lift tower as well as a new café. Inside the museum, *H.F. Bailey* will be the centrepiece of a series of new displays about the town's lifeboats. When the lifeboat has been moved out of the 1902 lifeboat house, where it has been housed since the early 1990s, this boathouse will be converted for the inshore lifeboat, so the ILB crew can be provided with greatly improved facilities.

During the summer of 2003, *Ruby and Arthur Reed II* went to Goodchild Marine, Burgh Castle, near Great Yarmouth, arriving on 12 July to have a new Pyrogen Fire System fitted. While she was away from station, relief 47ft Tyne *St Cybi II (Civil Service No.40)* (ON.1095) was on duty, and performed two services. Later in the year, Coxswain John Davies, who took up the post in October, went to the RNLI's headquarters in Poole so that he could see the new design of fast slipway lifeboat with which the station is to be equipped. The new Tamar class lifeboat, in planned development since 1994, had already extensively toured the country and visited many stations before Coxswain Davies, and other coxswains of Tyne lifeboats from around the country, looked at the boat. The prototype boat has been built mainly as an experimental craft as well as a test bed for a new system of computer-controlled boat management. The first Tamars are due to enter the RNLI fleet in 2005 and will offer considerable improvements over the Tyne class. At 16m in length, the new design is two metres longer than the Tyne and also considerably higher to provide better visibility when searching for a casualty, but the new boathouse at Cromer was built with the Tamar in mind. The Tamar, with a top speed of 25 knots in line with the new generation of fast afloat lifeboats, has an endurance of up to ten hours at full speed and all-weather capability that is a pre-requisite for all RNLI vessels.

The Tamar represents the future of Cromer lifeboat station and will, like the boats that have served since the station was established, provide the volunteer lifeboat crews with the best equipment and technology available. These volunteers have been ready to answer the call whenever it has come, whether the casualties are the sailing ships of the nineteenth century, the steamers of the twentieth or the pleasure yachts of the twenty-first. The lifeboats get ever more advanced and the station now boasts one of the RNLI's most modern lifeboat houses. However, the people involved with the running and management must take centre stage, for without them no lifeboat would operate. And so it is fitting that the crew, station officials and supporters were recognised in 2004 by the awarding of an RNLI Bicentenary Vellum. The presenting of this Vellum, an award decided during a meeting of the RNLI's Trustee Committee in November 2003, will mark 200 years of lifesaving and heroism. During these two centuries, the Cromer lifeboats and their crews have undertaken 1,318 services and saved 1,741 lives.

Left: *Billy Davies, coxswain from December 1999 to October 2003. (Paul Russell)*

Below: *Cromer lifeboat crew and station personnel, September 2003. (Paul Russell)*

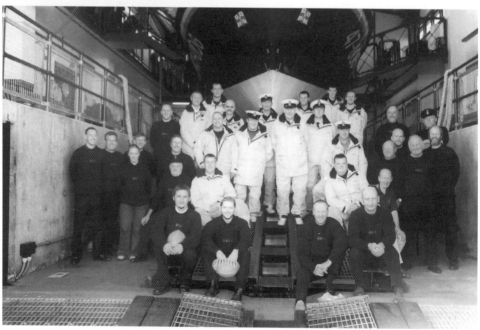

Appendix 1

Lifeboat Summary

On station	ON	Name Donor	Type Year built	Launches/ lives saved
Pre-RNLI lifeboats				
1805–30	—	[Unnamed] Norwich Mariners' Association.	25ft Greathead 1804	At least 5/31
1830–58★	—	[Unnamed] Norfolk Shipwreck Association.	31ft North Country 1830	At least 5/15

★ Taken over by the RNLI in 1857

On station	ON	Name Donor	Type Year built	Launches/ lives saved
RNLI lifeboats				
1858–68	—	[Unnamed] RNLI general funds.	34ft Peake self-righter 1858	6/5
1868–84	—	*Benjamin Bond Cabbell* Legacy of Mr B. Bond Cabbell, London.	34ft Self-righter 1868	9/31
1884–1902	12	*Benjamin Bond Cabbell* Legacy of Miss Ann Egdell, Alnwick.	35ft Cromer 1884	12/26
1902–31★	495	*Louisa Heartwell* Legacy of Miss E. Heartwell, London.	38ft Liverpool 1902	115/195

★ No.2 boat 1923 - 1931

On station	ON	Name Donor	Type Year built	Launches/ lives saved
No.1 station				
1923–24	670	*H.F. Bailey* Legacy of H.F. Bailey, Brockenhurst.	46ft 6in N & S (M) 1923	3/12
1924–35	694	*H.F. Bailey* As above.	45ft Watson (M) 1924	67/160
1928–29	714	*H.F. Bailey II* As above.	45ft 6in Watson (M) 1928	3/5
1935–45	777	*H.F. Bailey* As above.	46ft Watson (M) 1935	154/448
1945– 66	840	*Henry Blogg* RNLI Funds.	46ft Watson (M) 1945	99/149

On station	ON	Name Donor	Type Year built	Launches/ lives saved
Current station				
1967–84	990	*Ruby and Arthur Reed* Gift of Mrs R.M. Reed, Eastbourne.	48ft 6in Oakley (M) 1966	125/58
1985–96	1097	*Ruby and Arthur Reed II* Bequest of Mrs R.M. Reed, plus special local appeal, gifts and legacies.	47ft Tyne (M) 1985	75/29
1996–99	1189	*Her Majesty The Queen* (TSD) Appeal to Police Constabularies in UK with other gifts and legacies.	12m Mersey (M) 1993	19/6
1999–	1097	*Ruby and Arthur Reed II* Bequest of Mrs R.M. Reed, plus special local appeal, gifts and legacies.	47ft Tyne (M) 1985	

On station	ON	Name	Type	Launches/lives saved

No.2 station

1923–31	495	*Louisa Heartwell* Legacy of Miss E. Heartwell, London.	38ft Liverpool 1902	6/0
1931–34	514	*Alexandra* Freemasons of London.	35ft Liverpool 1903	3/0
1934–64	770	*Harriot Dixon* Legacy of Mr W. E. Dixon.	35ft 6in Liverpool (M) 1934	55/20
1964– Jun.1967	980	*William Henry and Mary King* Legacy of Miss J. G. King, Surrey, plus RNLI funds.	37ft Oakley (M) 1967	12/1

(M) indicates motor lifeboat   (TSD) indicates Temporary Station Duty

Inshore lifeboats

3.1967–10.1969	D-101	—	15'3" RFD PB16	19/4
1970–10.71	D-26	—	15'3" RFD PB16	16/6
3.1972–84	D-197	— Gravesend Branch.	15'3" RFD PB16	108/48
1984–8.92	D-307	*Spirit of Round Table* Sheringham and Cromer Round Table.	15'3" RFD PB16	81/30
12.8.1992 – 6.2001	D-436	*Chloe* Gift in memory of Chloe Long.	16'3" Avon EA16	54/6
20.6.2001 –	D-568	*Seahorse III* The Seahorse Ball.	16'3" Avon EA16	
1978-2003		Relief Inshore Lifeboats		40/3

Relief lifeboats on temporary duty

1931 & 1932	680	*City of Bradford*	45ft Watson (M)	1/0
1940 & 1941	694	*J.B. Proudfoot*	45ft Watson (M)	7/0
1958 & 1961	728	*Cunard*	45ft 6in Watson (M)	3/1
6-9.1964	834	*Jose Neville* (No.2 station)	35ft 6in Liverpool (M)	1/0
6-12.1965	778	*Edward and Isabella Irwin*	46ft Watson (M)	0/0
6.1973-3.74	821	*The Good Hope*	46ft Watson (M)	10/4
10.1978-4.79	849	*William Gammon - Manchester & District XXX*	46ft 9in Watson (M)	2/1
9.1984-12.85	926	*Guy and Clare Hunter*	46ft 9in Watson (M)	11/34
4-10.1987	1075	*Sam and Joan Woods*	47ft Tyne	1/0
11-12.1990	1122	*Owen and Ann Aisher*	47ft Tyne	0/0
8-12.1991	1122	*Owen and Ann Aisher*	47ft Tyne	0/0
3.1999	1075	*Sam and Joan Woods*	47ft Tyne	0/0
2-3.2000	1142	*Mariners Friend*	47ft Tyne	0/0
10-12.2000	1131	*City of Sheffield*	47ft Tyne	0/0
2-7.2002	1138	*Lord Saltoun*	47ft Tyne	5/0
7-8.2003	1095	*St Cybi II (Civil Service No.40)*	47ft Tyne	2/0

Appendix 2
Lifeboat Details

First lifeboat (not named)

Years on station	1805–1830
Record	At least 5 launches, 31 lives saved
Donor	Local subscriptions
Type	'Greathead' or North Country non-self-righter, ten-oared
Year built	1804
Builder	Henry Greathead, South Shields
Dimensions	Length 25ft, breadth 8ft 6in
Notes	Transferred to Wells 1830

Second lifeboat (not named)

Years on station	1830–1858
Record	At least 5 launches, 15 lives saved
Donor	Norfolk Shipwreck Association
Cost	£160
Type	North Country non-self-righter, twelve-oared
Year built	1830
Builder	Robson, South Shields
Dimensions	Length 31ft, breadth 9ft 6in, depth 3ft 9in
Disposal	Worn out 1858 and sold 1860

First RNLI lifeboat (not named)

Years on station	October 1858–August 1868
Record	6 launches, 5 lives saved
Donor	RNLI Funds
Cost	£212 16s 5d
Type	Peake self-righter, twelve-oared
Year built	1858
Builder	Forrestt, Limehouse
Dimensions	Length 34ft, breadth 8ft 3in
Notes	Damaged by fire at Forrestt's yard June 1858 but subsequently rebuilt
Disposal	Broken up 1868

Benjamin Bond Cabbell

Years on station	August 1868–September 1884
Record	9 launches, 31 lives saved
Donor	Legacy of Mr B. Bond Cabbell, of London
Naming ceremony	4 September 1868, christened by Miss Buxton, daughter of Dowager Lady Buxton of Cromer
Cost	£307
Type	Self-righter, ten-oared
Year built	1868
Builder	Woolfe, Shadwell
Dimensions	Length 34ft, breadth 8ft 9in, depth 4ft 4in
Disposal	Broken up May 1885

Benjamin Bond Cabbell

Years on station	September 1884–September 1902
Record	12 launches, 26 lives saved
Donor	Legacy of Miss Ann Egdell, Alnwick, Northumberland
Naming ceremony	29 September 1884, christened by Mrs Bond Cabbell
Cost	£365 3s 6d

Official Number	12
Type	Cromer non-self-righter, fourteen-oared
Year built	1884
Builder	James Beeching, Great Yarmouth
Dimensions	Length 35ft, breadth 10ft, depth 4ft
Disposal	Sold locally 1902

Louisa Heartwell

Years on station	4 September 1902–15 May 1931 (No.2 lifeboat 1923-31)
Record	115 launches, 195 lives saved
Donor	Miss Emily Heartwell, London
Naming ceremony	9 September 1902, christened by Lady Suffield
Cost	£981 12s 0d
Official Number	495
Type	Liverpool non-self-righter, fourteen-oared
Year built	1902
Builder	Thames Ironworks, Blackwall
Dimensions	Length 38ft, breadth 10ft 9in
Notes	No.2 lifeboat 1923-1931
Disposal	Sold on 20 May 1931 for £55 to Nathanial Green, of Stiffkey, and converted into a motor cruiser the following year by Warfolk Brothers at King's Lynn. She was renamed *Waiora* and was kept on the Norfolk coast for a number of years. She was later fitted with a single 125bhp Chrysler six-cylinder petrol engine and seems to have moved to Wales, as she was at Aberaeron in the 1960s and later moved to Barry Dock. By the 1990s she had become a houseboat on the Grand Union Canal, and was kept at Batchworth Moorings, near Rickmansworth. She later moved to the Chichester Canal where she remains in use as a houseboat on the Canal.

H.F. Bailey

Years on station	No.1 lifeboat, 26 May 1923–4 May 1924
Record	3 launches, 12 lives saved
Donor	Legacy of Henry Francis Bailey, Brockenhurst, Surrey, a London merchant, born in Norfolk, who died 1916
Naming ceremony	26 July 1923, christened by Lady Suffield
Cost	£10,993 6s 0d
Official Number	670
Type	Norfolk & Suffolk motor
Year built	1923
Builder	J. Samuel White, East Cowes, IOW
Dimensions	Length 46ft 6ins, breadth 12ft 9in, depth 5ft 3in
Engines	Single 80bhp Weyburn DE6, range 45 nautical miles
Notes	Transferred to Great Yarmouth & Gorleston in May 1924 and renamed *John and Mary Meiklam of Gladswood;* she served at Gorleston until 1939 and then spent more than a decade as a Reserve lifeboat.
Disposal	Sold out of service on 3 October 1952 for £950 to Captain J.D. Reed, BR Marine Deptartment, London. Renamed *Pen Cu,* she was used at Fishguard from 1952 as a British Rail workboat to embark or disembark pilots. In the 1950s she was fitted with a wheelhouse. During 1981 she sustained a damaged fender and was grounded on the quayside where a Dr Anderson found her 'in a rather sorry state.'. He bought her in June 1986 and she was then taken overland to Gorleston in July 1986 for restoration and display inside the Gorleston lifeboat house.

H.F. Bailey

Years on station	No.1 lifeboat, 19 August 1924–14 December 1935
Record	67 launches, 160 lives saved
Donor	Legacy of Henry Francis Bailey, Brockenhurst, Hants
Cost	£7,579 16s 3d
Official Number	694
Type	Watson motor
Year built	1924
Builder	J. Samuel White, East Cowes, IOW
Dimensions	Length 45ft, breadth 12ft 6in, depth 5ft 9in

Engines	Single 80bhp White DE.6 6-cylinder petrol
Notes	Renamed *J.B. Proudfoot* and transferred to the Reserve Fleet 1936.
Disposal	Sold out of service in September 1953 for £350 to Messrs Herd & MacKenzie, Buckie. She was rebuilt in 1957 as a single screw yacht by Herd & MacKenzie, and fitted with a single 94bhp Gardner six-cylinder diesel engine. Renamed *Gremarie*, she was registered in Newcastle-upon-Tyne. By the late 1970s she had moved to Puerto Estapona, Spain.

H.F. Bailey II

Years on station	No.1 lifeboat, 4 December 1928–14 May 1929
Record	3 launches, 5 lives saved
Donor	Legacy of Henry Francis Bailey, Brockenhurst, Surrey
Cost	£8470 5s 9d
Official Number	714
Type	Watson motor
Year built	1928
Builder	S.E. Saunders, East Cowes, IOW
Dimensions	Length 45ft 6in, breadth 12ft 6in
Engines	Twin 40bhp Weyburn CE4
Notes	Served at Cromer on temporary duty during the 1928-9 winter; then transferred to Selsey in 1929 and renamed *Canadian Pacific*. She served at Selsey until 1937, during which time she saved a further 30 lives.
Disposal	Destroyed by fire at the yard of Groves & Gutteridge, Cowes, on 18 June 1937.

H.F. Bailey

Years on station	No.1 lifeboat, 15 December 1935–20 December 1945
Record	154 launches, 448 lives saved
Donor	Legacy of Henry Francis Bailey, Brockenhurst, Surrey
Naming ceremony	27 August 1937, christened by Sir Samuel Hoare
Cost	£7,307 14s 0d
Official Number	777
Type	Watson cabin motor
Year built	1935
Builder	Groves & Gutteridge, Cowes, IOW
Dimensions	Length 46ft, breadth 12ft 9in, depth 6ft 3in
Engines	Twin 40bhp Ferry VE4 diesels
Notes	Transferred to Helvick Head in August 1946, where she served until 1960, launching 24 times on service saving 12 lives; she was then transferred into the Reserve fleet for a further 12 years.
Disposal	Sold in June 1973 for £3,001 to Leisure Sport Ltd, RMC House, Feltham, Middlesex, and displayed at Thorpe Water Park from 1973. Later returned to Cromer, she has been restored and placed on display in the Lifeboat Museum.

Alexandra

Years on station	No.2 lifeboat, 22 May 1931–July 1934
Record	3 launches, no lives saved
Donor	Freemasons of London
Cost	£944 14s 5d
Official Number	514
Type	Liverpool non-self-righter, fourteen-oared
Year built	1903
Builder	Thames Ironworks, Blackwall
Dimensions	Length 35ft, breadth 10ft, depth 4ft 2in
Notes	Previously stationed at Hope Cove from 1903-1930
Disposal	Sold out of service on 23 July 1934 and converted into a privately owned auxiliary ketch yacht named *Alexandra*; she was last reported at Port Bannatyne in Scotland in the 1960s but her current whereabouts are unknown.

Harriot Dixon

Years on station	No.2 lifeboat, 4 August 1934–15 June 1964
Record	55 launches, 20 lives saved

Donor	Legacy of Mr W.E. Dixon, Worthing
Naming ceremony	27 August 1937, christened by the Rt Hon Sir Samuel Hoare, Bt
Cost	£3,316 10s 2d
Official Number	770
Type	Liverpool motor
Year	1934
Builder	Groves & Gutteridge, Cowes
Dimensions	Length 35ft 6in, breadth 10ft 3in, depth 4ft 5in
Engines	Single 35bhp Weyburn AE6 diesel
Disposal	Sold out of service in December 1964 and converted into a cabin cruiser, moored initially at St Olaves on the Broads, and later moved to Blakeney. She was renamed *Sareter* and a deckhouse was added.

William Henry and Mary King

Years on station	No.2 lifeboat, 24 October 1964–22 June 1967
Record	12 launches, 1 life saved
Donor	Legacy of Miss Jane Graham King, Sutton, Surrey; in memory of her father and mother, plus RNLI funds
Naming Ceremony	8 July 1965, christened by HRH Princess Marina, The Duchess of Kent
Cost	£33,000
Official Number	980
Type	Oakley
Year	1964
Builder	J.Samuel White, East Cowes
Dimensions	Length 37ft, breadth 11ft 6in
Engines	Twin 52hp Parsons Porbeagle
Notes	Transferred to Bridlington in 1967 where she served until 1988.
Disposal	Scrapped in 1991 and taken to London to be used as a climbing frame at Childrens Culture Centre, Park School, Avron Road.

Henry Blogg

Years on station	No.1 lifeboat, 20 December 1945–3 April 1966
Record	99 launches, 149 lives saved
Donor	RNLI Funds
Naming ceremony	19 August 1948, christened by Sir John Cunningham
Cost	£15,241 17s 6d
Official Number	840
Type	Watson cabin motor, midship steering
Year	1945

Naming ceremony of William Henry and Mary King *on 8 July 1965 at the East Beach, the last No.2 lifeboat to serve the station. The Reserve lifeboat* Edward and Isabella Irwin *is on the slipway in the background. (From an old postcard supplied by Paul Russell)*

NAMING CEREMONY R.N.L.B. "WILLIAM HENRY AND MARY KING"

Builder	Sussex Yacht Company, Shoreham-by-Sea
Dimensions	Length 46ft, breadth 12ft 9in
Engines	Twin 40bhp Ferry VE4 diesels
Notes	Originally named *Millie Walton* and destined for Douglas, but reallocated to Cromer and renamed in 1946. After Cromer, she served in the Relief Fleet for ten years, during which time she saved 65 lives and launched 58 times on service.
Disposal	Sold out of service in April 1977 for £5,500 to Talbot H. Evans-Thomas, of Haverfordwest, and renamed *Blogg of Cromer*. Moored on the river Severn since the 1990s, she was based at Upton-on-Severn in 2003.

Ruby and Arthur Reed

Years on station	30 April 1967–4 September 1984 [Operational from June 1967]
Record	125 launches, 58 lives saved
Donor	Gift of Mrs R. M. Reed, Eastbourne, in memory of her husband of Stamford
Naming ceremony	21 June 1967, christened by Mrs R. M. Reed
Cost	£60,000
Operational Number	48-03
Official Number	990
Type	Oakley
Year	1966
Builder	William Osborne, Littlehampton
Dimensions	Length 48ft 6in, breadth 14ft
Engines	Twin 110hp Gardner 6LX diesels
Notes	Transferred to St Davids in 1985 where she served until 1988.
Disposal	Sold 30 September 1988 without engines to Hythe Village Marina, where she was placed on display outside as a static exhibit.

Ruby and Arthur Reed II

Years on station	16 December 1985–17 November 1996 and 24 March 1999–
Record	75 launches, 29 lives saved (1985-96)
Donor	Legacy of Mrs R.M. Reed and Local Appeal
Naming ceremony	20 June 1986, christened by HRH The Duke of Kent
Cost	£430,000
Operational Number	47-006
Official Number	1097
Type	Tyne
Year	1985
Builder	Fairey Marine, Cowes
Dimensions	Length 47ft, breadth 15ft
Engines	Twin 485 hp General Motors 6V-92-TA diesels
Notes	From August 1997 until November 1998 she served in the Relief Fleet while the new boathouse and slipway were constructed at Cromer; she served as a Relief lifeboat at Selsey, Shoreham, Padstow, St Helier and Appledore.

Her Majesty The Queen

Years on station	17 November 1996–4 March 1999
Record	19 launches, 6 lives saved
Donor	Appeal to all Police Constabularies in UK, with other gifts and legacies
Naming ceremony	16 July 1993, christened by HM The Queen at Ramsgate Harbour, Kent
Cost	£650,000
Operational Number	12-30
Official Number	1189
Type	Mersey
Year	1993
Builder	Hull moulded by Green Marine, Lymington; fitted out by Souter Shipyard, Cowes
Dimensions	Length 38ft, breadth 12ft 6in
Engines	Twin Caterpillar 3208T turbo-charged diesels
Notes	On Temporary Station Duty while the new lifeboat house and slipway were constructed; after service at Cromer returned to the Relief Fleet until December 1999 when she became the station lifeboat at Lytham St Annes.

Appendix 3

Service Summary

First Lifeboat

1810	Nov. 4	*Anna,* of Sunderland, saved 15
1823	Oct. 31	Brig *Esther,* of Shields, saved 12
1824	Oct. 13	Brig *Equity,* of Scarborough, saved 1
1825	Oct. 21	*Liberty,* of Boston, saved 3

Second Lifeboat

1836	Feb. 18	Steamship *Trent,* of North Shields, saved ?
1839	Oct. 28	Brig *Achilles,* of South Shields, saved 8
	Nov. 1	Galliot *Elizabeth Jacobi Tromp,* of Holland, saved 7

First RNLI Lifeboat (1858)

| 1867 | Dec. 4 | Brig *Wild Rose,* of Brixham, stood by |
| 1868 | Apr. 9 | Brigantine *Agenoria,* of Lowestoft, saved 5 |

Benjamin Bond Cabbell Lifeboat

1869	Oct. 22	Ship *William Fotheringham,* of New York, assisted to save vessel and 18
1870	Mar. 4	Brig *Emulous,* of Middlesbrough, saved 5
1875	April 9	Steam tug *Vixen,* of North Shields, assisted to save tug and 8
1879	April 10	Sloop *Hesperus,* of Copenhagen, saved sloop
	Nov. 20	Steamship *Moidart,* of Glasgow, stood by
	21	Steamship *Moidart,* stood by

Benjamin Bond Cabbell (second) Lifeboat

1888	Jan. 28	Brigantine *Jane Maria,* of London, saved 7
1893	Nov. 18	A fishing boat of Overstrand, saved 5
		A fishing boat of Runton, saved 3
1894	Oct. 26	Five fishing boats, landed 17
	Dec. 28-9	Schooner *Fair City,* of Gloucester, stood by and gave help
1897	Dec. 3	Ketch *Hero,* of Goole, saved 4
1901	Feb. 17	Steamship *Celerity,* of Yarmouth, saved vessel and 7

Louisa Heartwell Lifeboat

1903	Dec. 28-31	Steamship *Enriquetta,* of Grangemouth, stood by
1904	Oct. 8-10	Steamship *Rosalind,* of Newcastle, stood by, and assisted to save vessel and 17
	Dec. 8	Five fishing boats, of Cromer, stood by
1906	Feb. 1	Steamship *Newburn,* of Newcastle, stood by
	Sep. 17-8	Schooner *Zuma,* of Wisbeach, assisted to save vessel and 9
1907	Feb. 11	Steamship *Atbara,* of London, saved 12
	Dec. 14	Barge *Britisher,* of London, stood by and gave help
1908	Mar. 1	Barque *Ladore,* of Liverpool, stood by and gave help
	Oct. 24	Lugger *John Robert,* of Yarmouth, gave help
1909	Nov. 23	Barque *Alf,* of Laurvig, saved 2
	Dec. 21	Barquentine *Albatross,* of Lowestoft, saved 8
1910	Feb. 15	Barge *Resurga,* of London, gave help
	April 20	Steamship *Haakon,* of Arendal, stood by
	Dec. 17	Schooner *Desdemona,* of Thurso, assisted to save vessel and 5
1911	Dec. 4-6	Ship *Walkure,* of Hamburg, gave help
1912	Aug. 29	Trawler *St Antoine De Padoue,* of Nieuport, landed 21 from the Haisborough lightvessel
	Nov. 27	Hoveller *James and Ellen,* of Yarmouth, stood by while beaching
1913	Feb. 27	Ketch *Industry,* of Hull, assisted to save vessel
	May 6	Fishing boats *Katie, Harriet* and *John and Mary,* of Palling, saved boats and 9
1915	Jan. 8-9	Steamship *New Oporto,* of Hartlepool, saved 7
	18-20	Ketch *Thomas Stratton,* of Maldon, assisted to save ketch and 4

	Mar. 27-9	Steamship *Ida*, of Haugesund, assisted to save vessel
	May 27	Steamship *Bodil*, of Esbjerg, saved 14
	Sep. 17-9	Steamship *Mimona*, of Frederikstad, assisted to save vessel
1916	Jan. 14	Steamship *Havfru*, of Christiania, saved 1
	Mar. 16-7	Steamship *Lady Londonderry*, of Sunderland, assisted to save vessel
	28	Schooner *Ann*, of Goole, saved 5
	Aug. 30	Steamship *Mitcham*, of London, saved 22
	Dec. 21	Fishing lugger *Chieftain*, of Cromer, saved 3
1917	Jan. 9	Steamship *Pyrin*, of Piraeus, saved 16
	9-10	Steamship *Fernebo*, of Gothenburg, saved 11
	Nov. 27	Steamship *Kronprinsessan Victoire*, of Haugesund, saved 6
	Dec. 21	Motor fishing boat *Admiral Jellicoe*, of Yarmouth, stood by
	26	Steamship *Pollcrea*, of London, gave help
1918	Feb. 25-6	Motor barge *Innisbeg*, of Glasgow, assisted to save barge and 5
Sep. 30-Oct. 1		Steamship *Inna*, of Sunderland, assisted to save vessel and 1
1919	Nov. 17-9	HM Hired Steam Trawler *General Botha*, of Aberdeen, assisted to save vessel
	30	Steamship *Réfrigérant*, of Lorient (ex *War Coppice*, of London), rendered assistance
1920	Aug. 20-2	Steamship *Bavaria*, of Cologne, rendered assistance
	Sep. 6	Motor launch *Dot*, saved launch and 2
	24-6	Motor schooner *Danefolk*, of Copenhagen, assisted to save vessel and 23
	Oct. 10-4	Steamship *Inverawe*, of Leith, stood by and assisted to save vessel
1923	Jan. 14	Steam trawler *Lord Cecil*, of Grimsby, assisted to save vessel
	April 21	Steamship *Nystrand*, of Skien, stood by

H.F. Bailey Lifeboat

1923	July 19	Smack *Hepatica*, of Lowestoft, assisted to save vessel
1924	Jan. 1	Steamship *Nephrite*, of Glasgow, assisted to save vessel and 12

H.F. Bailey (second) Lifeboat

1924	Sep. 22	Auxiliary fishing cutter *Iona*, of Middlesbrough, landed 4 from Haisborough lightvessel
	Oct. 22	Steamship *Clansman*, of Lowestoft, saved 9
	Dec. 5	Steamship *Vojvoda Putnik*, of Split, assisted to save vessel and 41
	27	Smiths Knoll lightvessel, rendered assistance
1925	April 19	Steam drifter *Couronne*, of Lowestoft, saved 8
	June 12	Steamship *Equity*, of Goole, rendered assistance
	Oct. 14	Barge *Scotia*, of London, assisted to save vessel and 3
1927	July 9	Steam trawler *Anson*, of Grimsby, saved trawler and 9
	Nov. 21-2	Steam tanker *Georgia*, of Rotterdam, saved 15
	30	Lighter *Bertha*, of Goole, saved 4
1928	Jan. 25	Ketch *Harold*, of London, assisted to save vessel and 3

H.F. Bailey II Lifeboat

1928	Dec 11	Schooner *Thursonian*, of Wick, saved 5

H.F. Bailey (second) Lifeboat

1929	June 28	River steamship *Empress*, of Nottingham, saved vessel and 3
	Oct. 30	Four-masted schooner *Svenborg*, of Vardo, stood by
	Nov. 22	Motor yacht *Celia*, of Bridlington, landed 2
1930	Oct. 21	Steam drifter *Girl Evelyn*, of Fraserburgh, assisted to save vessel
1931	Feb. 17	Fishing boat *Welcome Home*, of Sheringham, saved 1
	Oct. 4	Steam trawler *Le Vieux Tigre*, of Boulogne, rendered assistance
	Nov. 20-2	Steamship *Zembra*, of Dunkirk, saved vessel
	Dec. 24	Steamship *Vikvall*, of Oskarshamn, rendered assistance
1932	Aug. 7	Motor trawler *Iverna*, of Galway, rendered assistance
	Sep. 3	Motor barge *Olive May*, of London, rendered assistance
	Oct. 11	Steam drifter *Alexandrine*, of Boulogne, stood by and gave help
	14-15	Steamship *Monte Nevoso*, of Genoa, saved 29
		Steam tug *Noordzee*, of Rotterdam, saved 1 from Monte Nevoso
	16	Steamship *Monte Nevoso*, of Genoa, saved a dog
	Nov. 28	Barge *Matilda Upton*, of Ipswich, assisted to save vessel and 3
1933	Mar. 1	Steamship *Mary Kingsley*, of London, rendered assistance
	Nov. 20	Motor barge *Goldcrown*, of London, rendered assistance
	Dec. 13	Barge *Sepoy*, of Dover, saved 2

1934	Nov. 24	Motor barge *Rian*, of Groningen, rendered assistance
1935	Feb. 13	Steamship *Campus*, of Cardiff, assisted to save vessel and 29
	May 31	Three-masted schooner *Six Sisters*, of Hull, rendered assistance

H.F. Bailey (third) Lifeboat

1936	Mar. 26	Steamship *Borée*, of Caen, landed 7 from steamship *Caduceus*
	April 2	Fishing boat *Little Madge*, of Sheringham, in tow of lifeboat *J.C. Madge*, of Sheringham, stood by and gave help
		Fishing boats *John Robert* and *White Rose*, of Cromer, gave help
	20	Barge *Will Everard*, of London, stood by
	Aug. 7-8	Steamship *San Francisco*, of Havre, rendered assistance
	8-10	Steamship *San Francisco*, of Havre, rendered assistance
	10-11	Steamship *San Francisco*, of Havre, rendered assistance
	Nov. 16-8	Steamship *Nesttun*, of Tvedestrand, rendered assistance
	18	Steam drifter *Pitagaveny*, of Banff, saved 10
	19	Steamship *Yew Forest*, of Glasgow, took out a doctor
		Steamship *Lindisfarne*, of Newcastle, rendered assistance
1937	Nov. 9	Spritsail barge *Hibernia*, of London, saved 3
1938	Feb. 10	Fishing boat *Urgent*, of Cromer, stood by
	May 30	Fishing boat *G.V.H.*, of Great Yarmouth, saved boat and 2
	Aug. 7	Motor vessel *John M*, of London, stood by
	Nov. 2	Steamship *Cantabria*, of Santander, saved 5
	Dec. 27	Steamship *Otto H*, of Pori, rendered assistance
1939	June 18	Rowing boat, of Cromer, landed 5
	Oct. 9	Steamship *Mount Ida*, of Piraeus, saved 29
	Dec. 1	Steamship *Realf*, of Moss, landed 32 and 10 Naval Ratings from *Santa Gata*
	8	Steamship *Corea*, of Goole, saved 7
	12	Steamship *Corbrook*, of London, stood by
	21	Motor vessel *Dosinia*, of London, assisted to save vessel and 51
1940	Jan. 9	Steamship *Upminster*, of London, stood by
	11	Steamship *Traviata*, of Genoa, landed 30 and saved 1
		HM Trawler *Holyrood*, gave help
	12	Light-vessel *No. 85*, saved a ship's boat and 3
	18	Steamship *Asteria*, of Piraeus, saved 11
		Lightvessel *No. 85*, saved a ship's boat and 4
	30	Steam trawler *Pelton*, of Grimsby, gave help

J.B. Proudfoot Reserve Lifeboat

| 1940 | June 16 | Steamship *Brika*, of Swansea, assisted to save vessel |

H.F. Bailey (third) Lifeboat

1940	Aug. 27	Aircraft, salved gear and wreckage
	Oct. 3	Motor vessel *Actuosity*, of London, saved 8
	Nov. 15	HM Trawler *Dungeness*, saved 11
	25	HM Trawler *Dungeness*, salved gear
	Dec. 7	Steamship *Royston*, of Newcastle, stood by
	12	Steamship *Royston*, of Newcastle, gave help
1941	Jan. 15	Steamship *Lieutenant Robert Mory*, of Belfast, landed 19 and gave help
	25	Steamship *Meriones*, of Liverpool, saved 101
	Mar. 8	Boat of steamship *Corduff*, of London, saved 13
		Steamship *Kenton*, of Newcastle, saved two boats
	13	Steamship *Essex Lance*, of London, gave help
	14	Steamship *Essex Lance*, of London, gave help
	15	Steamship *Essex Lance*, of London, gave help
	16	Steamship *Essex Lance*, of London, gave help
	26	Steamship *Kentwood*, of London, stood by
	July 24	Aircraft, salved rubber dinghy and picked up a body
	Aug. 6	Steamship *Oxshott*, of London, saved 16
		Steamship *Gallois*, of Rouen, saved 31
		Steamship *Deenwood*, of Lodon, saved 19
		Steamship *Betty Hindley*, saved 22
	Sep. 15	Motor vessel *Pontfield*, of Newcastle, gave help
	17-20	Steamship *Teddington*, of London, gave help

	21	Steamship *Teddington,* of London, gave help
	22	Steamship *Teddington,* of London, gave help
	23	Steamship *J.B. Paddon,* of London, landed an injured man
	24	Steamship *Teddington,* of London, gave help
	25	Steamship *Teddington,* of London, gave help
	29	Steamship *Teddington,* of London, gave help
	30	Steamship *Teddington,* of London, gave help
	Oct. 2-3	Steamship *Teddington,* of London, gave help
	5-9	Steamship *Teddington,* of London, gave help
	14-5	Steamship *Teddington,* of London, gave help
	16	British aircraft, landed a body
	17-8	Steamship *Teddington,* of London, gave help
	26	Steamship *English Trader,* of London, saved 44
	Nov. 6	Steamship *Teddington,* of London, took out officials
1942	Jan. 29	Rubber dinghy, saved 1
	Feb. 2	Motor vessel *Sedulity,* of London, landed an injured man
	Mar. 15	HMS *Vortigern,* picked up 11 bodies
	April 11	British aircraft, landed 6
	May 25	Yacht *Betty,* of Gorleston, gave help
	July 20	Aeroplane, gave help
	Nov. 18	Motor fishing boat *Silver Queen,* of Lowestoft, saved boat and 2
1943	Mar. 12	Barrage balloon, salved balloon
	July 26	Aircraft, saved 5
1944	June 20	Aircraft, salved wreckage
	July 29	Aircraft, salved gear
	Dec. 7-10	Steamship *Samnethy,* of London, saved 52
1945	Feb. 4	Motor fishing vessel *Valder,* of Hartlepool, gave help

Millie Walton Lifeboat

1946	Mar. 7	Steamship *Corcrest,* of London, assisted to save vessel and 22

The above lifeboat renamed *Henry Blogg*

1948	Jan. 4	Steam trawler *Balmoral,* of Grimsby, saved vessel and 11
	April 23	Motor yacht *Switha,* of Inverness, gave help
	July 8	Motor vessel *Francois Tixier,* of Dunkirk, saved 16
	Aug. 7	Rubber dinghy, saved dinghy and 1
	25-31	Steamship *Monte Nuria,* of Bilbao, stood by and gave help
	Sep. 2	Rubber dinghy, saved dinghy and 1
	10-12	Motor trawler *Georges Langanay,* of Fécamp, assisted to save vessel and 19
	Dec. 20-2	Motor vessel *Bosphorus,* of Oslo, gave help and saved 1
	23-5	Motor vessel *Bosphorus,* of Oslo, gave help
	28-9	Motor vessel *Bosphorus,* of Oslo, assisted to save vessel and 36
1949	Oct. 4	Yacht *Marjellen,* gave help
	Nov. 19	Steamship *Suntrap,* of London, landed an injured man
1950	Nov. 21	Barge *Thyra,* of Rochester, gave help
1951	Jan. 9	Cabin cruiser *Dimcyl,* of Lowestoft, gave help
1952	July 24	Meteor aircraft, gave help
	Aug. 1	Motor yacht *Zippalong,* of Boston, gave help
	Oct. 26	Steamship *Ask,* of Bergen, gave help
	Nov. 23	Steamship *Grove Hill,* of Middlesbrough, gave help
1953	June 11	Sea Cadet motor vessel *Norok,* of Goole, saved vessel and 16
1954	Oct. 2	Cromer lightvessel, landed a sick man, saving 1
	15	Fishing boat *Why Worry,* of Cromer, saved boat and 2
1955	Sep. 2	Bathers with rubber tyre, saved 3
1956	Feb. 19	Steamship *Corchester,* of London, landed a body
	Aug. 10	Yacht *Ambida,* of Hull, saved yacht and 7
1957	Sep. 9	Sailing dinghy, saved dinghy
	23	Fishing boat *Britannia V,* of Cromer, saved boat and 2
	Oct. 26	Trawler *John Willment,* of Lowestoft, took out a doctor

Cunard Reserve Lifeboat

1958	Feb. 2	Steamship *Hudson Bank,* of London, took out doctor and landed injured man, saving 1
	Mar. 2	Motor vessel *Continental,* of Hamburg, landed 5 from mv *Wansbeck,* of Newcastle

Henry Blogg Lifeboat

1958	May 31	RNLB *Foresters' Centenary*, of Sheringham, gave help
	Aug. 27	Yacht *Wima*, of Rochester, gave help
1959	Aug. 17	Yacht, saved yacht and 2
	Sep. 6	Motor launch *Gay Crusader*, of London, saved boat and 8
	Dec. 31	Aircraft, landed a body from motor vessel *Broughty*, of Dundee
1960	July 11	Steam trawler *Cradock*, of Grimsby, gave help
	Aug. 3	Rubber mattress, saved 1
1961	Feb. 16	Haisborough lightvessel, gave help
		Steam tanker *Wave Chief*, of London, gave help
	Mar. 8	Motor vessel *Corstan*, of London, landed a sick man
1962	May 29	Cabin cruiser *Mayfly*, saved cruiser and 5
	Sep. 23	Yacht *Elizabeth Ann*, saved yacht and 4
	Nov. 2	HM survey vessel *Scott*, landed a sick man
	24	Motor vessel *Viscount*, of Groningen, gave help
1963	April 9	Haisborough lightvessel, landed a sick man
	May 12	Sailing dinghy, saved dinghy and 1
	June 11	Motor vessel *Warwickbrook*, of London, landed a doctor
	Dec. 23	Motor fishing boat *Four Brothers*, of Lowestoft, gave help
1964	Mar. 11	Motor vessel *Joika*, of Oslo, gave help
	July 5	Yacht *Sally Brown*, of Boston, saved yacht and 2
1965	Dec. 28	Oil rig *Sea Gem*, stood by
1966	Jan. 16	Steam salvage tug *Octopus*, of Ijmuiden, escorted vessel
		Motor vessel *Start*, of Groningen, escorted vessel
	April 3	Oil rig *Constellation*, stood by

Ruby and Arthur Reed Lifeboat

1967	July 4	Motor fishing vessel *Renovate*, stood by
	20	Motor vessel *Alme*, of Meppel, took out a doctor
	Sep. 3	Haisborough lightvessel, landed a sick man
	Oct. 10	Crab boat *Lewis James*, of Cromer, gave help
	29	Motor Vessel *Assurity*, of London, landed a sick man saving 1
	Dec. 19	Trawler *Rotha*, of Lowestoft, landed a sick man saving 1
1968	Feb. 4	Dinghy, saved dinghy and 3
	Mar. 2	Motor launch *Pinnace*, of Poole, saved launch and 2
	31	Steamship *Alice Bowater*, of London, landed a sick man saving 1
	May 11	Fishing boat *Provider*, of Cromer, saved boat and 2
	13	Tug *Workman*, of Hull, stood by tug with warhead on board
	June 30	Cabin cruiser *She's a Lady*, assisted to save cruiser and 3
	July 11	Motor vessel *Ramso*, of Copenhagen, escorted
	Aug. 23	Trawler *Filby Queen*, of Lowestoft, landed sick man
	30	Yacht *Stilalisanin*, landed 1 and saved yacht
	Sep. 18	Trawler *Rock Fish*, of Lowestoft, took out a doctor
	Nov. 15	Gas rig *Hewitt Alpha*, gave help
1969	Jan. 3	Motor vessel *Friederike*, of Brake, landed a sick man
	14	Trawler *Suffolk Kinsman*, of Lowestoft, landed a sick man
	22	Motor fishing boat *Thistle*, saved boat and 3
	May 10	Motor fishing boat *Kindly Light*, gave help
	21	Pipe laying vessel *W.D. Tideway*, of London, landed sick man
1970	June 26	Motor fishing boat *Normanby*, of Bridlington, gave help
	Nov. 12	Fishing boat *My Beauty*, of Cromer, escorted
1971	May 15	Cabin cruiser *Nadine Leah*, gave help
	June 13	Yacht *Gentle Nimbus*, gave help
1972	May 5	Two fishing boats, stood by
	20	Trawler *Boston Viscount*, of Lowestoft, landed injured man
	Aug. 21	Fishing boat *Cossack*, saved boat and 4
	Sep. 12	Cabin cruiser *New Prince of Wales*, saved cruiser and 3
	Oct. 25	Fishing boat *Provider*, of Cromer, saved boat and 4
1973	Mar. 22	Sick man on board motor vessel *Silver Sands*, landed a sick man, thereby saving 1

The Good Hope **Reserve Lifeboat**

	Nov. 5	Crab boat, escorted boat
	15	Injured man on board fishing trawler *Boston Jaguar*, of Lowestoft, took out doctor
	30	Fishing vessel *Katrina Ann* R.91, saved 4
1974	Jan. 3	Fishing boat *The Duncan*, of Yarmouth, escorted boat
	4	Fishing boat *Amanda Ann* YH.443, of Yarmouth, gave help
	Feb. 6	Container ship *Leila*, of West Germany, in tow of Trinity House vessel *Patricia*, escorted
	Mar. 2	Motor fishing vessel *Henri Jeanine*, of Belgium, stood by

Ruby and Arthur Reed **Lifeboat**

	Aug. 31	Sick man on board lightvessel LV.22, landed a sick man
	Sep. 10	Motor vessel *Langstone Tern*, escorted boat
	Nov. 1	Injured man on board motor vessel *Dutch Sailor*, landed an injured man
1975	Feb. 21	Cargo vessel *Fortuna II*, landed an injured man
	May 22	Sick man on board HMS *Shevington*, gave help
	Sep. 8	Yacht *Irishman*, saved boat and 10
	Oct. 26	Cruiser *Andruss*, saved boat and 2
	Dec. 12	Freighter *Alexandria*, stood by vessel
	14	Freighter *Alexandria*, stood by vessel
1976	Feb. 6	Injured man on board trawler *Suffolk Conquest*, took out doctor
	June 23	Cargo vessel *Garden Saturn*, stood by vessel
	Aug. 7	Fishing vessel *Albert*, saved vessel and 2
	18	Injured man on board Haisborough lightvessel, landed an injured man
	Sep. 15	Yacht *Mr Micawber*, saved boat and 2
	Oct. 18	Fishing boat *Sea Green*, gave help
1977	Feb. 19	Cargo vessel *Atlantic Duke*, stood by vessel
	22	Catamaran *Katabatic*, gave help
	24	Chemical carrier *Thorodland*, of Panama, stood by vessel
	Mar. 18	Cargo vessel *Femmy Lian*, of Cyprus, gave help
	Apr. 18	Cargo vessel *Star River*, of France, gave help
	July 27	Injured man on board cargo vessel *Heye-P*, of West Germany, gave help
	Sep. 9	Yacht *Autumn Liz*, gave help
	Nov. 14	Cargo vessel *Nimrod*, of Jersey, saved 1
	Dec. 24	Cargo vessel *Rafaela*, of Panama, stood by vessel
1978	Aug. 16	Fishing boat, gave help
	Sep. 4	Fishing boat *Charles Perkins*, gave help

William Gammon – Manchester and District XXX **Relief Lifeboat**

1979	Mar. 6	Haisborough lightvessel, took out doctor and landed an injured man, thereby saving 1

Ruby and Arthur Reed **Lifeboat**

	May 22	Missing crewman from fishing vessel *Concorde II*, landed a body
	June 6	Yacht *Victoria George*, gave help
		Tug *Englishman*, stood by vessel
	20	Oil rig standby vessel *Boston Hornet*, took out doctor and landed a sick man
1980	Jan. 5	Fishing vessel *Ellen*, of Great Yarmouth, gave help
	17	Cargo vessel *Lendoudis Evangelos*, of Greece, gave help
	April 8	Fishing boats, escorted boats
	May 3	Motor fishing vessel *Bess*, of Denmark, saved boat and 4
	June 23	Motor cruiser *Jenny Glen*, of Kings Lynn, saved boat and 2
1981	Jan. 30	Cargo vessel *Ems*, of West Germany, and cargo vessel *Undine*, of Belgium, in collision, recovered liferaft
	June 2	Fishing boat *Provider*, of Great Yarmouth, gave help
	Aug. 2	Cabin cruisers *Lancer* and *Falcon*, gave help
	13	Helicopter, gave help
	Nov. 30	Oil rig supply vessel *The Cuttlefish*, saved 2
1982	Sep. 17	Skin diver, gave help
	21	Fishing vessels *Provider*, of Cromer, and *Elizabeth Kathleen*, of Wells, escorted
	Dec. 12	Motor boat *Trade Winds*, saved boat and 3
1983	July 12	Injured man on board fishing boat *Ventura*, of West Runton, landed an injured man
1984	Feb. 15	Cargo vessel *Camilla Weston*, of London, landed 5
	May 9	Sick man on board cargo vessel *Marie Anne*, of West Germany, landed a sick man

July 12   Aircraft, recovered wreckage
13   Fishing boat *G.N.D.,* of Great Yarmouth, saved boat and 2
Aug. 15   Injured man on board cargo vessel *Emily P.G.,* of Shoreham, landed an injured man
Sep. 4   Fishing boat *Provider,* of Great Yarmouth, escorted boat

Guy and Clare Hunter Lifeboat

1985   April 4   Cargo vessel *Klaas I,* of Panama, stood by vessel
May 13   Fishing boats, escorted
July 15   Fishing boat *Sarah Jane,* of Great Yarmouth, gave help
22   Fishing vessel, gave help
28   Yacht *Helm Spray III,* saved boat and 2
Aug. 11   Rafts, saved 30
19   Cabin cruiser *Moby Dick,* gave help
Sep. 28   Sick man on board diving support vessel *Orelia,* of Aberdeen, landed sick man
29   Motor boat, saved boat and 2

Ruby and Arthur Reed II Lifeboat

1986   Jan. 24   Tanker *Orleans,* of Lowestoft, gave help
Rig standby safety vesssl *Boston Sea Stallion,* of Lowestoft, escorted
Aug. 29   Fishing vessel *Nicholas,* of London, saved boat and 2
Sep. 26   Yacht *Blythe Andora,* gave help

Sam and Joan Woods Relief Lifeboat

1987   June 4   Fishing vessel *Sonjan,* of Peterhead, gave help

Ruby and Arthur Reed II Lifeboat

1988   Feb. 8   Tug *Anna B,* gave help
June 15   Fishing vessel *Sparkling Star,* saved boat and 3
July 10   Yacht *Kass-A-Nova,* saved vessel and 4
15   Coaster *Luminence,* gave help
17   Lost diver, gave help
23   Fishing vessel *Two Sisters,* saved boat and 1
Aug. 4   Fishing vessel *Ever Hopeful,* of Great Yarmouth, gave help
29   Skin divers, landed 5
Sep. 19   Fishing boat *G.N.D.,* of Great Yarmouth, escorted
Sep. 29   Yacht *Phaedra,* of Whitby, saved boat and 2
Oct. 1   Fishing vessel *Courageous,* of Inverness, gave help
1989   Feb. 14   RoRo cargo vessel *Tor Gothia,* of Sweden, gave help
May 30   Fishing boats, escorted boats
June 30   Yacht *Serena,* saved boat and 2
Yacht *Martlet,* saved boat and 2
Oct. 10   Fishing vessel *De Vroun Melanie,* of Lowestoft, stood by
1990   May 6   Motor boat, escorted boat
June 20   Yacht *Meander,* gave help
Aug. 6   Standby safety vessel *St Mark,* saved 2 vessels
30   Floating drifting rig *Rouville,* gave help
Sep. 16   Fishing vessel *Mar Tigre,* stood by vessel
Nov. 21   Cargo vessel *Stavroula,* gave help
1992   Jan. 12   Motor boat *Sara B,* escorted vessel
Feb. 19   Sick man on board vessel *Bressay Sound,* landed a sick man
June 10   Yacht *Tassella,* gave help
July 20   Yacht *Illyria,* saved boat and 1
29   Yacht *Cherokee II,* gave help
Aug. 21   Gas survey vessel *Fortissimo,* landed 3 and saved vessel
Oct. 14   Fishing vessel *Isobel Kathleen,* saved boat and 4
24   Barge *Rock,* gave help
Dec. 5   Yacht *Milford,* of Otley, saved boat, two dogs and 1
1993   Oct. 13   Yacht *Happy Bear,* saved casualty and 5
Nov. 5   Small motor vessel, gave help
Dec. 7   Rig standby vessel, stood by
1994   July 28   Motor cruiser *Heather Down,* gave help
30   Two skin divers, landed 2
Sep. 22   Cargo vessel *Nescio,* took out doctor and landed a sick man

1995	Mar. 12	Cargo vessel *Nordstar* in collision, escorted
	June 27	Salvage vessel *Putford Puffin*, took out doctor and landed a sick man
	July 5	Diving support ship *Ocean Stephaniturm*, stood by boat
1996	April 1	Fishing vessel *Juliet*, one person and craft brought in
	23	Motor cruiser *Blue Lancer*, two persons and craft brought in
	July 21	Two divers, gave help
	24	Yacht *Giselle*, saved craft and 2
	Aug. 15	Motor cruiser *Ocean Diver*, saved craft and 3

Her Majesty The Queen Lifeboat

1997	Feb. 25	RoRo cargo vessel *Inowroclaw*, gave help
	Mar. 16	Cargo vessel *Oakland*, gave help
	July 9	Diver support craft *Crusader*, escorted craft
1998	April 17	Pipeline guard vessel *Laurids Skomager*, landed 4 and craft brought in
	Aug. 12	Yacht *Only Me*, gave help
	16	Yacht *Christina 2*, saved craft and 3
	Sep. 4	Helicopter, gave help
	23	Cabin cruiser *Kirkvik*, gave help
	Nov. 6	Yacht *Tange*, of Whitby, saved craft and 3
	Dec. 5	Fishing vessel *Ocean Explorer*, escorted craft

Ruby and Arthur Reed II Lifeboat

1999	July 10	Six divers, six persons brought in – saved by another lifeboat
		Dive support craft *Desert Moon*, eight people and craft brought in
	Sep. 10	Yacht *Halcyon Oak*, two people and craft brought in
	Oct. 3	Yacht *Lady Patience*, gave help
	Dec. 16	Powerboat *Samphire of Wells*, gave help
	22	Body in sea, gave help
2000	Mar. 11	Passenger ferry *Norstar*, stood by
	May 27	Yacht *Coquette*, escorted craft
	June 16	Diver support craft *Crusader*, landed 4 and a dog
	July 10	Ex-trawler *Excelsior*, saved craft and 9
2001	Jan. 14	Tug *Golden Cross*, four people and craft brought in
	Feb. 16	Dinghy *Maximum Exposure*, one person and craft brought in
	25	Tanker *Zanita*, escorted craft
	May 17	Dinghy *Maximum Exposure*, one person and craft brought in
	June 5	Powerboat *Whirlwind*, two people and craft brought in
2002	Jan. 9	Fishing vessel *Zuider Zee*, gave help

Lord Saltoun Relief Lifeboat

	Mar. 13	Tug *Jack Rose*, landed 3 and craft brought in
	April 29	Coaster *Alserbach*, stood by
	June 20	Cabin cruiser *One Chance*, two people and craft brought in
	20	Whale, gave help
	July 5	Dive boat *Gudivar*, three people and craft brought in

Ruby and Arthur Reed II Lifeboat

| 2003 | May 7 | Yacht *Ngataki*, three people and craft brought in |
| | 24 | Yacht *Rambling Rose*, one person and craft brought in |

St Cybi II (Civil Service No. 40) Relief Lifeboat

| | July 26 | Yacht *Black Duck*, four people and craft brought in |

Ruby and Arthur Reed II Lifeboat

| | Sep. 7 | Sloop *Just Joia*, gave help |

No.2 lifeboats

Louisa Heartwell Lifeboat
1923   Dec. 21   Schooner *Gotha*, of Bergqvara, stood by

Harriot Dixon Lifeboat
1939	Mar. 20	Motor vessel *Fosna*, of Bergen, landed a sick man
	Oct. 9	RNLB *H. F. Bailey*, of Cromer, gave help and landed 29 saved from *Mount Ida*
	12-3	Steamship *Linwood*, of Middlesbrough, saved 12
	Dec. 12	Steamship *Corbrook*, of London, stood by
1940	Feb. 13	Tanker *British Triumph*, of London, saved two boats
	Nov. 18	HM Trawler *Dungeness*, gave help
	20	HM Trawler *Dungeness*, gave help
	Dec. 10	Steamship *Royston*, of Newcastle, gave help
1941	Mar. 11	Steamship *Kenton*, of Newcastle, salved gear
	April 1	HM Trawler *Valexa*, landed 1
	14	HM Trawlers *Madden* and *Tamora*, took out doctor and landed 4 injured men
	Aug. 6	Steamship *Taara*, of Parnu, saved 8
	Oct. 1	Steamship *Teddington*, of London, gave help
	19	Steamship *Teddington*, of London, gave help
	21-2	Steamship *Teddington*, of London, gave help
	Nov. 21	Steamship *Teddington*, of London, gave help
1942	Nov. 24	HM Trawler, brought papers ashore
1943	Dec. 3	Fishing boat *Morning Star*, of Cromer, escorted
1947	Oct. 26	Motor vessel *Gold Gnome*, of London, stood by and gave help
1948	April 1	Speedboat *Day II*, landed 2 from steamship *Dynamo*
	Sep. 11-2	Motor Trawler *Georges Langaway*, of Fécamp, gave help
1949	Jan. 26-7	Motor vessel *Farndale*, of Middlesbrough, gave help
1950	Feb. 6	Three fishing boats, of Cromer, and one of Runton, escorted
	June 17	Motor vessel *Glamis*, of Dundee, landed a sick man
1953	May 31	HMS *Cheerful*, landed passengers
	June 5	Fishing boats *Miss Cromer* and *Why Worry*, of Cromer, escorted
	Sep. 15	Fishing boat *Why Worry*, of Cromer, escorted
1955	Sep. 28	Steamship *Moonwood*, of London, took out doctor
	Dec. 17	Three fishing boats, of Cromer, escorted
1957	July 22	Yacht *Pococita*, stood by
1960	April 16	Fishing boat *June Rose*, of Sheringham, escorted
1961	Jan. 13	Motor vessel *Jura*, of Groningen, gave help
	Aug. 15	Crab boats *Friendship*, *Black Beauty*, *William Robert* and *English Rose*, of Cromer, escorted
1963	April 5	Steamship *Hudson Sound*, of London, landed a sick man

Jose Neville Reserve Lifeboat
| 1964 | June 29 | Crab boat *George William*, of Cromer, gave help |
| | | Crab boat *Young Fisherman*, of Cromer, escorted |

William Henry and Mary King Lifeboat
1965	Nov. 27	Fishing boat *Young Fisherman*, of Cromer, gave help
		Fishing boats *Charles Perkins*, *George Robert*, *Black Beauty* and *Lewis James*, of Cromer, escorted
1966	Feb. 1	Admiralty motor vessel *Universal Dipper*, gave help
	June 2	Cabin cruiser *Shellduck*, of Ipswich, gave help
	10	Yacht *Vole*, gave help and landed 3
	Aug. 5	Crab boats *My Beauty*, *Autumn Rose*, and *Lewis James*, of Cromer, stood by
	Dec. 8	Trawler *St Lucia*, of Lowestoft, landed an injured man
	11	DUKW amphibious vehicle, saved DUKW and landed 9
1967	May 30	Motor fishing vessel *Karin Hoegh*, landed a sick man, thereby saving 1

Inshore lifeboat services

1968	May 15	Motor fishing boat *Allison Jane*, gave help re injured man
	June 3	Dinghy, gave help
	22	Bather, saved 1
	30	Catamaran, gave help
	July 2	Bathers, saved 2
	Aug. 22	Sailing canoe, gave help
	30	Yacht *Stilalisanin*, gave help, saved 1
1970	June 30	Bather, saved 1
	Oct. 18	Two fishing boats, escorted
		Dinghy *Lucy Jane*, landed 3 and escorted
		Dinghy, escorted
1971	June 13	Yacht *Gentle Nimbus*, gave help
		Dinghy, gave help and landed 1
	July 16	Crab boat, gave help
	19	Dinghy, saved dinghy and 4
	24	Dinghy, saved dinghy and 1
	Aug. 7	Canoe, landed 1
	10	Cabin cruiser *Zippalong*, gave help
1972	July 24	Canoe, saved canoe and 1
1973	Apr.17	Motor cruiser *Jubilee*, gave help
	June 4	Cabin cruiser, escorted boat
	Aug. 7	Dinghy, saved boat and 4
	Sep. 11	Bather in difficulty, saved 1
	Oct. 5	Motor fishing vessel, gave help
1974	June 1	Motor fishing vessel, gave help
	4	Injured man on board dredger *Marinex V*, landed injured man
	Aug. 10	Canoe, saved boat and 2
	Sep. 30	Landed an injured man
1975	June 15	Dinghy, gave help
	July 10	Dinghy, saved 3
	Aug. 10	Dinghy, saved 2
	17	Dinghy, gave help
1976	July 6	Swimmer, saved 1
	11	Yacht, gave help
		Yacht, gave help
	15	Sailing dinghy *Gurgle*, saved boat and 2
	Aug. 13	Dinghy, escorted boat
	15	Sailing dinghy, saved boat and 2
	Sep. 5	Rafts, gave help
	12	Rafts, gave help
1977	April 19	Rowing boat, gave help
	July 23	Inflatable dinghy, gave help
		Sailing dinghy, saved boat and 2
	Aug. 12	HM submarine *Sea Lion*, landed 22
	14	Air bed, gave help
		HM submarine *Sea Lion*, landed 2
	16	Gemini tender to HM submarine *Sea Lion*, saved boat and 2
	29	Dinghy, saved 1
	Oct. 30	Inflatable dinghy, saved boat and 5
1978	June 25	Catamaran, saved boat and 2
	July 9	Injured man on board cargo vessel *Camilla Weston*, landed 1
		Cargo vessel *Camilla Weston*, gave help
1979	May 28	Yacht *Lotus*, gave help
	June 11	Motor launch *Enterprise*, gave help
	July 6	Swimmer, saved 1
	16	Motor cruiser *Snow Goose II*, gave help
	22	Cargo vessel *Frederika*, gave help

	Aug. 6	Speedboat, gave help
	28	Man fallen from cliff, gave help
	Sep. 16	Sailing dinghy, saved boat and 2
	30	Canoe, saved canoe and 1
1980	July 12	Yacht *Taber*, gave help
	Aug. 9	Motor cruiser *Star Wind*, gave help
	14	Rubber dinghy, escorted boat
		Swimmer, saved 1
	30	Motor boat *Boy Jummu*, escorted
	Sep. 7	Airbed, saved 1
		Rubber dinghy, saved 2
		Rubber dinghy, saved boat and 2
		Speedboat *Shakespeare*, saved boat
1981	May 1	Fishing boat *George William*, saved 2
	June 1	Motorboat *Tiki*, escorted boat
	4	Dinghy, saved boat and 2
	8	Yacht *Dux*, gave help
	15	Tender to Royal Navy survey vessel HMS *Echo*, gave help
	19	Swimmer, saved 1
	22	Fishing boat *Denise David*, escorted
	24	Fishing vessel *Paternoster*, gave help
1982	April 10	Fishing boats, escorted boats
	July 18	Rubber dinghy, gave help
		Raft *Parcel Express*, saved 2
		Injured man from raft *Parcel Express*, on board support boat, landed 1
	25	Motor boat *Maisie*, landed 1
	Aug. 6	Rubber dinghy, gave help
	29	Sailboard, saved board
		Rubber dinghy, saved boat
		Sailboard, landed 1 and saved board
	Oct. 24	Speedboat, gave help
1983	May 4	Motor cruiser *Lady Barbara*, gave help
	June 5	Two rafts, escorted
	Aug 10	Swimmer, saved 1
1984	June 24	Sailboard, escorted
	July 8	Yacht *Karelia*, gave help
	12	Aircraft, recovered wreckage
	Aug. 15	Injured man on board cargo vessel *Emily PG*, took out doctor
	19	Rubber dinghy, gave help
1985	May 30	Yacht *Deodato*, gave help
	July 21	Sailing dinghy in tow of speedboat, escorted
		Rubber dinghy, gave help
	26	Fishing vessel *Our Boys*, escorted
	Aug. 11	Sailing dinghy, saved boat and 2
		Rafts, saved 21
		Sailing dinghy, gave help
		Raft, saved raft
		Two rafts, gave help
	15	Sailboard, saved board and 1
	19	Fishing boat *Kathleen*, gave help
		Cabin cruiser *Moby Dick*, gave help
	22	Dinghy *Osprey*, gave help
	Sep. 29	Motor boat *DGM*, gave help
1986	July 13	Canoe, saved boat
	23	Sailing dinghy, saved boat and 3
	Aug. 4	Rubber dinghy, saved boat
	17	Man fallen from cliff, stood by

	18	Fishing boat, escorted boat
	29	Fishing boat *Sally Elizabeth*, stood by
		Fishing boat *Jonathan James*, escorted
1987	May 10	Cabin cruiser *Candy II*, gave help
	July 25	2 fishing vessels, escorted
	Aug. 11	Motor boat, craft brought in
	20	Sailboard, saved board and 1
	Sep. 22	Cargo vessel *Funk*, gave help
		Cargo vessel *Funk*, gave help
1988	July 10	Rubber dinghy, saved craft
	17	Divers missing, landed 3
	Sep. 4	Sailboard, escorted
1989	May 22	Fishing vessel, landed craft
	30	Fishing vessel, escorted
	31	Cabin cruiser, gave help
	June 21	Fishing vessel, escorted
		Fishing vessel, escorted
	Aug. 8	Sailboard, saved board and 1
	13	Sailboard, saved board
	15	Animal in sea, gave help
	17	Sailboard, saved board and 1
1990	May 2	Swimmer, saved 1
	June 18	Motor boat, escorted
	Aug. 20	Sailboard, saved board and 1
	30	Rig, gave help
1991	April 6	Sailboard, landed 1
	11	Motor boat, landed 2
	June 29	Fishing vessel, stood by
	July 21	Swimmers, landed 2
	30	Fishing vessel *Norfolk Girl*, saved craft and 3
	Aug. 2	Motor boat, landed craft
	15	Rubber dinghy, saved craft
	Nov. 10	Fishing vessel *Norfolk Girl*, saved craft and landed 1
1992	July 17	Jet ski, landed craft
	Aug. 5	Motor boat *Triton*, landed craft
	19	Bather, saved 1
	June 6	Fishing vessel, landed craft
	Sep. 3	Rig *Sir Robert McAlpine*, landed 2
	12	Motor boat *Infield Diver*, landed craft
1993	June 6	Fishing vessel, landed casualty
	Sep. 3	Rig, landed 2
	12	Motor boat, landed craft
1994	May 28	Power boat out of fuel, craft landed
	June 24	Small fishing vessel, escorted casualty
	Aug. 13	Sailboard, saved board and 1
	Sep. 10	Dog in sea, saved dog
		Man overboard from jet ski, saved jet ski and 1
	Oct. 2	Speedboat, two persons and craft brought in
1995	May 28	Speedboat, landed 3, craft brought in
	June 24	Fishing boats, escorted

	July 24	Sailboard, landed 1, brought in board
	31	Two persons overboard from jet ski, landed 2 and saved jet ski
	Sep. 26	Fishing boat *Mel-Y-Mor*, landed 3 and craft brought in
	Oct. 6	Canoe, saved boat and 1
1996	April 2	Sick man onboard motor cruiser *Braywood Hawk*, landed sick man and gave help
	May 2	Fishing vessel *Valerie Theresa*, escorted
	June 9	Diver support craft, four persons and craft brought in
	Aug. 20	Injured youth at Cromer Lighthouse, landed an injured youth
1997	May 12	Motor boat, one person and craft brought in
	July 9	Sheringham Atlantic 75 lifeboat B-702, gave help
		Fishing vessel *Laura Ann*, gave help
	24	Rubber dinghy, landed 2 and craft brought in
	Aug. 24	Speedboat *Speedy*, three people and craft brought in
1998	Aug. 6	Conveyed sick youth from beach to ambulance
1999	Aug. 18	Jet ski, landed 2 and craft brought in
	Oct. 2	Two people in the sea, saved 1
	3	Yacht *Lady Patience*, gave help
2000	Mar. 8	Speedboat *Just Chasing P.*, one person and craft brought in
	May 14	Person overboard from jet ski, saved 1
	June 17	Surfboard, one person and craft brought in
	Aug. 25	Person in danger of drowning, assisted to save one
	Oct. 17	Man stranded on beach, gave help
	Dec. 11	Sick man on board merchant vessel *Maria*, gave help
2001	May 7	Fishing vessel *Gladiator*, gave help
	June 12	Dog in sea, gave help
	July 29	Jet ski, one person & craft brought in
	Aug. 15	Speedboats, gave help
	15	Inflatable dinghy, craft brought in
	25	Inflatable, craft brought in
2002	July 10	Sick crewman on board survey vessel *Commander Subsea*, one person brought in
	17	Dead seal in water, gave help
	Aug. 14	Person ill on beach, gave help
2003	May 11	Motor boat *Alali*, five people and craft brought in
	31	Two children trapped under pier, assisted to save 2
	July 11	Fishing vessel *Carrie Ann*, one person and craft brought in

Appendix 4
Personnel Summary

Honorary Secretaries

Henry Sandford	1858-1869
William G. Sandford	1869-1898
George S. Rust	1898-1905
Charles E. Bond	1905-1908
Frank H. Barclay	1908-1935
Major E. Peter Hansell	1935-1963
T.H. Baldwin	1939-1945
Dr Paul S. Barclay	1963-1974
Douglas L. Snelling	1974-1978
Jim J. Smith	1978-1999
Chris T. Barnes	1999-2002
Richard J. Leeds	2002-

Coxswains

Robert 'Bully Bob' Allen	1858-1874
James Davies	1874-1893
John James Davies	1893-1902
James 'Buttons' Harrison	1902-1909
Henry George Blogg	1909-1947
Henry T. 'Shrimp' Davies	1947-1976
Richard W. Davies	1976-1999
W.T. 'Billy' Davies	1999-2003
John James Davies	2003-

2nd Coxswains

John James Davies	1863-1874
Benjamin Allen	1874-1875
John James Davies	1875-1893
M. James 'Buttons' Harrison	1893-1902
Henry George Blogg	1902-1909
G. 'Buckram' Balls	1909-1933
J.J. 'Jack' Davies	1934-1943
W.T. 'Captain' Davies	1943-1947
Lewis B. 'Tuner' Harrison	1947-1953
R.C. 'Bob' Davies	1953-1957
J.R. 'Dick' Davies	1957-1968
Lewis B. 'Tuner' Harrison	1968-1975
Richard W. Davies	1975-1976
W.T. 'Billy' Davies	1976-1999
John James Davies	1999-2003
John Allen Balls	2003-

Mechanics

Ernest Amis	1923
T.H. Rayner	1923-1924
R. 'Bob' Davies	1924-1933
H.W. 'Swank' Davies	1933-1961
John R. Allen	1961-1972
Ralph H. Amey	1972-1978
Donny F. Abbs	1979-1987
Robert J. Hannah	1987-1992
Paul J. Wegg	1992-

Bowman

Robert Davies	1893-1894
George Rook	1894-1902
George 'Buckram' Balls	1902-1909
J.J. 'Jack' Davies	1909-1933
W.T. 'Captain' Davies	1934-1944
Henry T. 'Shrimp' Davies	1944-1947
Robert C. 'Bob' Davies	1947-1953
Sidney C. 'Kelly' Harrison	1953-1969

Coxswain (No.2 lifeboat)

Henry George Blogg	1934-1947
J.W. 'Jimmy' Davies	1947-1953
Lewis B. 'Tuner' Harrison	1953-1967

Mechanic (No.2 lifeboat)

H.V. 'Joe' Linder	1934-1954
Dennis G. Gaff	1954-1967

Bowman (No.2 lifeboat)

Sidney C. 'Kelly' Harrison	1953-1967

ILB Senior Helmsmen

Edward J. Luckin	1967-1978
Frank H. Muirhead	1978-1983
Sean Bradley	1984-1985
Alan Keyworth	1986-1987
David J. Pope	1988-1997
Adrian Woods	1998-

Appendix 5
Medals and Awards

1839   28 October: *Achilles*, of South Shields, saved 8

Norfolk Shipwreck Association Silver medal to Captain Francis Pank.

1867   21 July: *Sutcliffe*, of Harwich

Silver medal to the Honorable Auberon Herbert.

1894   18 August: Swimmer, saved 1

Royal Humane Society Bronze medal to Coxswain John James Davies.

1917   9-10 January: Steamship *Fernebo*, of Gothenburg, saved 11

Gold medal to Coxswain Henry G. Blogg; Silver medal to Acting Second Coxswain William T. Davies and Private Stewart Holmes; Bronze medals (first issue) to George Allen, James Allen, E.W. Allen, William Allen, Henry Balls, Charlie Cox, George Cox, L.J. Harrison, Thomas Kirby, G. Mayes, Walter Rix, and William Rix. Thanks on Vellum to J.S. Allen, W. Allen snr, Herbert Blogg, James Davies, Ben Harrison and George Rook, who went out twice saving 11 from *Fernebo* and 16 from *Pyrin*.

1924   March: in recognition of lifeboat work

Empire Gallantry medal to Coxswain Henry G. Blogg, replaced by the George Cross in 1940, presented to surviving Gold medal winners during the RNLI's centenary year.

1927   22 November: Steam tanker *Georgia*, of Rotterdam, saved 15

Gold medal to Coxswain Henry G. Blogg; Bronze medals to Second Coxswain George Balls, mechanic Robert Davies, John J. Davies snr, W.T. Davies, L.J. Harrison, E.W. Allen, J.W. Davies, H.W. Davies, S.C. Harrison, Richard J. Barker, George Cox, and J.J. Davies jnr. Queen of Holland also sent a gold watch for Blogg and silver watches for the crew.

1931   17 February: Fishing boat *Welcome Home*, of Sheringham, saved 1

Bronze medal to Bowman John J. Davies snr.

1932   14-16 October: Steamship *Monte Nevoso*, of Genoa, saved 29 and a dog

Silver medal to Coxswain Henry G. Blogg, Thanks on Vellum to Second Coxswain George Balls, mechanic Robert Davies, J.J. Davies snr, W.T. 'Captain' Davies, E.W. Allen, J.W. Davies, H.W. Davies, Robert Blogg, J.J. Davies jnr, Arthur Balls, George Cox, Robert Cox. In 1935, the Italian Government sent a Silver medal and Diploma for Blogg, and Bronze medals and Diplomas to each of the crew. Blogg was also awarded a Canine Defence Silver medal for saving the ship's dog.

1933   13 December: Barge *Sepoy*, of Dover, saved 2

Silver medal to Coxswain Henry G. Blogg; Thanks on Vellum to Second Coxswain G. Balls, mechanic H.W. Davies, Bowman John J. Davies, snr, 2nd Mechanic William T. Davies, James W. Davies, William H. Davies, John J Davies, jnr, Charles P. Cox, Robert Cox, Edward W. Allen, Sidney Harrison and L.B. Harrison; also to Acting Coxswain R. Davies in No.2 Lifeboat.

1939   9 October: Steamship *Mount Ida*, of Piraeus, saved 29

Silver medal to Coxswain Henry G. Blogg; Bronze medals to Second Coxswain J.J. Davies snr, mechanic H. W. Davies, second mechanic J.W. Davies; Thanks on Vellum accorded to signalman H.T. Davies, R.C. Davies, F. Davies, J.J. Davies jnr, W.H. Davies, J.R. Davies, R. Cox and G. Cox.

1941   6 August: Convoy 559, saved 88

6 August: Steamship *Taara*, of Parnu, saved 8

Gold medal and British Empire medal to Coxswain Henry G. Blogg; Silver medal to Second Coxswain J.J. Davies; Bronze medals to Mechanic Henry W. 'Swank' Davies; Thanks on Vellum accorded to J.W. Davies, W.T. Davies, Henry T. 'Shrimp' Davies, J.R. Davies, Charles Cox, S.C. Harrison, Edward W.

Allen, J.J. Davies jnr, W.H. 'Pimpo' Davies, R.C. 'Bob' Davies, George Cox, Charlie Brakenbury, Lewis B. Harrison. Bronze medals to Second Coxswain Leslie J. Harrison and mechanic H. Linder of the No.2 lifeboat.

1941   26 October: Steamship _English Trader_, of London, saved 44

Silver medal to Coxswain Henry G. Blogg; Bronze medals to Second Coxswain John .J. Davies, snr, Mechanic H. W. Davies, second mechanic James W. Davies, Bowman William T. Davies, John J. Davies, jnr, Sidney C. Harrison, signalman Henry T. Davies, William H. Davies, Robert C. Davies, James R. Davies; signalman Edward W. Allen was posthumously awarded Bronze medal.

1948   8 July: Motor vessel _Francois Tixier_, of Dunkirk, saved 16

French Government Maritime Cross to Coxswain Henry T. Davies, French lifesaving medal to Second Coxswain Lewis B. Harrison, mechanic H.W. 'Swank' Davies, J.R. 'Dick' Davies, R.C. 'Bob' Davies, J.J. 'Jack' Davies jnr, Frank Davies, S.C. Harrison, George Cox, Tom Jonas, and George Rook.

1953   June

Queen's Coronation medal awarded to Coxswain Henry G. Blogg.

1970   January: for services to the RNLI, announced in New Year honours

British Empire medal to Coxswain Henry T. 'Shrimp' Davies, presented in March 1970.

1973   15 November: Fishing trawler _Boston Jaguar_, of Lowestoft, took out doctor

Bronze medal to Dr P.S. Barclay, Thanks on Vellum to Coxswain Henry T. Davies and R.W. Davies.

1981   1 May: Fishing boat _George William_, saved 2

Bronze medal to Helmsman Clive Rayment, plus certificates to the crew.

1988   29 September: Yacht _Phaedra_, of Whitby, saved 5

Thanks on Vellum accorded to Coxswain Richard W. Davies, plus certificates to the crew.

1993   13 October: Yacht _Happy Bear_, saved 5

Bronze medal to Coxswain Richard W. Davies, plus certificates to the crew.

1998   6 November: Yacht _Tange_, of Whitby, saved 3

Thanks on Vellum accorded to Second Coxswain Billy Davies, Vellum service certificates to the crew of seven.

1999   2 October: Swimmer, saved 1

Thanks on Vellum to Coxswain Richard W. Davies, and Vellum service certificates to the inshore lifeboat crew.

Three award-winning coxswains with the bust of Henry Blogg at the East Gangway: Richard Davies, Billy Davies and Henry 'Shrimp' Davies after the retirement of the latter in 1976.
(By courtesy of Eastern Counties Newspapers)

Appendix 6

Cromer Lifeboat Families

Throughout the past century and a half, Cromer's lifeboats have been crewed by men from families the names of which have become synonymous with the station and many of the famous rescues performed over the years. Probably the best known of all is the Davies family, members of which have been manning the lifeboat probably since the station was established, and who continue to do so. James Davies was the first Davies to be coxswain when he took charge of the pulling lifeboat in 1874. He remained coxswain until 4 December 1893 when sadly he died while at sea fishing with George Allen and Henry Balls, members of other well-known lifeboat families.

James was succeeded by his son John James Davies, who remained as coxswain until 1902 and married Ellen Blogg, Henry Blogg's mother. Blogg took over as coxswain in 1909 and, since his retirement in 1947, the four coxswains have all been from the Davies family. It was therefore fitting that, as the station was preparing to celebrate its bicentenary, John Davies was appointed coxswain in October 2003 to become the sixth Coxswain Davies. His appointment ensures that the link between the Davies family and every official Cromer coxswain since the RNLI took over the station in the 1850s continues. Like many other members of the Davies family, John, who followed his cousin Billy and father Richard as coxswain, is a fisherman, having been at sea since the age of fifteen.

Various generations of the Harrison, Allen and Balls families have also served in the lifeboat. George 'Buckram' Balls, second coxswain under Henry Blogg until 1933, was great grandfather of the current second coxswain, John Balls. Their names can often be found in the crew lists, together of course with many Davies. The accompanying family tree provides details of successive generations of the Davies family who have served in the Cromer lifeboat. Unfortunately, space does not allow for a complete detailed family tree.

W.T. 'Captain' Davies
1886-1949
Second Coxswain 1945-47

J.R. 'Dick' Davies 1921-90
Second Coxswain 1957-68

Second Coxswain Richard Davies (left) with Coxswain Henry 'Shrimp' Davies, 1975. Since Henry Blogg retired in 1947, a Davies has been coxswain of Cromer lifeboat, with Richard succeeding 'Shrimp' a year after this photograph was taken and Richard's cousin 'Billy' Davies taking over in 1999. Richard's son John was appointed coxswain in October 2003. (By courtesy of Eastern Counties Newspapers)

The Davies Family Tree

[Note this family tree represents only those members of the family who have been officers of the lifeboat. Other members of the family have also served but space does not permit their inclusion]

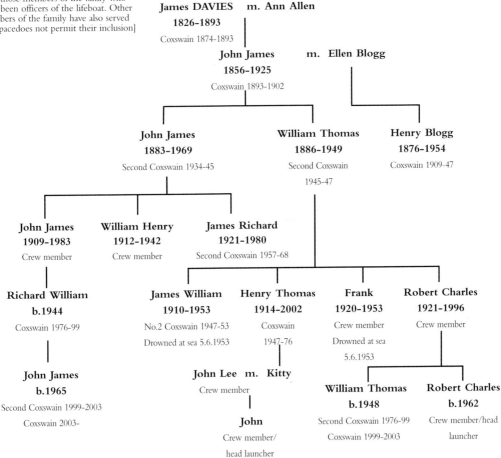

James DAVIES   m. Ann Allen
1826–1893
Coxswain 1874-1893

John James   m. Ellen Blogg
1856–1925
Coxswain 1893-1902

John James
1883–1969
Second Coxswain 1934-45

William Thomas
1886–1949
Second Coxswain
1945-47

Henry Blogg
1876–1954
Coxswain 1909-47

John James
1909–1983
Crew member

William Henry
1912–1942
Crew member

James Richard
1921–1980
Second Coxswain 1957-68

Richard William
b.1944
Coxswain 1976-99

John James
b.1965
Second Coxswain 1999-2003
Coxswain 2003-

James William
1910–1953
No.2 Coxswain 1947-53
Drowned at sea 5.6.1953

Henry Thomas
1914–2002
Coxswain
1947-76

Frank
1920–1953
Crew member
Drowned at sea
5.6.1953

Robert Charles
1921–1996
Crew member

John Lee   m.   **Kitty**
Crew member

John
Crew member/
head launcher

William Thomas
b.1948
Second Coxswain 1976-99
Coxswain 1999-2003

Robert Charles
b.1962
Crew member/head
launcher

*John James Davies, snr
Second Coxswain
1934-45*

*H.W. 'Swank' Davies
Mechanic 1933-61*

*James William 'Jimmy'
Davies
No.2 Coxswain
1947-53*

*Robert Charles Davies
1921-1996
Second Coxswain
1953-57*

Appendix 7
The Lifeboat Museum

The Henry Blogg Lifeboat Museum at Cromer is housed in the former No.2 lifeboat house at the bottom of the east gangway. The last lifeboat to use this building was the 37ft Oakley *William Henry and Mary King* (ON.980), which left in June 1967. Since then, the building has been converted for use as a museum by the Cromer Branch and contains many interesting exhibits relating to the station's history with an emphasis on the exploits of Coxswain Henry Blogg. Several major exhibits have been at the museum, but since 1991 the centrepiece of the Museum has been *H.F. Bailey* (ON.777), on station for only ten years but one of the most famous lifeboats to serve the station because she was used by Coxswain Blogg to perform many of his most famous lifesaving feats.

The 18ft 6in McLachlan inshore lifeboat A-507 on display outside the museum. This lifeboat was one of only a few such craft built by the RNLI in the late 1960s and early 1970s. This example served at Peel (IOM) and Plymouth, and was at the museum from 1984 to 1989. (Paul Russell)

37ft Oakley Valentine Wyndham-Quin (ON.985) was displayed outside the Lifeboat Museum from 1989 to 1991 and was then moved to Harwich for further display at the old Lifeboat House Museum on The Green. She served at Clacton-on-Sea and Clogher Head during her service career. (Paul Russell)

Appendix 8

What Became of the Lifeboats?

Louisa Heartwell
Sold out of service in May 1931 to Nathanial Green, of Stiffkey, Loiusa Heartwell was converted by Warfolk Bros at King's Lynn into the motor cruiser Waiora. She was initially based on the north Norfolk coast and later moved to Wales, being kept at Aberaeron and Barry Dock. By the 1990s, she was at Rickmansworth and later moved to the Chichester Canal, where she is pictured as a houseboat. (Nicholas Leach)

H.F. Bailey (ON.694)
Sold out of service in September 1953, H.F. Bailey was converted into a single screw yacht by Herd & MacKenzie at Buckie and later renamed Gremarie. She was moved to Spain and based at Puerto Estapona, where she was pictured in October 1997. (Philip Simons)

Harriot Dixon
Sold out of service in December 1964, Harriot Dixon *was converted into a motor boat and renamed* Sareter. *She was moored originally at St Olaves on the Broads but was later moved to Blakeney where she has been since the 1970s. She can usually be seen either moored at Blakeney Pit or, as pictured, out of the water in a field to the west of Blakeney village. (Paul Russell)*

Henry Blogg
Sold out of service in April 1977 for £5,500 to Talbot Evans-Thomas of Haverfordwest, she was stripped, re-engined and completely rebuilt with a large cabin over three years. She was renamed Blogg of Cromer *and was kept at a number of different places. By the mid-1990s, she was based on the river Severn at Kempsey, near Worcester, and was moved to Upton-on-Severn in about 2000. She is pictured moored on the Severn at Upton in October 2003. (Nicholas Leach)*

Ruby and Arthur Reed
Ruby and Arthur Reed *was sold out of service in September 1988 without engines for £5,000 for display at Hythe Village Marina, Southampton Water, in the middle of a roundabout. (Nicholas Leach)*

Bibliography

Bensley, Mick (2001): *The Rescues of Henry Blogg* (Bengunn).

Cox, D.C. (nd): *The Saga of the Sepoy* (privately published).

Holden, C. Crawford (nd): *History of Cromer Lifeboats* (unpublished manuscript).

Jolly, Cyril (1958): *Henry Blogg of Cromer* (George C. Harrap; new edition Poppyland Publishing, 2003).

Jolly, Cyril (1981): *The Loss of the English Trader* (Acorn Editions).

Leach, Nicholas (2001): *Never Turn Back: An Illustrated History of Caister Lifeboats* (Tempus Publishing, Stroud).

Lee, Kitty (1991): *The History of the Cromer Lifeboats and crews* (Kitty Lee).

Malster, Robert (1974): *Saved from the Sea* (Terence Dalton, Lavenham, Suffolk).

Malster, Robert & Stibbons, Peter (1979, 1981, 1986, 1994): *The Cromer Lifeboats* (Poppyland Publishing).

Mayes, W.J. (nd): *For Those In Peril* (W.J. Mayes).

Savin, A.C. (1937): *History of Cromer* (Rounce & Wortley).

Stibbons, Peter; Lee, Katherine; and Warren, Martin (1983): *Crabs and Shannocks* (Poppyland, 1983).

Temple, C.R. (1974): *East Coast Shipwrecks* (Wensum Books).

Thiele, C. (1939): *The History of the Cromer Lifeboats* (Rounce & Wortley).

Wake-Walker, Edward (1992): *Gold Medal Rescues* (David & Charles, London).

Warner, Oliver (1974): *The Lifeboat Service* (Cassell, London).

Warren, Martin (1995): *Around Cromer* (Alan Sutton Publishing).

Wiltshire, Roger (1994): *Norfolk's Lifeboats* (SB Publications).

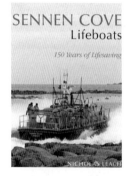

Sennen Cove Lifeboats
NICHOLAS LEACH

Land's End has seen many shipwrecks over the past two thousand years, where the treacherous waters of the Atlantic meet those of the English Channel. In 1853, the RNLI established a lifeboat station at nearby Sennen Cove and the people of this small Cornish village have been saving lives ever since. This is the story of Sennen's lifeboats and volunteer lifeboat crews, the first comprehensive history of the lifeboats and wrecks off the tip of Cornwall.

0 7524 3111 0

Never Turn Back An Illustrated History of Caister Lifeboats
NICHOLAS LEACH

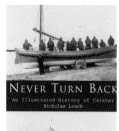

The Caister lifeboat station is one of the most famous in the country, largely due to the lifesaving exploits of its nineteenth-century lifeboatmen, and to the tradgedy of 1901 when their lifeboat capsized, killing nine of the crew. Nicholas Leach covers all aspects of the station at Caister from its establishment to the stationing of the current lifeboat, *Bernard Matthews*. Many of the outstanding rescues are described, as are the lifeboats that have served this station for more than 150 years.

0 7524 2146 8

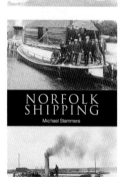

Norfolk Shipping
MICHAEL STAMMERS

The county of Norfolk is surrounded by water, with the North Sea to the east and north, the Great Ouse, Little Ouse and River Waveney to the west and south, and for hundreds of years ships have played a vital role in the economy of the county. Norfolk Shipping shows 200 photographs and images of just some of the many craft that have plied both the North Sea off the coast and inland to the Broads and along the county's main rivers, from sailing craft and steam ships to tugs and pleasure steamers.

0 7524 2757 1